THE CULTURAL PRODUCTION OF INTELLECTUAL PROPERTY RIGHTS

Sean Johnson Andrews

THE CULTURAL PRODUCTION OF INTELLECTUAL PROPERTY RIGHTS

Law, Labor, and the Persistence of Primitive Accumulation

TEMPLE UNIVERSITY PRESS
Philadelphia • Rome • Tokyo

TEMPLE UNIVERSITY PRESS
Philadelphia, Pennsylvania 19122
tupress.temple.edu

Published 2019

Library of Congress Cataloging-in-Publication Data

Names: Johnson Andrews, Sean, author.
Title: The cultural production of intellectual property rights : law, labor, and the persistence of primitive accumulation / Sean Johnson Andrews.
Description: Philadelphia, Pennsylvania : Temple University Press, 2019. | Includes bibliographical references and index.
Identifiers: LCCN 2018030217 | ISBN 9781439914298 (cloth : alk. paper)
Subjects: LCSH: Intellectual property. | Intellectual property—Cultural aspects. | Cultural property—Protection—Law and legislation.
Classification: LCC K1401 .A959 2019 | DDC 346.04/8—dc23
LC record available at https://lccn.loc.gov/2018030217

♾ The paper used in this publication meets the requirements of the American National Standard for Information Sciences—Permanence of Paper for Printed Library Materials, ANSI Z39.48-1992

Printed in the United States of America

9 8 7 6 5 4 3 2 1

To Jill

Contents

Acknowledgments

From conception to publication, this book has taken more than a decade to complete. In that time, I have read and spoken with more people than I can count about the issues and concepts I discuss here. I have also written another book (*Hegemony, Mass Media, and Cultural Studies* [2016]) and nearly a dozen articles and book chapters—again, with input and assistance, direct and indirect, from many other people, some of whom I thank below.

Throughout this whole process, I am grateful to have had the support of my wife, Jill—from supporting me financially as a graduate student, to moving across the country several times as I made my way along the tenure track, to yet again helping make time for multiple revisions, corrections, indexing, and more. And in the middle of all of this, we lost a son, the grief transforming us permanently: as I read back through the book, the words I have written touch the scars of wounds inflicted in adjacent moments of our history. But I am also reminded of the many joys we have shared: the main conceit of this book came to me while relaxing on a weekend trip with my wife. Whatever help the people below provided, there would be no book before you if not for Jill. So I thank her first.

This project began its life as a dissertation, and I am grateful to my committee—Tim Gibson, Peter Mandaville, and Paul Smith—for helping me turn it into a defensible project. Each of them helped me explore the ideas in this book in seminars, independent studies, and other conversations over many years. Likewise, Dina Copelman, Katrina Irving, David Kaufman, and

Marilyn Mobley McKenzie at George Mason University; Anantha Babbili at Texas Christian University; and James Mittelman at American University aided my understanding of key texts, thinkers, and concepts. Denise Albanese pointed me to valuable resources and gave me essential feedback in the first revisions. I wish Peter Brunette were still here to thank for the same—especially for an independent study where we read the early Birmingham Centre for Contemporary Cultural Studies work on media.

Being any sort of leftist at George Mason University also allowed for quite a bit of opposition research. I learned much from attending several years of David Levy's Summer Institute for the Preservation of the History of Economics and from speaking with Tyler Cowen, Peter Bottke, and Dr. Bottke's colleagues on the Austrian Economics Blog. Chapter 3 bears on many of the debates and dialogues I participated in there, particularly around the time of the 2008 financial crisis.

I also owe thanks to the other faculty, staff, and students in the Cultural Studies Program at George Mason. It was a fantastic crucible of ideas and arguments, and I appreciate all the conversations I have had with colleagues there over the years. Ludy Grandas, Michelle Meagher, Katy Razzano, and Lia Uy-Tioco all helped me work out the conception of culture in one way or another. Michelle Carr's vital bureaucratic navigation and support—as well as her occasional stern word of motivation—also pushed this project to its first-level approval. Two fellowships from the College of Humanities and Social Sciences helped sustain the research and writing; before that, my experience teaching at New Century College helped me develop some of the basic ideas included herein. For that, I must thank Nance Lucas and Janette Muir, as well as Mick Beltz, Kelly Dunne, Sarah Sweetman, and Sue Woodfine.

Since I moved to the tenure track, the faculty and students of the Cultural Studies Program and Humanities, History, and Social Sciences Department at Columbia College Chicago have offered me many questions to consider in relation to this concept and have helped me hone the general argument of the project, especially Carmelo Esterrich—who also provided feedback on the cover—Zack Furness, Ann Gunkel, and Robert Watkins. Jaafar Aksikas has been my constant comrade and collaborator, and I have benefited greatly from our work together, particularly in developing our collection on law and culture but also in our work with the Cultural Studies Association (CSA), where he served as president and I as treasurer for several years. I have had many fruitful conversations about ideas developed in this book at CSA meetings over the past decade, particularly with Andrew Culp, Lisa Daily, Rob Gehl, Zach McDowell, Gavin Mueller, and Gil Rodman. And I presented portions at the Union for Democratic Communications, aided by Lee Artz, Rob Carley, and Steve Macek.

I also thank James Arvanitakis and Martin Fredriksson, who have been long-time supporters and collaborators, particularly on issues of piracy and my fusion of cultural studies, history, and political theory. I developed key ideas in conversations with Nick Couldry, Doug Henwood, Vincent Mosco, Janice Peck, Michael Perelman, Carol Stabile, Ted Striphas, and Siva Vaidhyanathan, as well as with various contributors to the lbo-talk and Pen-L Listservs. I also received extremely helpful advice from Jordan Hatcher, Jens Klenner, Chris Piper, Joel Rice, Robyn Ross, Lesley Smith, and Fan Yang; Bryan Alexander gave his stamp of approval to a recent draft, as well as essential feedback along the way. In Ecuador, Yury Guerra provided valuable, informative guidance through the intricacies of politics, culture, and property there.

At Temple University Press (TUP), Micah Kleit was a long-time champion of this project, and Sara Jo Cohen ultimately shepherded it—and me—through the process. I appreciate her help, feedback, and patience throughout. Assistant Editor Nikki Miller, Ann-Marie Anderson in the Marketing Department, and many others helped see this project to completion. Joan S. P. Vidal with TUP and Heather Wilcox with Second Glance Editorial provided indispensable guidance and improved this manuscript in innumerable ways.

The photo on the cover was taken by Solomon D. Butcher, an American photographer who spent the bulk of his career documenting the life of U.S. pioneers. Taken from his collection *Pioneer History of Custer County*, this photo is a reenactment of "settlers taking the law in their own hands—cutting 15 miles of the Brighton Ranch fence." I was struck by the fact that in addition to touching on this book's larger theme of the relationship between law, informal coercion, and cultural legitimacy, Butcher's photograph includes a copyright claim, scrawled at the end of his caption. The event he describes is purported to have occurred in 1885, the year before the signing of the Berne Convention in Switzerland, which guaranteed copyright across national borders. In keeping with the spirit of the pioneer wire cutters, the United States did not sign the agreement for more than a century, refusing to honor European intellectual property rights. I elaborate on the analogy between copyright piracy and fence cutting in Chapters 3 and 4 and on the continuity between real property and intellectual property throughout the book. I thank Mary-Jo Miller, with the Nebraska State Historical Society, who helped facilitate the license for what I find to be a very fitting cover image.

For their help and support, I also thank friends, family, and colleagues who are not mentioned here. Their love, care, and occasional critique fostered the development of this project in untold ways.

And I thank you, dear reader, for your thoughts and feedback on the ideas here. All errors and omissions are ultimately my own, but I hope our disagreements can be the site of an increasingly fruitful conversation on the topics herein.

THE CULTURAL PRODUCTION OF INTELLECTUAL PROPERTY RIGHTS

Introduction

Intellectual Property, Neoliberalism, and the Trump-Branded Triple Movement

I began this study as a pirate, but I ended up more of a property abolitionist. I never used Napster, but BitTorrent permanently altered my feelings about intellectual property rights. This perspective was partially self-serving—it is easier to violate the law when you simply do not believe in it. And I did violate the letter of copyright law, although I would assert that the behavior of torrenters is generally closer to its original spirit. The purpose of copyright—at least in the U.S. Constitution—is intended "to promote the progress of science and useful arts." If you had ever waited hours for a 100MB file to download over a DSL connection (circa 2003), BitTorrent was a revelation. And the behavior itself transformed into a whole underground culture with a new ethic. It was clear that a distributed cultural commons could work; by launching a torrent in a tracker, I joined many others in a swarm to feed each other pieces of the same file—a single file magically exploded into hundreds or thousands of different packets, taking a multitude of different paths through the network, making full use of the distribution of the (then, at least) neutral Internet. It was hard to look at the serious gap between the legacy media rights holders and their integration with the Internet and not believe that the use of copyright was simply a guard against any "progress" if that meant competition to their business model.

My earliest experiences with file sharing over those networks were of people distributing media that media companies were not willing or yet able to distribute: broadcast news, late-night TV (e.g., *The Daily Show*, *The*

Colbert Report, network and basic cable programs with no archive of past episodes or realistic hope of future distribution), BBC documentaries, out-of-print musical recordings (a mainstay of Napster), and of course mashups. This era was before the existence of YouTube or similar streaming sites for sharing video or SoundCloud for sharing music—a time when, once a TV program aired, getting access to a recorded copy was usually an official affair, with forms to complete or telephone calls to make. This system was radically democratized with the advent of digital video recorders (DVRs) to aid in time shifting, new recording standards to retain a program's sound fidelity even when encoded in a very compact file, and of course the Internet and file-sharing sites and technologies. Some of these sharing sites—Pirate Bay being the most famous and long-standing, although many others existed at the time—were also linked up with groups formed to ensure that certain programs were recorded and shared, especially those that might be of political or cultural importance.

In the context of the start of the 2003 U.S. war in Iraq, the legitimacy of the law itself seemed up for discussion: old agreements we had made as a society—like those against surveillance, torture, and war—were now openly violated, apparently as part of the political strategy to shore up U.S. power, domestically and abroad. Not only did breaking property laws seem minor by comparison; distributed file sharing was a way to circulate information about the war, the coverage of the war, and examinations of the politics of the moment—information that often was not being circulated otherwise, on- or offline. Once you become deeply identified with breaking one law, it throws into relief the equivocal legitimacy of all other laws, especially if that legitimacy is already in crisis. The economic crash of 2008—the massive, unpunished financial crimes and bankrupt economic ideologies behind it—then overwhelmed me during what became the first draft of this book.

In short, what started as an examination of the debate about copyright and intellectual property (IP) broadened to consider the entire ideological and institutional apparatus of Western neoliberal capitalism. This mode of production taxes resources of the entire planet for the tremendous benefit of a few; yet even in its moments of crisis, finance capital is bailed out—the valorization of its assets secured—while the majority of the population suffers from the long-term effects of what I call the reified culture of property. The fact that the hegemonic, reified culture of property allowed no radical alternative suggested the extreme likelihood that forces of reaction would step into the fray.

In the first weeks of Donald Trump's presidency, he released a series of executive orders, issued daily to seed the news cycle and make the most of the media attention that each announcement generated. And while not all of them generated the same amount of interest, the most controversial in the first week of his term was certainly the "Executive Order: Protecting the Nation from Foreign Terrorist Entry into the United States," colloquially understood as the "Muslim Ban" he had promised throughout his campaign. The policy—rolled out in a haphazard manner with little oversight or discussion with the relevant government agencies charged with reviewing or executing the charge—inspired thousands of protesters to descend on airports across the country. The following Monday, a spokesperson for former president Barack Obama echoed sentiments expressed by commentators across the political spectrum: "Citizens exercising their constitutional right to assemble, organize and have their voices heard by their elected officials is exactly what we expect to see when American values are at stake" (J. Davis 2017).

But what are the "American values" at stake? This book considers this question obliquely by looking at the contemporary conceptualization of and debates over intellectual property rights (IPR) and how they are produced—as a juridical category and as the meaningful precipitate of a much larger cultural process. IP is justified, controlled, enforced, and valorized as simultaneously democratic and capitalist, almost from its first instances in the English Civil War, to our era of cloud-based, networked, global, neoliberal capitalism. But in the balance between liberty and property, property always wins. In the contemporary U.S. context, IPR—like property rights in general—are some of the most important American values; protecting the corporate capitalist oligopolies that currently control American IP is rarely up for debate in the political establishment—certainly far less often than the nearly endless debates about the rights of immigrants, the ability of women to control their own bodies, and the ability of black people to walk down the street without the threat of death or destitution by the police.

By viewing the prehistory of the dominant understanding of intellectual property rights as part of the larger system of capitalist violence, I hope, in the words of Slavoj Žižek, "To step back, to disentangle ourselves from the fascinating lure of this directly visible 'subjective' violence, violence performed by a clearly identifiable agent" (2008, p. 8). By stepping back, we direct our attention to the larger system of capitalist expropriation that has bipartisan support, unpacking especially the role of copyrights and trademarks in its struggle for hegemony—and the way the now hegemonic Law and Economics ideology guiding our approach to IPR reifies them as just another form of private property to be ruthlessly protected by the capital-oriented state.

Much of this book was written during the Obama years, when the hegemonic political horizon was a version of what Nancy Fraser (2013a) has recently termed "progressive neoliberalism." In that context, I consider several of Obama's University of Chicago colleagues—Cass Sunstein, who briefly served as "regulatory czar" for Obama (much to TV pundit Glenn Beck's consternation), and especially Lawrence Lessig, who is most well-known for critiquing copyright and its effect on what he has called the "creative commons." Lessig honed his approach to IP in an earlier series of legal journal articles, in which he synthesizes progressive conclusions out of the right-wing Law and Economics tradition he took to be a ground truth. He followed the work on copyright and IPR I discuss here by targeting what he saw as the underlying problem of political corruption in Washington (a neoliberal version of what Trump referred to as "draining the swamp"), including an attempt to run for president in 2016 and a brief campaign to deny Trump the electoral college votes (offering pro bono advice for electors who wanted to vote "their conscience" rather than honor the mandate of their states).

Focusing on IPR may seem quaint in the Trump era, when policies appear to be written with the aid of subtly shrouded (or maybe "hooded" is the correct term) white supremacists, including Attorney General Jeff Sessions and one-time White House chief strategist (and former *Breitbart* editor) Steve Bannon. But Obama and Lessig's liberalism helped pave the way for the Trump ascendency. As I outline in this book, theirs is a liberalism that cedes the ground of acceptable debate and politics to the resurgent right. According to Ellen Meiksins Wood (1981, 1991, 2002), in this "pristine culture of capitalism," the economic is separated from the political; the neoliberal ideology asserts that nothing can be done politically to transform the economic problems created by the capitalist mode of production other than to make it slightly more humane or "rational" or "balanced" around the edges.

Thus, in crafting his signature health-care policy, President Obama and his legislative advocates never fundamentally (or, in the end, at all) questioned the idea that health care should be a commodity supplied by a market exchange of some sort. In eventually crafting a plan nearly identical to those proposed by the right-wing Heritage Foundation, liberal legislators claimed that this approach was circumscribed by politics, but it is more accurate to say that they abstained from politics. It was not just that they refrained from fighting the hard political battle for something like a public option or socialized medicine but that they agreed such an option was politically impossible because "the economy" could not sustain it—an argument contradicted by the existence of some form of national health care in nearly every other industrialized country.

This underlying political economic assumption informs the progressive neoliberalism of the Democratic Party, such that even when there was a clear political will for change in a more socially democratic direction—as evidenced by the primary campaign of Vermont's senator Bernie Sanders—the party resisted policy changes that would actually be an easy sell to many voters. In the heat of the 2016 presidential campaign, when Trump had made a Mexican border wall and criticisms of free-trade agreements, including the North American Free Trade Agreement (NAFTA) and the Trans-Pacific Partnership, cornerstones of his pitch, Obama penned an op-ed declaring that "building walls to isolate ourselves from the global economy would only isolate us from the incredible opportunities it provides." With barely a nod to the U.S. Rust Belt that has felt most harmed by these "incredible opportunities," he declared, "The world has changed" (Obama 2016). All that we can do is try to make the rules work in our favor, for no fundamental change is possible. This opinion was a far cry from Obama's own campaign rhetoric of hope and change—and a great contrast to the populist promises of Sanders and Trump.

Limiting the range of political economic options is fundamental to the modern, capitalist conception of the state, dating back to John Locke's *Second Treatise of Government* but rearticulated in the present era in what Chantal Mouffe (2000) calls "the democratic paradox," which is a hegemonic stabilization of the inherent tension between liberty and equality. Mouffe asserts that "the unchallenged hegemony of neo-liberalism represents a threat for democratic institutions":

> Neo-liberal dogmas about the unviolable [*sic*] rights of property, the all-encompassing virtues of the market and the dangers of interfering with its logics constitute nowadays the "common sense" in liberal-democratic societies and they are having a profound impact on the left, as many left parties are moving to the right and euphemistically redefining themselves as "centre-left." In a very similar way, Blair's "third way" and Schroder's "neue Mitte," both inspired by Clinton's strategy of "triangulation," accept the terrain established by their neoliberal predecessors. (Ibid., p. 6)

This study focuses especially on the dogma of "the unviolable rights of property" and the ways in which the leaders of the balanced copyright movement—including Lessig and other neoliberal stalwarts—have gone out of their way to affirm what I call the reified culture of property, even as they present evidence of the social production of value that should challenge the moral and philosophical foundations of this dogma. Following Georg Lukács's (1971) elaboration of the concept, by reification I mean the epistemological fallacy whereby processes and relations between people are perceived as natural, ahistorical, thingly obstacles to be navigated rather than social constructs to be negotiated or altered. And, as I show herein, since the early days of English capitalism, its advocates have argued that its preferred social property relations are rooted in "natural law," unchangeable by people, politics, and, especially, the law or the state.

From one perspective then, this book is not about IPR. Instead, it concerns the mainstream debate over IPR and what that debate reveals about what I call the reified culture of property that pervades Western capitalist societies. The debate about IPR is usually centered on the way digitization and globalization have changed how the properties in question are produced and distributed and their owners remunerated, but the rupture created by these global, digital processes should inspire broader questions regarding the social production of value and the liberal (or neoliberal, as it is often discussed) defense of law and the state.

I argue that the opening created by globalization and digitization and evidenced by the debate over IPR allows us to reevaluate this broader culture surrounding property, its social valorization, and the role of the state in its protection. The early rhetoric of globalization and digitization promised amazing, liberatory possibilities: Technological progress! The spread of democratic freedoms! A more humane, environmentally friendly labor and production process! As usual, the myths of the global village and the "end of work" have yet to be realized: this book argues that tugging at the political, economic, cultural, and technological threads woven through the concept, laws, and practices surrounding IPR is an important start toward the creation of a more democratic, humane society, to paraphrase Stuart Hall.

To engage in this evaluation, I argue, we must develop a conceptualization that helps us more deeply understand the relationship between culture—and cultural studies—and the law. Building on recent work (Aksikas and Johnson Andrews 2014, 2016; Johnson Andrews 2016), I approach these questions at different registers simultaneously to consider what cultural studies can, or maybe should, be able to contribute to the conversation about IPR—or indeed the law itself—as a "cultural production." As Rosemary Coombe (1999) points out, the concept of culture has been uncritically deployed by legal studies scholars at precisely the moment that such fields as anthropology and cultural studies have developed a more nuanced and problematized understanding of that concept. This is especially the case in conversations about IPR, since the collective process of meaning making is more obvious and visible. Audience-focused research on fan/slash fiction, Internet prosumption, Wikipedia, crowdsourcing, and a wide variety of emergent practices has recalled earlier work by Dick Hebdige, Janice Radway, and especially Henry Jenkins (who, as discussed later, figures centrally in Lessig's book *Remix*), leading legal scholars of copyright to the idealized connotation of culture, in the words of Raymond Williams, "as a noun of process" (2011, p. 77).

The dominant neoliberal ideology articulates this "culture as a process" to the free market, which it sees as the only true source of meaning, power, and value. Economic freedom—meaning the *laissez-faire* limitation of state protections of anything other than property—comes to stand in for formal democratic processes, and the "electronic freedom" of the new information infrastructure presumes democracy as an automatic outcome of the technology. As Jodi Dean puts it, "The proliferation, distribution, acceleration and intensification of communicative access and opportunity, far from enhancing democratic governance or resistance, results in precisely the opposite—the post-political formation of communicative capitalism" (2005, p. 53). But Dean would likely agree that the fantasy of the Internet and Web 2.0 as being essentially democratic is only partially a return of the ever-present myths that Vincent Mosco recounts in *The Digital Sublime* (2004); instead, following Žižek, the fantasy is "directly due to the depoliticization of economics, to the common acceptance of Capital and the market mechanisms as neutral tools/procedures to be exploited" (2000, pp. 353–354).

The politics of cultural representation remain important, but in that framework, the issues of class, labor, and the reproduction of capitalism become themes to discuss and critique alongside an array of others: the norms of race, gender, sexuality, and other categories of identity have presented even more pressing concerns, in theoretical terms and in terms of the social movements of the time. In the words of Mouffe, whose pivotal text *Hegemony and Socialist Strategy* (written with Ernesto Laclau; 2001) helps outline the political and theoretical necessity of this shift, "The driving force behind it was a political question, at a time when both the social-democratic left and traditional marxism seemed incapable of understanding the specificity of the new movements that had developed since 1968, such as feminism, the environmental movement, anti-racist struggles, and against discrimination on the grounds of sexuality" (Mouffe and Errejón 2016, p. 15). While the site of this struggle was often the informal grounds of culture rather than changes in policy or law, the latter eventually began to reflect those concerns.

If scholars of the law were influenced by cultural studies' understanding of culture, there was little reciprocal interest among scholars of cultural studies to reconsider the structuralist questions of determination by law or economics. The work by Austin Sarat and Jonathan Simon (2001), for instance, which attempts to synthesize these fields, offers an important opportunity for cultural studies to help legal scholars get "Beyond Legal Realism." The authors rightly point out that cultural studies could help legal scholars consider the way representations of the law influence its function as well as "[widen] the moments of subjectivity that are even considered in the analysis of law and legality" (ibid., p. 12). But their interest in these moments of subjectivity and what they call the "cultural turn" in legal studies has been instigated by what they describe as "the general decline in confidence in virtually every institution, reform movement, and program of knowledge gathering attached to the social" (ibid., p. 6). This "decline of the social" parallels a dramatic increase in exactly the kind of material and economic inequality that legal realists, such as Robert Hale, had hoped to combat. The notion of getting "beyond legal realism" is premised on the existence of a legal realism to get beyond, yet the contemporary Law and Economics movement has been instrumental in fomenting that "general decline in confidence" and has been successfully trying to get us beyond the progressive outlook of legal realism for several decades, a historical context that I explore more fully herein and they barely mention.

Even such scholars as Coombe, who straddles both fields, are more inclined toward what Hall and others would call a culturalist—rather than structuralist—interpretation of the relationship between law and culture: her collection of essays on IPR is infused with the spirit of its epigraph, which features a quote from Michel de Certeau's *The Practice of Everyday Life* (1998). Certeau, Coombe, and many in the culturalist tradition highlight the dynamic forms of agency that still exist despite (or even because of) the force of the law, the state, and other institutions of seemingly intractable power. David Harvey argues in his *A Brief History of Neoliberalism* that this left-libertarian ethos was easily appropriated by the reactionary right in the service of dismantling the welfare state, an ethos that we can certainly see reaching its pinnacle with Trump and Bannon's "Deconstruction of the Administrative State" (Harvey 2005; Rucker and Costa 2017). But if it is the pinnacle, it is a deeply contradictory one: the misogynistic, antigay, white-supremacist articulation of Trump's political discourse is as deviant from the dominant culture as is his protectionist rhetoric on trade and neo-Nazi critique of bankers and the media. Yet the articulation of "progressivism" with neoliberalism in the Bill Clinton and Obama eras made this reaction all too inevitable in the U.S. cultural context.

IPR may seem like a tangential object to this renewal and this critique, yet I would argue that they are an important locus around which we can organize all the above. For one thing, as Naomi Klein has recently observed, "to understand Trump you really have to understand the world that made him what he is, and that, to a very large extent, is the world of branding" (2017, loc. 350).

Trump is a brand: few of the buildings bearing his name are the result of his work as a real estate developer, and, as commentators like John Oliver noted during the presidential campaign, his association with wealth and success is less related to his business prowess than to the fact that "he's spent decades turning his own name into a brand synonymous with success and quality and he's made himself the mascot for that brand" ("Donald Trump" 2016). Like the globalized corporations Klein criticizes in *No Space, No Choice, No Jobs, No Logo* (2002),

> rather than building and owning the structures himself, as he had earlier in his career, Trump realized that he could make far easier money simply by selling his name to developers around the world, who would use his celebrity to attract buyers and customers for their office buildings, condos, and hotels. The outside developers would do the construction and carry all the liabilities. If the projects failed (as they frequently did), Trump still collected his licensing fee. And the fees were enormous. According to the *Washington Post*, on a single hotel-condo project in Panama, "Trump has earned at least $50 million on the project on virtually zero investment." (Klein 2017, loc. 446)

The majority of Trump's revenue comes from leasing his name—his trademarked brand—which he not only rents to luxury hotel developers but also famously plasters over clothing, steaks, houseware, and even a (now failed) university.

Klein highlights the way this cultural value and power has now intersected with more conventional notions of political and economic power. On the one hand, Trump's brand is ruthless power and success: achieving control of the U.S. state serves as a validation of the tenets of the brand. On the other hand, the state itself is essential to the security of that brand as IP—a security that is practically difficult to achieve in the era of globalization, but which is facilitated when you are the so-called leader of the free world. Klein cites a *New York Times* report from April 2017 pointing out that Trump's corporation, "now run by his two adult sons, has 157 trademark applications pending in 36 countries" (Klein 2017, loc. 557).

Meaning, Power, and Value: Cultural Studies, Postindustrial Property, and the Neoliberal Crisis of Sovereignty

In terms of his legal status as a trademarked brand, Trump is the perfect embodiment of the ways in which cultural meaning, political power, and economic value are immanent elements, each mutually constituting the other and working together to secure hegemony. By "meaning," I refer primarily to what others might call the specifically cultural elements: the common set of connotations and signifiers through which communication and the transmission of ideas occur. Trump is unique in this regard because in many cases, as political writer Farhad Manjoo observes, "He is no longer just the message. In many cases, he has become the medium, the ether through which all other stories flow" (Manjoo 2017). In this way, Trump is a synecdoche for the other intellectual properties that now form the medium of our collective consciousness and cultural production. Manjoo realized this by trying to ignore all coverage of Trump in the first week of February 2017, finding it increasingly hard to find any message not using him as a springboard for some argument, observation, or product pitch. While we could chalk this observation up to Trump's ability to stir up controversy, it is also the result of a media system that aims for the largest possible audience, a tendency that creates a self-sustaining cycle: encoding messages using the dominant, hegemonic frameworks and signifiers simultaneously produces meanings and interpellates viewers who feel compelled to know those meanings (even if they do not agree with them). For legacy media, this cycle means more advertising dollars; for social media, it means more likes and shares, which can also mean a great deal of money. Some of the amateur purveyors of fake news in the run up to the 2016 election were making $10,000 per month in ad revenue (Dewey 2016), many of them primarily targeting Trump voters with false stories about Hillary Clinton.

This information reveals the other two elements that are directly intertwined with the first: economic value and political power. One metric of economic value is Trump's "earned media," which helped him tremendously in the primary and the presidential election but was even more valuable during his first month in office. Manjoo cites data from the advertising analytics firm mediaQuant, which

> counts every mention of a particular brand or personality in just about any outlet, from blogs to Twitter to the evening news to *The New York Times*. Then it estimates how much the mentions would cost if someone were to pay for them as advertising. In January, Mr. Trump broke mediaQuant's records. In a single month, he received $817 million in coverage, higher than any single person has ever received in the four years that mediaQuant has been analyzing the media. [. . .] In fact, Mr. Trump gets about $100 million more in coverage than the next 1,000 famous people put together. (Manjoo 2017)

Although it is true that much of this coverage and these mentions were negative from the perspective of the dominant culture—related to the massive demonstrations following his inauguration, the botched travel ban and protests at airports across the country, and the incidents of white-supremacist terror that the Southern Poverty Law Center reported were spiking in the early days of his presidency—they were fully in line with his brand image and therefore served to reinforce the political power among his supporters.

Jason Read, following Louis Althusser, develops the concept of immanence to describe the ways in which what I call meaning, power, and value are mutually constituted by one another in contemporary capitalism:

> It is no longer possible to separate capital, as the producer of goods and commodities, from what used to be called the superstructure: the production of ideas, beliefs, perceptions, and tastes. Capitalist production has today either directly appropriated the production of culture, beliefs, and desires or it has indirectly linked them to the production and circulation of commodities. [. . .] If everything is immanent, both cause and effect, then it is no longer possible to understand the superstructure, the ideas and production of consciousness, as simple effects emanating from, or reflecting, the conflict between forces and relations of production. They must be understood as causes as well, as the constitutive conditions of the reproduction and the dissolution of a particular economy, or mode of production. (2003, pp. 2, 8)

In my most recent book (Johnson Andrews 2016), I outline the immanent relationships between meaning, power, and value more extensively, especially in terms of how they relate to the concept of hegemony.

Cultural studies scholars primarily look at hegemony in the dimensions of meaning and power: how does ideology help cement political power by establishing the legitimate common sense? Most critiques of IP within the field begin from this perspective: copyright, trademark, and other restrictions on our common semiotic materials serve to limit democratic conversation and demotic cultural production, particularly in an era when it is more possible than ever to be a one-person mass culture start-up. As I discuss in Chapter 2, this position is also a good reason to look at the origins of copyright in the era of the English Civil War, when the main purpose of copyright was to crack down on pirate publishers peddling proto-Communist Protestant pamphlets advocating political and economic "Levelling." Of course, then as now, the most dangerous of these populist alternative visions threatened the legitimacy of dominant capitalist order. The cultural legitimacy of the dominant economic model is essential: the state can use force to compel its subjects to take their place in that order for only so long before it threatens the legitimacy of the law and the state itself. It is not a coincidence that Trump has emerged at a moment when #BlackLivesMatter, #Occupy, and other movements are challenging decades-long expansions of the police and prison-industrial complex. Loïc Wacquant (2009) and others have described this expansion of the carceral state as "punishing the poor." Thomas Piketty (2014) argues that all these forms of resistance are predictable since, when inequality is on the rise, the potential for political insurrection rises as well. The proportion of the population we would need to lock away to maintain order grows exponentially, and soon the poor have, quite literally, nothing to lose but their chains.

Property as a social relationship relies on a state that is seen as legitimate, and the sovereignty of the liberal state is simultaneously legitimated and limited by an ideology that articulates how the value of property is produced and should be defended. Central to this liberal state is the Lockean understanding of natural law, and central to Locke's model is a particular conception of value and its relation to property, the division of labor, and the state. The debate over IPR potentially undermines this culture of property because the metaphorical extension of property rights to immaterial objects illuminates the inadequacy (and malleability) of this concept of value and the state charged with protecting it. The debate about IP is therefore really a debate about how value is produced and distributed relative to the legal owners of property—which is the central debate of the capitalist economic model from its inception.

The very notion that "the economy" exists is itself an ideological commonplace of what Ellen Meiksins Wood (1991) calls the "pristine culture" of capitalism. In presenting the "economy" as disembedded from society, this discourse pretends it is a natural phenomenon that no political action could fundamentally alter. And in our present, postindustrial, neoliberal era, even an analytical distinction between culture, politics, and the economy is difficult to maintain. The ideological apparatus itself is a source of economic value. Hegemony is therefore not only about the cultural suture articulating antagonistic political economic property relationships; insofar as those property relationships are hegemonic, the cultural content can itself become a source of value qua profits. Indeed, since the economy itself is said to be "cultural," it means that IPR increasingly serve as enclosures around the means of production in much the same way as the fences of Early Modern England.

But the parallels to that earlier era also alert us to something that early practitioners of cultural studies saw as fundamental to their project: the role of labor in producing meaning, value, and ultimately power. In their early incarnation, cultural studies and the New Left framed questions of labor in relation to the way automation, deskilling, and incorporated unions had robbed workers of their creative potential. Realizing that the economic also had an ideological component, early cultural studies scholars, born as they were from the New Left, assumed that the gains of the unionized workplace and social democratic welfare state would easily muffle the potential political power of the working class. So the argument shifted: postwar industrial capitalism had sheared the mental and manual capacities from one another not only through the social division of labor but even within the workers themselves. As Andrew Ross (2009, 2010) has recently argued, the search for "meaning in work" is valid, and we should not let it go even as the current generation is offered precarity in exchange for the demand to, in the words of Angela McRobbie (2016), "be creative." Forced into the fissured workplace (Weil 2014) by the increasingly disembedded market, these skilled mental laborers see the value they produce expropriated in the same ways in which factory workers of yore did, but this time facilitated with legal contracts assigning the IP they create to the companies that hire them (A. Ross 2000). In short, the problems faced by contemporary mental and manual laborers are more similar than they have been in a century, in part because of IPR and the ways in which these rights help intensify capitalist social relations in the face of digital and global disruption.

In the spirit of Michael Denning's (2004) recent call for a "labor theory of culture," I aim to employ this immanent understanding of meaning, power, and value to understand the complex articulation of IPR—in law and practice—and how these rights operate in and explain the current crisis of neoliberalism. If Trump as a brand embodies many of the important trends and contradictions of globalization, as a populist leader, he opposes many features of globalization and its liberal democratic notions of sovereignty. As we will see, although the ideology of neoliberalism claims that the state should have less power—the political should be separate from the economic—the legitimacy of the state is ultimately based on its exceptionally strong protection of property. And the latter is bound up with the Lockean assumption that the *owner* of that property did the work—the labor—to create its value, an assumption that Trump has exploited to build his political, economic, and cultural career. At the same time, in opposing the tenets of progressive politics, Trump's political appeal points to the uneven alliances that cultural studies scholars have made since the advent of neoliberalism and suggests the need for a more direct attack on the culture of property he still represents.

Progressive Neoliberalism and the Triple Movement

Other scholars, including Mouffe and Fraser, discuss elements of what I call a reified culture of property using the concept of neoliberalism. Neoliberalism is a useful concept because it points to the ways in which this culture of property has been articulated—and rearticulated—in the postindustrial era. Neoliberalism is haunted by what Jefferson Cowie and others have termed the "great exception" of the New Deal in the United States and the rise of social democracy in Europe (Cowie 2016). These midcentury breaches of this long-standing "culture of property" were driven by what Karl Polanyi (2001) calls a "double movement," whereby society rises up to demand protection by the state from the ravages caused by the disembedded market.

In turn, neoliberalism can be seen as what Mark Blyth (2002) calls a "*counter* double movement." Central to the neoliberal movement is a theoretical and philosophical imperative to recommodify what have increasingly become social wages or social goods—in short, by reasserting the political, economic, and ultimately cultural and moral legitimacy of the culture of property. Blyth convincingly argues that, while the double movement that pressed for the New Deal and the counter double movement of neoliberalism had specific social interests behind them, the key to their hegemonic rise was the coherence of their economic ideas at the time of their ascendency. Thus, in the 1970s, there were alternatives—for instance, the Regulationist Economics School in France and other leftist critiques of corporate capitalism—to the theories of Milton Friedman, Friedrich von Hayek, supply-side economics, rational choice theory, and the Laffer curve. But the leftist critics of embedded capitalism were less successful in defining the crisis of stagflation and proscribing a solution that would be attractive politically. This political-ideological crisis was compounded by what Fraser (2013a, 2013b) has termed a "triple movement" for emancipation.

In her most recent collection of essays, Fraser outlines her concept of "the triple movement," which "conceptualizes capitalist crisis as a three-sided conflict among forces of marketization, social protection, and emancipation" (2013a, loc. 5342). If Polanyi sees the double movement as being a demand for social protection against "the disintegrative effects of marketization," the triple movement of emancipation is a reaction against "the entrenching domination" of the social protection provided by the welfare state. The concept of the triple movement is triply useful: first, it helps categorize the social movements of the 1950s, 1960s, and 1970s in relation to the dominant culture and political economy, which helps explain the particular political and theoretical direction of cultural studies and their ancillary fields; and, I would argue, insofar as the concept of the triple movement helps us understand the ways in which progressive, emancipatory politics relates to the midcentury double movement and the counter double movement of neoliberalism, it explains the most reactionary tendencies of Trump and other populist leaders as a *counter* triple movement.

Fraser uses the "triple movement" to categorize the "vast array of social struggles that do not find any place within the scheme of the double movement":

> I am thinking of the extraordinary range of emancipatory movements that erupted on the scene in the 1960s and spread rapidly across the world in the years that followed: anti-racism, anti-imperialism, anti-war, the New Left, second-wave feminism, LGBT liberation, multiculturalism, and so on. Often focused more on recognition than redistribution, these movements were highly critical of the forms of social protection that were institutionalized in the welfare and developmental states of the postwar era. (Fraser 2013b)

The development of cultural studies as a field emerged from the New Left and was infused with the political and theoretical precipitates of these related movements. The (official) site of labor was incorporated into the system via the alliance between corporate capitalism, large unions, and the state, so critical focus shifted to culture and representation as sites of struggle and emancipation (Aksikas and Johnson Andrews 2014; Johnson Andrews 2016). As C. Wright Mills argues in his "Letter to the New Left," it appeared that the earlier reliance on labor as the source of revolutionary progress should be abandoned: "Such a labour metaphysic, I think, is a legacy from Victorian Marxism that is now quite unrealistic" (1960, p. 22). Instead, the New Left should think about the role of the cultural apparatus, which was seen as "manufacturing consent" to the political economic order and, in the words of Althusser, reproducing the relations of production (Althusser 2014; Hall 1982).

The crisis of progressive liberalism should take us back to the bread-and-butter issues of labor, class, and social protection that have largely been left to one side in favor of the emancipatory socialist strategy advocated by such theorists as Laclau and Mouffe (2001)—although not without recognizing the very real need to continue those emancipatory struggles as such. As Mouffe observes, "Nowadays we have to defend the social-democratic institutions we previously criticised for not being radical enough. We could have never imagined that the working-class victories of social democracy and the welfare state could be rolled back. In 1985 we said 'we need to radicalise democracy'; now we first need to restore democracy, so we can then radicalise it; the task is far more difficult" (Mouffe and Errejón 2016, pp. 22–23).

Scholars have come to some broad, if still ambivalent, agreement on the failures of the New Left and cultural studies in the neoliberal era. In looking at the different movements to radicalize social democracy, Fraser notes that "in each case, the movement disclosed a type of domination and raised a corresponding claim for emancipation. In each case, too, however, the movement's claims for emancipation were ambivalent—they could line up in principle either with marketization or social protection" (2013a, loc. 5388). In the event, she argues, in most of these movements—including the feminist movement and the New Left:

> The ambivalence has been resolved in recent years in favour of marketization. Insufficiently attuned to the rise of free-market forces, the hegemonic currents of emancipatory struggle have formed a "dangerous liaison" with neoliberalism, supplying a portion of the "new spirit" or charismatic rationale for a new mode of capital accumulation, touted as "flexible," "difference-friendly," "encouraging of creativity from below." As a result, the emancipatory critique of oppressive protection has converged with the neoliberal critique of protection per se. In the conflict zone of the triple movement, emancipation has joined forces with marketization to double-team social protection. (Fraser 2013b, p. 130)

McRobbie (2008) has recently reflected on this miscalculation in her earlier work, where she had argued that consumer feminism was a space of liberation; in reality, that liberation was inherently premised on reproducing young women's neoliberal subjectivity. On the other hand, McRobbie (2016)—along with many other cultural studies scholars—has also been well attuned to the insidious emergence of precarious, immaterial, largely feminized, and unpaid labor that is central to the "creative economy" and the ways in which this affective meaning making creates not only power but also value.

In short, well before the emergence of Trump and the wave of other populist movements around the world, critics on the left were awake to the limits of marketization. But in many cases, as with the liberal critics of IPR I discussed throughout this book, most recent leftist critics see something unique about the political economy of immaterial or digital or affective labor rather than focus their attention on the larger culture of property that helps the capitalist class siphon surplus value across the system.

It would be obtuse to suggest that there are not differences between material and immaterial property, as the Motion Picture Association of America (MPAA) did in its infamous antipiracy campaign, comparing the "theft" of a movie to stealing a car or a purse. But campaigns like that one are the precipitate of a larger ideological struggle, led by capitalist conglomerates that have invested hundreds of billions of dollars in purchasing (and occasionally producing) cultural commodities. These immaterial property owners would like the state to protect their property with the same vigor as it protects real property, particularly in a global, digital economy where IP is often a more fundamental asset than retail real estate or factory equipment. In this context, it is essential to not only protect but to extend the reified culture of property.

By a culture of property, I mean a culture whose social relations are ever more deeply commodified; where the ultimate goal is to subject *all* social interaction (not just those of commerce) to the market system's individualistic understanding of the social process of valorization, geared as it is toward the accumulation of privately held properties; where the primary role of the state is held to be the protection of that process—and especially the value it produces—according to the already existing ownership and distribution patterns; where the owners of property are presumed to have created the value protected by the state; where the state protection of this property is held to be natural and/or scientifically necessary and thus beyond democratic reorientation; and, finally, where this formal legal environment helps determine a culture such that individuals respond to the functional discipline of the market as if it were a force of nature rather than a historically contingent social relation.

The staunchest defenders of this reified culture of property paradoxically argue the state is ultimately unnecessary. They rely on the unquestioned cultural efficacy—a deep and determining cultural belief—of the value and legitimacy of private productive property, assuming the neoliberal model of society as a universal set of norms so guaranteed of hegemonic, political stability that the state is unnecessary. They assume the legitimacy of the status-quo distribution; overlook previous rounds of coercive, state-led primitive accumulation and the direct disciplinary force of the state in preserving the property acquired in that process; and deny the political function of the state and the law in crafting a social order and population that more closely resemble the pure model that they argue is a natural state of affairs.

The efficacy of this culture is tied to an ideal subject: *homo economicus*, or what Paul Smith (2007) has referred to as "the subject of value." This subject features centrally in Hayek's (1945) mythical understanding of how the market should operate as a communication mechanism: transmitting prices *qua* information to buyers and sellers through a nonhierarchical, unplanned, global network and helping them make decisions about where to place their investments. This rationally calculating, self-organizing subject is best served by deregulation and recommodification: regulations are futile attempts at state planning that will never be as efficient at communicating actual supply and demand as the market. But the market can communicate accurate information only if everything—including Polanyi's fictitious commodities of labor, land, and money, along with air, water, health, life, the past, the present, and the future—is given a price and sold to the highest bidder. In our present era, "everything" especially includes immaterial, cultural property that is covered by patents, trademarks, and copyrights. The latter are central to the global capitalist regime of accumulation, facilitating the offshore production, commodity chains, financial arbitrage, and tax havens that make the hegemonic model of globalization possible and profitable.

So in a sense, this book is not really about IPR, or at least not *only* about them. Instead, it is about the ways in which the debates about IPR are so focused on the marginal trees of media that they miss looking at the neoliberal forest floor that nurtures them. It considers what the debates about copyright, trademarks, patents, and other varieties of IP tell us about property in relation to what I describe above as meanings, power, and value in the early twenty-first century. The bulk of this study is spent conceptualizing the relationship between hegemony, law, and culture; historicizing the hegemonic struggle over the Lockean culture of property, which legitimates the capitalist protection of "real" and intellectual property; and positing the ways in which the debate over IPR, labor, and the creative commons can be extended to what seem to be settled understandings of real property rights and the state. It seeks to uncover the political, economic, and ideological roots that make the culture of property so fundamental—and then argues that it might be best to tear them out of the ground.

With the emergence of what Henry Jenkins (2006) calls the "convergence culture" of new media, and the extension of these rights in tangible and intangible property to other cultures through globalization, this reified foundation is fracturing. The forceful projection of IPR onto other countries through such treaties as the now-defunct Trans-Pacific Partnership and such institutions as the World Trade Organization (WTO) shows the narrow cultural relevance and specific cultural history of the general concept of property and the political institution that protects it—namely, the liberal state. Likewise, the exciting discovery of the participatory, social production of value around so-called IP—especially in the crowdsourced, social factories of Web 2.0—has given new life to the Marxist observation that all value is produced socially. I ultimately argue that it is in this temporal, technological, and spatial opening, facilitated by the uneven distribution and development of globalization and digitization, that we can see the already vibrant alternatives to the current configuration of property and intellectual property rights.

IPR is an attempt to secure decisive rights to the otherwise fluid cultural properties at the national and international levels. But this attempt serves only to highlight the amorphous nature of these rights—especially the possibility of fair use and public domain—and the massive primitive accumulation of our cultural patrimony and the power entailed by the unequal access to legal resources between major corporate owners and the average users. Insofar as the law and the state protect these unequally distributed rights, the law and the state themselves risk losing their legitimacy, a possibility productively explored in the recent work of Eduardo M. Peñalver and Sonia Katyal (2007, 2010). And the more aspects of the culture—and cultural practices—that fall under the protection of these policies, the more opportunities there will be to encourage "property outlaws" of all kinds, opening up ever more generalized threats not only to ownership but also to the sovereignty of the state that protects it.

Indeed, as I have argued elsewhere, the dramatic return of the quintessential bad subject—the pirate—in myth and reality, the high seas and the dark web, should reignite our discussions about the liberal state and its relationship to property, primitive accumulation, labor, and culture (Johnson Andrews 2014, 2018). After all, the original copyright pirates (discussed in Chapter 2) were ultimately challenging the enclosure of the commons, the imposition of capitalist social relations, and the newly hewn political ideologies and institutions shoring up this new hegemonic consensus. In our own era, one can draw a fairly straight line from Napster to #Occupy to Trump—or at least to a version of the populist character Trump played on the campaign trail. Each of these points has challenged the fundamental culture of property for which neoliberal politicians and economists have long claimed that "there is no alternative." As Angela Nagle (2017) argues in her recent account of the rise of the alt-right on Internet chatrooms and social media, part of the appeal of Trump—particularly among young white men—is in the ways in which his campaign and the culture around it were framed as transgressions of the dominant social and cultural norms, a framing that is normally associated with the left but was adroitly appropriated by the right.

The xenophobic character of Trump's populism is indisputable, as it is in the political appeals of Marine Le Pen and Rassamblement National in France, Nigel Farage and the UK Independence Party in the United Kingdom, and elsewhere. But this character is articulated with a rhetorical turn toward autarky and protectionism that is indicative of a politics of the double movement akin to Polanyi's original concept. Adolf Hitler and the Nazis are most often coded in terms of their white-supremacist and anti-Semitic appeals. But for Polanyi, as an economic anthropologist, the more important feature of the rise of fascism in the 1930s was the centralization of state authority in a leader that promised to provide social protection from the ravages of the market. Polanyi finds the rise of a form of authoritarian populism in Russia, Germany, and the United States to be similar in important ways: "the purport of fascism or socialism or new deal is part of the story itself," but "the origins of the cataclysm lay in the utopian endeavor of economic liberalism to set up a self-regulating market system" (2001, loc. 1320). In short, as in that earlier emergence of the double movement, Trump and his cohort are clearly drawing on angst in response to neoliberalism—shuttered factories, laid-off workers, precarity, misery, and "deaths of despair" (Monnat 2016).

The difference is that, just as neoliberalism was a counter response to the earlier double movement for social protection against the ravages of the market, Trump and company have articulated their politics as a response to what Fraser calls the "triple movement" for emancipation—the cultural movements pressing for the expansion of civil rights and liberties, particularly along lines of race, gender, and sexuality. Because these movements for emancipation were articulated with the "Third Way" neoliberal politics of Clinton, Tony Blair, and others, Trump's reactionary articulation represents what we might call a "counter triple movement" against the identity politics, egalitarianism, and pleas for tolerance and inclusion that have become prominent features of not only the academic and cultural left but also neoliberal capitalism itself.

While there were massive protests against the travel ban at the end of his first week, Trump's executive order pulling the United States out of the Trans-Pacific Partnership and his demand to renegotiate the terms of NAFTA earlier in the week were all but uncontroversial. Right or wrong, these neoliberal policies have long been blamed for the erosion of jobs and livelihoods. And despite the fact that the U.S. Democratic Party has long made peace with neoliberalism as the dominant hegemonic ideology, it was the radical right—from Hayek and Friedman to Barry Goldwater, Ronald Reagan, and Margaret Thatcher—that instantiated the fundamentalist culture of property, often by implicitly and explicitly articulating their policies as a form of resistance to the progressive movements for liberation.

While Fraser and other critics from the left see this articulation as conjunctural—and the "cultural left" as being responsible for this reaction—I find this periodization somewhat suspect. White supremacy is (and has been) intrinsic to the legitimacy of the U.S. state since before the Declaration of independence and the Constitution, through the Civil War and unfinished Reconstruction, and to today. As Ira Katznelson discusses in his book *Fear Itself* (2013), most of the New Deal policies were crafted to win the approval of southern lawmakers, who refused to allow those policies to equally help black and white Americans. Cowie adds to this discussion the acknowledgment that the United States of the 1930s had some of the most restrictive immigration policies of its history, due to the 1924 legislation restricting immigration from anywhere but the (mostly white) countries of Western Europe. In his troubling book *Hitler's American Model: The United States and the Making of Nazi Race Law* (2017), James Q. Whitman notes that the Nazi lawyers attempting to draft their own white-supremacist laws looked to U.S. racial codes and this 1924 law (among other legislation). Thus, while it is upsetting that the current U.S. Attorney General Jeff Sessions stated his admiration for that 1924 law in a radio interview with Steve Bannon a few months before the 2016 election, it is less an aberration from U.S. history than a key component of its mainstream. If the New Deal was a "great exception" to the protection of property rights and the rule of capital over labor, then the "triple movement" for the more egalitarian distribution of those protections is the great exception to the white-supremacist patriarchy that usually walks hand in hand with these capitalist premises.

Indeed, it would be more accurate to see the economic aspects of the counter double movement of neoliberalism to be of a piece with the political and cultural movements running counter to the triple movement of emancipation. Richard Nixon, Reagan, and now Trump have all been guilty of playing up these reactionary impulses, but it is more accurate to see them as savvy politicians capitalizing on already existing anxieties than instigators of these more fundamental cultural impulses and political forces. Cultural studies scholar Jayson Harsin (2010, 2012) has noted that the political support for New Deal policies began to evaporate once it became clear that they would help more than just white people. And in her recent controversial history of the origins of the Koch-funded Law and Economics institutions at George Mason University (GMU), Nancy MacLean (2017) argues that the neoliberal political economic thought of James Buchanan and others was initially developed in Virginia as an intellectual challenge to desegregation, branding the federal efforts at integration as a form of government coercion and an infringement on private property. Maclean traces the intellectual origins of this neoliberal movement to John C. Calhoun, who developed his version of these arguments as a senator from South Carolina during the run-up to the

Civil War, when more millionaires lived in Mississippi than in New York and the value of slaves as capital was greater than that of the railroads. But we could as easily trace it to the author of South Carolina's original colonial charter: John Locke.

In Chapter 2 I look at the Lockean origins of this culture of property, and in Chapter 3 I examine the Law and Economics movement that has helped rearticulate these ideas for the present era. While the stated mission of that interdisciplinary enterprise is simply to bring economics and the law into conversation, the conversation is limited to using what people outside the movement would identify as libertarian, Austrian, classical liberal, or, following Friedman, "neoliberal" understandings of economics. This viewpoint means seeing the state's role as limited to the protection of property of all kinds. Thus, like the liberal capitalist view of property rights, IPR maximalists are an interest group and an ideological position. The advocates for maximalist IPR therefore form just one division of the "Neoliberal Thought Collective" that Philip Mirowski (2013) describes, but it is an important one. The Law and Economics movement, like the maximalist advocates for copyright, was inspired by a set of conjunctural circumstances: the transformation of U.S. law and the economy during and after the New Deal. Seeing the New Deal as an affront to the natural laws governing the relationship of state and economy, this insurgent group of lawyers, economists, and political scientists set out to reorient the U.S. state toward classical liberal principles.

Fraser argues that these recent articulations of the counter movement should alert us to the need for a movement that will combine the impulses behind the social protection from neoliberalism and the emancipation from resurgent misogyny, racism, and xenophobia. I agree that the current conjunction—and especially the U.S. context—demands just this approach. However, given the recent emphases of cultural studies on issues of emancipation and liberation in terms of these diverse categories of subjectivity, I contend that it is most important to consider the ways in which neoliberalism and the culture of property have influenced the category that most of us have in common: that of laborers. As Christopher May says in his critique of the idea of "the information society":

> Most of us still need to go to work, where there remains an important division between those who run the company and those who work for it, not least in terms of rewards. When we look at what allows some of us to become rich and the rest of us to get by on our pay and pensions, this still has something to do with who owns what. (2002, p. 2)

My critique of IPR (and of the so-called Free Culture movement of Lessig and others) understands these rights' expansion in scope and scale as part of a larger neoliberal assault on the rights of citizens and workers and of the reactionary reorientation of the U.S. state (and, through the WTO, the International Monetary Fund [IMF], and the World Bank, the direction of many other states) toward the protection of capitalist profits over the needs of the larger society. Insofar as we now live in a society that claims culture as part of the economy, and insofar as our legal system is increasingly structured to prioritize the needs of capitalist property owners, there is nothing unique about the value produced around IP or the protection of that value by the neoliberal state. The Free Culture movement has identified the renewed visibility of the social production of value, which should inspire a deeper reflection on property rights and neoliberalism more generally. The only way to truly challenge the increased rule and role of IPR, therefore, is to challenge the "propertarian ideology" (Travis 2000) of the neoliberal state. This challenge, in turn, will provide the grounding for precisely the kind of multipronged movement to combat not only the resurgent white-male supremacy but also the crippling economic policies that have created the inequality, carceral discipline, and diseases of despair that are likely to be the scourge of all in the coming years.

Culture, Property, and the Myth of Balance

We have good reason to be alarmed at the changes underway in the policies of IPR: the laws that proscribe IPR have been expanded in *scope* and *scale* on the domestic (U.S.) and international levels. Within the United States, a sampling of this expansion includes the criminalization of circumventing digital rights management (DRM) in the Digital Millennium Copyright Act (DMCA) of 1996; the extension of copyright terms by an additional twenty years through the Copyright Term Extension Act of 1998; the Prioritizing Resources and Organization for Intellectual Property (PRO-IP) Act of 2007, which increases civil and criminal penalties for copyright and trademark violations and creates a cabinet-level position for the national and international enforcement of IPR; and a slew of highly public court cases and civil lawsuits against so-called music and movie pirates, trademark infringers, and patent violators. The now infamous Stop Online Piracy Act (SOPA)—which public protests and private lobbying managed to beat back—was not signed into law in 2012, but different iterations of its most toxic aspects continue to circulate. Most of these increase only the *scope* of the protection—for instance, the length of time the IPR is protected, the move to making piracy or DRM circumvention a criminal (as opposed to merely civil) offense, the increased resources in executive and judicial institutions for the laws' enforcement, and the transformation of small elements of copyrighted materials, such as a quote from a movie script, whose length would not usually qualify for protection, into trademarked properties.

At the international level, this increased scope is applied at a greater *scale*. The Trade-Related Aspects of Intellectual Property Rights (TRIPS) rider was made essential in the reincarnation of the General Agreement on Tariffs and Trade (GATT; i.e., the WTO) to supplement the treaties and rules administered by the United Nations' (UN's) World Intellectual Property Organization (WIPO). As May (2007) and others have argued, the latter laws were seen as too soft on developing countries, kowtowing to their needs and lacking clear enforcement mechanisms. TRIPS was intended, in no small part, to give countries like the United States (and their multinational corporations and investors operating abroad) some clout in forcing these increased rules in other countries. TRIPS is connected to the WTO's "dispute resolution" mechanisms, which allow for retaliatory enforcement procedures—such as trade sanctions—when countries fail to protect IPR.

Each of these developments represents a move to more forcefully protect IPR. I call maximalist the above legislation, the interest groups that support it, and its corresponding ideological position within the larger debate. The term *maximalist* in relation to IPR in this book should be understood as a position advocating the protection of "intangible" IPR in as stringent and forceful a manner as "tangible" property rights, increasing in scope and scale. Although this maximalist position in the debate over IPR is an ideological position, supported by various legal and economic theories explored throughout this study, it is also peopled by well-defined interest groups. Like the condition known as globalization, maximalist protection of IP was brought about through policies written and implemented by a handful of powerful actors. Peter Drahos and John Braithwaite interviewed a senior U.S. trade representative in 1994 who claimed that "probably less than 50 people were responsible for TRIPS." Key players in the U.S. pharmaceutical, computer-chip, and media-content industries were given key positions in the advisory committees setting the U.S. trade agenda in the Uruguay Round; they then partnered with European and Japanese conglomerates to draft the "intellectual property principles that became the blueprint for TRIPS" (Drahos and Braithwaite 2003, p. 12). The work of lobbyists behind the scenes has become a mainstay of U.S. trade and IP policy making: leaked documents recently showed that Hollywood lobbyists helped the Office of the U.S. Trade Representative (USTR) draft arguments opposing WIPO's Marrakesh treaty, a policy that would help provide access to their content for the visually impaired (Masnick 2013), and lobbyists for content and pharmaceutical industries had similar input in the secret drafting of the Trans-Pacific Partnership, with both groups looking to dilute equivalent fair use and public-domain uses of their products (Liebelson 2015).

As Drahos and Braithwaite point out, these interest groups consistently enlist the "analytical backing and justification" of such think tanks as the Heritage Foundation, the American Enterprise Institute, and the Hoover Institution by funding conferences, bankrolling specific projects, and making direct financial contributions (2003, p. 70). These think tanks and their financial backers generally support a maximalist view of protecting IPR, a view often held alongside a commitment to the supposedly fundamental and inviolable principles of private ownership, free markets, and limited state regulation.

This ideological, legal, and occasionally repressive effort at reforming the cultural norms and social practices of countries around the world is matched by attempts to materially control what Lessig calls "the technology to capture and spread tokens of culture," using DRM, encryption, digital signatures on commodities produced in global commodity chains, and other methods (2008, p. 116). By making it harder to transfer and copy—and making it *legal* to make it harder to transfer and copy—the maximalists seek to transform the ideological position that IPR is property into a natural principle of modern culture. In other words, they hope to reify it, making it an obstacle to be navigated rather than a culturally constituted juridical fiction to be negotiated, employing civil lawsuits, criminal law, and even trade sanctions to force the emergent practices of piracy and counterfeiting back into obscurity and social disrepute.

While I do not agree with this maximalist position in the least, it is not because I see IPR as being unique. Instead, I find maximalists to be the latest in a long chain of apologists for commodification, primitive accumulation, and the social division of labor and value—and I assert that we should resist this longer process first. The more complete privatization of U.S. popular culture was one of the most important processes of the twentieth century. As I have examined at length (Johnson Andrews 2016), the cultural studies tradition was at least partially founded to challenge and understand the implications of the commodification of popular culture. This commodification has itself been increasing in scale and scope since the beginning of industrial capitalism, but especially since the middle of the twentieth century. Therefore, it is not surprising that, having saturated our "lifeworld" with these privately owned commodities for the past half century or so, the erstwhile owners of said properties have returned to claim their pound of our collective consciousness.

Yet if we look at the principles of liberalism as they have operated throughout the history of Western capitalism regarding productive property in relation to the state, I would argue it makes perfect sense that maximalists are asking for protection from the states of the world for the valuable property they now own, even if that property is "cultural." Liberal capitalism is founded on the principle of using the state to protect the socially created value embodied in private property, particularly property in the means of production. This principle has come to the fore in Western culture in the era of neoliberal retrenchment (aided by the Law and Economics movement mentioned above); in the policies advancing what we now understand as globalization, this principle was explicitly emphasized above all others.

Unfortunately, a majority of the scholars criticizing this maximalist position go out of their way to uphold this reified culture of property. Most of these critics of the maximalist position are primarily interested in "the issues that stem from assuming a metaphorical relationship between property and intellectual property" (May 2000, p. 11). They say that IP's unique characteristics demand different considerations than those of property more generally. IP is intertwined with what they call "culture," and there we must tread lightly and "balance" the need for protection and incentives with the need for openness. Among others, issues of free speech (which rely on the free use of the public domain) and economic development (which are supposed to be different in the "information economy") mandate against this regulation. Further, the expansion of digitization means that more aspects of the social and natural world can be understood as "information" and, therefore, "property." This situation requires what they call a "balanced" view: property rights in general are inviolable, but extending these property rights to IP should be done with caution and balance. I explore these arguments but am more concerned with their foundational principle—that the reified culture of property rights is beyond question.

Most participants in this debate presume that its impetus stems from the processes unleashed by the political and technological projects of globalization and digitization. The distributed production of global commodity chains and peer-to-peer (p2p) networks helps make visible, on the one hand, the social production of value and, on the other, the arbitrary boundaries of the legal fiction of property. While there are obviously material differences between these forms of production and more tangible production processes, there is continuity to the enclosure of both, particularly in light of globalization and digitization.

For instance, balanced IPR critic and legal scholar Yochai Benkler (2007) has drawn attention to the U.S. Federal Trademark Dilution Act of 1995, arguing that material transformations are driving the further enclosure of our cultural commons. Traditional trademark law protected trademarks from *infringement*, meaning that companies making similar products could not use similar names, logos, or other identifying symbols because doing so would confuse the customer. This law was not for the benefit of the company but the customer, who needed to have faith that products branded with the same mark were made by the same company. The 1995 antidilution law changed this intent, because it saw trademarks, in Benkler's words, as communicating "cultural" rather than "commercial" meanings.

The law restricting *dilution* expanded this protection to encompass *any* product that had a mark, logo, or the like that was similar to the trademark owner's, regardless of whether there could be any confusion, particularly in the case of well-known brands. Benkler says this expansion is evidence that "the product sold in these cases is not a better shoe or shirt—the product sold is the brand. And the brand is associated with a cultural and social meaning that is developed purposefully by the owner of the brand so that people will want to buy it" (2007, p. 448). The capitalization of seemingly immaterial social and cultural meaning, however, is not just a randomly generated necessity: it is the product of a material transformation in the global economy (Lury 2004). The problems Benkler identifies in the 1995 act were arguably exacerbated by the Trademark Dilution Revision Act of 2006, as it is especially geared toward protecting the global industrial trademarks most deeply intertwined with our cultural ways of knowing.

These material transformations, often understood in terms of globalization, are interwoven with concerns over IPR. A U.S. Government Accountability Office (GAO) report often cited as an early landmark in U.S. anxiety over international IPR presents the counterfeit of U.S. trademarked products as a primary concern:

> The recent increase in concern over inadequate protection of U.S. intellectual property rights is associated largely with the economic development of several newly industrialized countries. Many businesses in these countries have attained the capability for mass production and distribution but lack name brand recognition and find it difficult to compete with established products. Therefore, they often resort to reproducing products already well known in the world marketplace. (1987, p. 2)

The report warns against counterfeiting as a strategy used by foreign corporations to leapfrog, expediting a move "up the value chain"—a concern that is contingent on seeing the United States and U.S. corporations as sitting at the top of a value chain, where the "ideas" are produced.

Certainly it is possible that foreign firms posed legitimate threats in this regard. Robert Brenner (2006) sees this leapfrogging as a primary cause of the falling profitability of U.S. firms on a global scale, but he situates this concern in the early 1970s and focuses on the gains of technology transfer rather than IPR violations per se. The strategy at the time was initiated by Western corporations aiming to employ cheaper, less-organized labor through global sourcing. The trade initiatives of the 1970s and 1980s—primarily concerned with the sourcing of U.S. apparel and computer technology—were also instrumental in the early articulation of what later became the blueprint for global IPR protection. Drahos and Braithwaite (2003) cite the Reagan-era Caribbean Basin Initiative as one of the first tarries in the IPR war; Ellen Israel Rosen (2002) says that the same trade regime transformed the import/export ratios between the Caribbean countries and the United States, and eventually between Mexico and the United States, particularly in relation to apparel goods. These trade regimes gave preference to what Jane Collins (2003) calls "branded marketers." Unlike traditional branded clothing manufacturers, which might own factories somewhere, these firms focus on the "high-value-added" work of developing brand identity—work that becomes extremely profitable when the products to which the brand is attached are produced through contracts to foreign firms that assume all the risk of purchasing brick-and-mortar factories and dealing with the complications of low-paid laborers. To paraphrase Benkler, the trade regime gave preference to companies that thought of themselves as selling only a brand.

The same firms concerned with trademark dilution in the United States are concerned with trademark dilution *and* trademark infringement abroad. Benkler's observation about the material changes in the ways in which brands are considered is rooted in this global contingency—that the value of the brand is produced in a longer cultural process of meaning making, analogous to the ways in which the branded products are themselves produced through a global chain of production. In both cases, the IPR owner sits at the top of the hierarchy of value. Protecting this immaterial value is a key policy priority, but the profitable exploitation of this mark is ultimately based on very material realities. And all of this is related not just to a random set of new precedents or of technological change (Lessig and Benkler mostly consider the latter) but to global neoliberal capitalism as the dominant political economic system.

If globalization demands the expansion of the scale of IPR protection, digitization and innovations in science and technology allow for the expansion of its scope. For instance, the ability to capture the essence of a living organism in a sequence of DNA creates the possibility that intrinsically different aspects of nature and human culture can be classified under the signifier of "information." So software programs (copyright), corn-seed varieties (patents), and the visual signifier of the Coca-Cola Company (trademark) are all protected under the same kind of rubric. Legal scholar James Boyle calls this a "homologization of forms of information," a rhetorical move justified (in the dominant discourse) because of "their liquidity, in the monetary sense of easy conversion from one form to another" (1996, p. 7). In other words, because they can all be captured digitally, they can be considered essentially identical as "information." Homologizing these varied objects under the heading of "information" or "intellectual property" means that "ideas originally applied to one 'information area' seem to apply to another, first in metaphor and then in technological reality. The same problems arise in area after area and, increasingly, solutions are borrowed too" (ibid.). In other words, as May notes, the problem is the expansion of the scope of this metaphorical homologization between information and tangible property to include more and more elements of social and cultural life. In a review of Boyle's book, Mark Lemley agrees, saying that the problem is not just with the homologization of information but also that "there is currently a strong tendency to 'propertize' everything in the realm of information" and that "the power the intellectual property owner has over those rights is increasing," tendencies that he attributes to the now hegemonic Chicago School Law and Economics movement (1997, p. 873).

While balanced IPR critics try to limit their observations to an analytical distinction between material and immaterial property, maximalist advocates recognize the contemporary continuity between the production of value in tangible and intangible property and demand that the liberal state protect all these forms of value as property of the legal owners. I assert that proponents of the balanced position are challenging the continuum of property from the wrong direction: instead of trying to stem the downstream torrents of privatization, it is better to begin closer to the source—at the more fundamental culture of property and the liberal state that protects it. The conflict that Boyle and others see between the amazing potential of globalization and digitization and the maximalist attempt to channel this potential according to the dictates of the reified culture of property is not just a contemporary phenomenon but a recurring tension in capitalist modernity.

In short, the conflict over IPR highlights what Ellen Meiksins Wood argues are two different visions of modernity: one sees modernity as an ongoing process that requires balance, democratic participation, and rational inquiry, which allows for the universal improvement of the human condition in all its particularity; the other sees improvement not in terms of the improvement of humanity but in terms of "the improvement of *property*, the ethic—and indeed the science—of profit, the commitment to increasing the productivity of labor, the production of exchange value, and the practice of enclosure and dispossession" (2002, pp. 188–189; emphasis original). The latter is most clearly articulated in the principles of classical liberalism, and its tension with the other face of modernity—the more innovative, democratic energy—is recognized as a problem by critics of IPR. However, the more fundamental culture of property is so deeply engrained as a cultural dominant at the heart of the neoliberal resurgence of global capitalism that it often inspires critics of the maximalist position to see more liberalism as the only answer to too much property.

Despite this basic similarity between the maximalists' position and that of its balanced critics, many of these critics have also developed powerful arguments about the ways in which value is produced in IPR that are strikingly similar to criticisms made of property in general a century and a half ago. For instance, the peer-to-peer (p2p) process of social valorization championed by balanced IPR scholars, including Lessig and Benkler, is crucial evidence in their case against the maximalist position: they just seem unaware of how these arguments could be as easily applied to material production. Because they see the division between mental and manual labor as natural, they are unable to see the continuity of this social valorization in material production processes—and its expropriation by what could be argued are invalid owners. Their *lacunae* are all the more true when the properties in question are deemed to be key components of the productive economy, as they are in the so-called information society. By making visible the social process of valorization, they help undermine the softest, yet most important, pillars of this reified culture of property: value. These critics, therefore, act as a paltry opposition to the maximalist position and as the other key foil for the arguments of this book.

Un-Locke-ing Culture: Labor, Value, and the State

In her article "Copyright as Myth," Jessica Litman discusses "the problem of unintentional or inadvertent infringement" of previously published works. Contrasting the mandates of copyright law (which would require permissions from all sources of inspiration) with those of the creative process of authorship, she declares that "all authorship is fertilized by the work of prior authors" (1991, p. 243). Declarations of this kind are commonplace in the arguments against maximalist intellectual property rights: the labors of the creative individual that intellectual property rights are supposed to sanctify with ownership are inevitably the product of a variety of other socially produced inputs. This description is also true for other forms of productive property and of the individual most often cited as inspiring the philosophical justification for property rights in general: John Locke. Locke's defense of private property and the liberal state is infused with the ideas of a myriad of sources that he synthesizes from what Williams might call an emergent "structure of feeling" in seventeenth-century thought. Chief among these, as Chapter 2 elaborates, was the ideology of "improvement" central to the natural science movement known as the Invisible College that included Sir Francis Bacon. I follow a convention in the literature of property rights in attributing authorship of this idea to Locke, but it should be understood that he is just the most-oft-cited representative of a wider cultural formation.

As I outline in subsequent chapters, scholars have a renewed interest in Locke's defense of property precisely because of the conjunctural struggle over IPR and property rights in general as a result of globalization and digitization. I argue that this interest is due to the centrality of the concepts of labor and value within his *Treatise*. Locke's defense of property is really a defense of the fundamental culture of property that is under threat and that maximalist IPR—which relies on Lockean assumptions about ownership, value, and its protection by the state—is meant to rescue. Likewise, balanced critics of the maximalist position reproach the maximalists for their overreach in applying Locke's defense of property to IP. Both, in other words, see Locke as germinal to the debate about IPR. The harmony of their views exists because the debate about IPR is really a debate about the basic culture of property in Anglo-American society.

Locke bases his defense of the liberal state on what he calls a "natural law" and partially articulates this theory in response to Robert Filmer. Filmer begins from the then-popular biblical claim that God gave everyone the land in common; thus, the only way for private property to exist would be for a God-appointed "patriarch" (or monarch) to legitimate its removal from that common. A democratic government would begin with property held in common, parceled out by popular mandate: private property would necessitate a God-appointed monarch or an everlasting series of plebiscites. To Locke, who was arguing for a parliamentary monarchy, the prospect of a return to absolutism was unacceptable, yet he believed that property must be privately held. On this count, Locke also had to argue against the religiously oriented popular movements that emerged during the English Civil War, especially those of the Levellers and the Diggers: drawing from pirated Protestant pamphlets, they asserted that, insofar as there was a natural law, it was that "God is no respecter of persons." This view was taken, in its most extreme versions, to mean that political *and* economic democracy should exist, meaning that all people should have the vote and that the enclosures of the previous century should be reversed—and maybe the property system should even be dismantled (McNally 1989).

In writing his treatise, Locke had to argue for property in a secular, parliamentary, political democracy in a way that would justify both while limiting the possibility of economic democracy. His solution is to make one contingent on the other: government could be democratic, but only insofar as it supported property. Rights to property, Locke insists, were given by a natural law, which preceded the state; instead, private ownership of property flowed from the individual labor of appropriation. To paraphrase, even though God might have given everyone the world in common, there was a natural law that said that once someone had "improved" a piece of land through his or her labor, this individual could claim exclusive ownership over it. On this basis, Locke says that a democratic government could exist provided that the government protected this natural law; insofar as the government failed to protect private property, that government was illegitimate.

The role of value in this argument pivots on the curious idea of the labor of "improvement" that lies behind Locke's claim. While he was interested in matters of politics, Locke was more driven to lay down a new economic model. As mentioned above, he was inspired by the Baconian idea of improvement that had justified much of the enclosures and the transformation of swamps and other spaces of the English countryside into supposedly more efficient farmland. His secondary goal in the *Treatise* was to advocate for more efficient farms and a more frugal gentry running them. In Locke's argument, the labor of improvement referred not to the laborers themselves, many of whom increasingly had no land of their own; instead, the natural law of the appropriation extended from the laborers one employed back to the owner of the property. In short, the justification of private property still held if the labor of improvement and appropriation was done by the owner's servants or tenants rather than the owner. Since the more efficient farms that Locke advocated required a good number of these laborers, paid in wages, the economic dimension of this value creation was increasingly hypothetical. Little of the labor of appropriation was done by the people claiming ownership in the improved property. The value that was produced—the improvement of the land through the labor of appropriation—did not come from the individual laborer but instead took place through a much wider process.

Karl Marx found this wider process of social valorization essential to understanding the true nature of capitalist property relations. After all, if the economic argument for improvement necessitated the state-enforced enclosure of the commons, the dispossession of the cottagers, and the collective use of their labor in capitalist farms, it hardly followed that this argument justified a government that protected the individual property owner on the basis of "natural law." However, as in the maximalist defense of IPR today, Marx notes that the defenders of the reified culture of property in his own time

> like to present every attack on the capitalist *form of appropriation* as an attack on the other kind of property, the property that has been worked for, indeed an attack *on all property*. [. . .] The general *legal* conception, from Locke to Ricardo, is therefore that of *petty-bourgeois property*, while the relations of production they actually describe belong to the *capitalist mode of production*. [. . .]
>
> 1) economically they oppose private property resting on labour, and show the advantages of the expropriation of the mass [of workers] and the capitalist mode of production;
> 2) but *ideologically and legally* the *ideology* of *private property resting on labour* is transferred without further ado to property resting on the *expropriation of the direct producer*. (1977, pp. 1083–1084; emphasis original)

By illuminating the extended process of reproduction—ignored by the economic and political defenses of Lockean property—and the illegitimate legal title to the collectively produced value, Marx hoped to undermine this culture of property more generally and the system containing "this fixation of social activity, this consolidation of what we ourselves produce into an objective power above us, growing out of our control, thwarting our expectations, bringing to naught our calçulation" (Marx and Engels 2011, p. 53).

Marx was looking at the industrial form of capitalism, but many of the presumptions about this culture remain. The power of capital in relation to labor and the assumption that laborers are less important to the production of value is central to the contemporary capitalist order. As the copyright critic and legal scholar Boyle points out, "intellectual property and its conceptual neighbors may bear the same relationship to the information society as the wage-labor nexus did to the industrial manufacturing society of the 1900s" (1996, p. 13). Boyle says that the relationship between IPR and the information society has been underanalyzed, which may have been the case before his path-breaking work. But now the need is to analyze the analogy he raises between the basic structure of capital and property in both ages—and how we should therefore understand the push to instantiate the maximalist position in the present day. In both times, the legal structure demanded that all the benefits of the economy of scale flow to owners concentrated at the top, and in both times a concerted effort was made to create the cultural and ideological legitimation for a state that so nakedly gave preference to a small handful of owners instead of the majority of precariously employed workers.

The ideology justifying this circumstance is still based on the notion that the law protects and incentivizes the individual entrepreneur. This entrepreneur/owner, like the owner of a large farm in Locke's time, is taken, legally and culturally, to be the producer of all the value contained in a property; the only possible role for the state in this liberal conceptualization is one that protects this individual property, even in what are socially produced values. Liberalism thus makes the law protecting property, which is supposed to be based in some way on a democratic agreement, an apolitical fact of life. As I detail in the conceptual framework in Chapter 1, instead of there being a mutual constitution between law and culture, law becomes a reified structure: it reifies the cultural process that could reform the law and make it fit the transformed social relation.

Critics of IPR are most attuned to this process of valorization in relation to digitization or what Jenkins calls *Convergence Culture* (2006). In *Remix*, his 2008 book on copyright, Lessig builds on Jenkins's descriptions of online "participatory culture." In relation to the cross-platform, multimedia environment inhabited by the so-called digital natives of the early twenty-first century, Jenkins says that we should begin to think differently about how media—and meaning and value—are produced and consumed: "Rather than talking about media producers and consumers as occupying separate roles, we might now see them as participants who interact with each other according to a new set of rules that none of us fully understands" (2006, p. 3). Therefore, the rules that are currently in place are being slowly undermined, and the reified culture of property is becoming suspect. Lessig and others hope to help craft this new set of rules—but only in relation to intangible, intellectual property, especially copyright. Recognizing this extended process of valorization should also undermine the legitimacy of the broader reified culture of property.

In terms of so-called real property, this reified culture remains, but the struggle over IPR is helping throw it into greater relief. As the critic Lessig maintains in his book *Free Culture*:

> We live in a world that celebrates "property." I am one of those celebrants. I believe in the value of property in general, and I also believe in the value of that weird form of property that lawyers call "intellectual property." A large, diverse society cannot survive without property; a large, diverse, and modern society cannot flourish without intellectual property. (2004, p. 33)

But he undermines his own argument, saying, "But it takes just a second's reflection to realize that there is plenty of value out there that 'property' doesn't capture. I don't mean 'money can't buy you love,' but rather, value is plainly part of a process of production" (Lessig 2004, p. 28).

Critics of maximalist IPR recognize this extended process of production, and I argue that this recognition is one of the primary challenges to the Lockean understanding of value within the culture of property. Although Lessig and others place a limit on the conclusions they can derive from recognizing this extended process of production, if we take seriously the rediscovery of the social production of value, we should see that social production of value as relatively widespread, far beyond these recently commodified dimensions. The notion that there is "value out there that 'property' doesn't capture" is something one could argue about most of the value that markets claim to measure and distribute. But to move in this direction would require a much more fundamental critique of the capitalist culture, which assumes private property as an inviolable concept. As we will see in the case of digitization and globalization, this assumption is true even when it is obvious that the gains in efficiency are due not to the owner but to the extended process of valorization he or she is able to hook into. Lessig focuses on digitization, but the expanded process of production through commodity chains and the international division of labor has a similar effect—and, in actuality, has more at stake in the projection of IPR on a global scale.

Critics of the expansion of IPR within the United States, the United Kingdom, Canada, and Australia rightly point out the multitude of contradictions in current IPR policies. Even if enforcement were workable, they point to the impact that it would have on culture. Here they mean "culture" in the narrowest possible sense: the free exchange of information and ideas and the archive of previously exchanged content that we build on. The limited reach of the coercive forces of the law and the mercurial exchange and mutual elaboration of meaning through media content are important elements of the crisis, but they get nowhere near its fundamentals. To get there, we must talk about culture—and think about property and value—in a deeper way. This means understanding the mutual constitution of law and culture—and the fundamental crisis created when they no longer link up in a relation of efficacy. Imparting this understanding is my primary goal in Chapter 1.

These circuits of valorization are made more visible by the "participatory culture" made possible by media convergence and digitalization *and* the distributed production of economic globalization. Just as value is produced through an extended process of valorization in the networked, digital environment, the extended process—and myriad of positions—in the production of globalized commodities more generally also undermines the culture of property, showing it to be the product of a narrow, insular worldview of a particular society. These processes together undermine the culture of property in general, and this resulting crisis calls for the imposition of IPR on a global scale. As Marx said long ago, "Whenever, through the development of industry and commerce, new forms of intercourse have been evolved (e.g., ensurance [*sic*] companies, etc.), the law has always been compelled to admit them among the modes of acquiring property" (Tucker 1972, p. 188). This pattern has held true today with the supposed arrival of the postindustrial, information economy: the novel process of extending these rights inevitably reveals the political nature of the rights to property and the naked force required to implement one allocation of value over another. In reference to the rights of labor and capital to the value produced through the process of production, Marx reveals how different positions within that process view their just proportion of the final product differently. Capital insists that it should be able to use the commodity of labor as it sees fit, but "the peculiar nature of the commodity" (i.e., that it is the product of a living human, producing in common with others) gives it rights as well. Each right cancels the other out, creating "an antinomy" "of right against right, both equally bearing the seal of the law of exchange. Between equal rights, force decides" (Marx 1977, p. 344). When the cultural efficacy of law breaks down, when the visible antinomy of these rights undermines the Lockean ideology, the law and the police are used as a last-resort blunt instrument. Many IP scholars are keen to highlight the extended circuits of valorization in the "digital natives" of the first world; few connect these circuits with their counterparts in distributed production on a global scale. Yet it is only by understanding them together, as dual contagions to the culture of property, that we can see the problem—and consider the possible solutions. This book is an attempt to do so.

Outline of Chapters

The conflict over IP is best seen as a conflict over property rights in general. In both cases, the legitimation of the juridical culture of property is underpinned by a specific understanding of the proper political economy of ownership and valorization. As I have argued, this culture of property is undermined by two changes: digitization and globalization. Contemporary critics of IPR are unable to properly articulate the terms of this debate because they readily accept the ideological essentials of the reified culture of property, even as they are able to reverently describe the expanded process of valorization they see in the creative process for the goods protected by this legal regime. On the one hand, seeing the expanded process of valorization through p2p, "remix," and "convergence" culture has exposed the ways in which value is produced more generally to a wider investigation. On the other hand, IP is necessary to preserve the dominance of certain property holders in the domestic sphere as well as the positions of the United States and Western Europe in the international division of labor. Trying to secure these roles through various treaties has resulted in exposing them to the differences in culture throughout the world.

This book is an attempt to outline this culture of property and its origins, permutations, and implications for the global, digital environment. In Chapter 1, I develop the concept of cultural efficacy, which more thoroughly evaluates the questions involved in presenting a "cultural inside." I argue that the field of cultural studies is due for a reexamination of questions of class, property, and capitalism as well as questions of the law and the state in relation to culture. The latter form some of the strongest channels through which the enigmatic "culture as a process" is forced. Until the reification of the latter is questioned and critiqued, cultural studies cannot effectively claim to be a project of global importance or scope; instead, the field will remain a loose kaleidoscope that merely finds ways to describe the apparently chaotic interplay of cultural elements on the ground level rather than ever being able to note the effective closures that determine this process.

Chapter 2 gives an extended history of four processes: the consolidation of the nation-state; the construction of law in relation to culture; the development of the Lockean definition of property in terms of natural law in contrast to other competing ideas about the relationship between property, value, and the state; and the process of primitive accumulation that has allowed this definition to appear legitimate and effective. This history of capitalist private property is more fundamental to the expansion of IPR than to the history of IPR themselves. However, there is a parallel development in both that coincides with a more fundamental cultural construct. Coeval with property rights and IPR is the birth of the modern nation-state. The unitary law of the sovereign nation-state was initially legitimated by the religious patriarchy common to most of the feudal cultures of Western Europe. In the context of England, its earlier separation from the Roman Catholic Empire unsettled this hierarchy of legitimation. Copyright first emerged as a way of controlling the competing religious ideas that might threaten this central authority.

In the brief moment of English absolutism, the expanding authority of the central state was used to force capitalist social relations based on private property onto an unwilling population. The revolution that overturned the feudal hierarchy resulted briefly in a resistance to this imposition; in short order, the unitary rule of law that was supposedly necessary to restrain the limited authority of the central government also restrained the restive population and governed them based on the cultural articulation of "natural law." Copyright joined with other restrictions on movement and religious freedom to reduce the resistance to this imposition. The late Lockean justification of the federal authority in the defense of property rights thus followed a century of developing the ideological apparatuses to legitimate the repressions necessary for primitive accumulation. The erasure of this history serves as a common component of the liberal defense of property, as does the pattern of primitive accumulation that preceded it.

Chapter 3 follows Chapter 2's argument with a discussion of the specific content (i.e., culture) of that law in England and the United States. It describes a more recent struggle over the idea of natural rights to property and the reaction of the Law and Economics movement to the results of this struggle—that is, the welfare state and legal justification of the New Deal. The Law and Economics movement has informed the current legal hegemony in the United States and Lessig's critique of IPR. This chapter argues that the central premise of this movement is faulty because it takes as natural what is actually political and cultural in the legal institution of private property rights and neoclassical economic relations. It takes for granted the cultural efficacy of the system of private property, deriving it from nature instead of a specific articulation of the utilitarian economics and formal power of the state—both of which are overtly criticized from within the movement for attempting to reshape culture according to positive rights.

If the previous chapter looks at the political/legal defense of a certain economic model, Chapter 4 continues by exploring the obverse: the economic arguments in defense of a certain political/legal model. It highlights a disconnect between neoclassical indexes of value (e.g., price) and the social process of valorization from which they are abstracted. Although critics of IPR are able to see the latter with regard to "creative" work, their observations would apply to the products of most other kinds of labor. The chapter outlines the ways in which some concepts from Marx—commodification, primitive accumulation, and the division of labor—help describe, on the one hand, the inadequacy of this index and, on the other hand, the historical, social, and material process whereby it came to appear descriptive in the U.S. context. It develops more fully the concept of "cultural efficacy" to denote the process whereby top-down programs and products gain bottom-up legitimacy. It argues that the implementation of IPR in its current form is indeed a form of unjust appropriation, but this injustice is not limited to intangible property—it is intrinsic to the system that critics of this program otherwise defend.

On this ground, we can turn to the global, digital spaces of the limited reification of the culture of property in general and the culture of IP in particular—and the attempts by policy makers to impose both through trade agreements and other forms of international law. In the end, this is what Herbert Schiller and others meant by cultural imperialism: the attempt to completely transfer the cultural framework of capitalism throughout the developing world, resulting in the global rule of capitalist social relations and the international protection of private property rights, capital investment, and "shareholder value." But only by recognizing this cultural formation, only by working from a coherent, complete conceptualization of culture, with the animating and attenuating dialectics outlined above, can this complete system, idealized in theory and coercive in practice, be critically engaged—nor can the resistance to its imposition be fully comprehended.

The paradox between liberalism and democracy remains salient at this level, and, in part, the uneven development of these processes creates the conflicts that continue to stall the smooth imposition of a global legal environment that would serve capital and property alone. Locally conceived alternatives, emerging in indigenous communities and what Ankie Hoogvelt terms the "post-development" countries of Latin America, are able to witness the limits of the liberal culture of property and rethink the contours of this model in their own context. This resistance, termed "irrational" or "autocratic," also opens a contradictory space of counterhegemonic struggle. The lesson for scholars of cultural studies is not that these areas will produce an alternative model to be applied from the top down elsewhere but that the more deliberative, collaborative understanding of culture—and value and, therefore, property—that emerges from these struggles can inform our criticism of the dominant culture of the hegemonic core. In other words, the lessons to draw from the space where this culture of property is yet to become reified can clarify the limits that current critics of IP set on the prospects for social change. On the other hand, the fact of uneven development should alert us to the continued expropriation of the periphery for the benefit of the core—and show that the simple suturing of the IP regime at the global scale for the benefit of core, postindustrial economies is unethical and unsustainable.

1

Culture, the State, and (Intellectual) Property Rights

The world's largest living organism is mostly invisible. The rhizomorphs and underground networks of mycelia of a honey fungus spread across 3.7 square miles in the Blue Mountains of Oregon, looking for new hosts to consume. The only way it can be seen is through the patterns of its destruction—visible via aerial photographs of dying trees—or by the small, yellow-brown mushrooms that appear above ground, which are the delicious, fruiting bodies of this much larger organism.

Culture and language are often thought of in much the same way: while it is difficult to see the underlying structures that unite the fruiting bodies, it is easy to imagine that they exist. The Swiss linguist Ferdinand de Saussure expressed this methodological problem in the dichotomy between the *langue*, or language system, and the *parole*, or individual speech act: the only way to see the underlying system of language is through the buds of the individual speech acts. Speech is individual, but "language exists perfectly only within a collectivity": "If we could embrace the sum of word-images stored in the minds of all individuals, we could identify the social bond that constitutes language" (Saussure 1961, p. 14).

In the past, capturing "the sum of word-images" of all individuals was a time- and labor-intensive process, such as that of compiling the recently completed *Dictionary of American Regional English*. The bulk of the data for this study were collected between 1965 and 1970 by eighty fieldworkers sent to 1,002 communities to collect answers to a 1,847-item questionnaire. It took five years for the 2.3 million answers provided by nearly three thousand people on reel-to-reel tape recorders to be converted into computer punch cards and another ten years to produce the first volume of the dictionary (Schuessler 2012).

By the time the fifth and final volume of the dictionary was published in 2012, aggregate, geotagged conversations on Twitter had begun to provide linguistic researchers an unprecedented dataset to comb through and identify similar regional variations—such as whether people in different parts of the country are more likely to use the word "uh" versus "um," "soda" versus "pop," or "hella" versus "very" (Lee 2011; Parry 2011; Sonnad 2014; Springer 2012). With a little fine-tuning, these analysts have been able to produce maps of speech spreading into language akin to the aerial photos identifying the destructive signature of the honey fungus.

In their introduction to theories of communication, Armand Mattelart and Michèle Mattelart (1998) note a recurring trend in the use of biological metaphors to describe the relationship between human societies and the systems of meaning, power, and value through which they reproduce and sustain a collective order. In sociology, perhaps the most famous example comes from Herbert Spencer, who coined the phrase "survival of the fittest" in his *Principles of Biology*, suggesting that the success of the rich and the death of the poor were akin to the process of natural selection revealed in Charles Darwin's *Origin of the Species*. Like Karl Marx, Spencer predicted a withering away of the state, but the mechanism for this decline would be the evolution of society as "the spontaneous, integrated growth and not a manufacture, an organically evolving context for the development of heterogeneity and differentiation among the individuals who compose it" (Sciabarra 2006, p. 404). In his understanding:

> Industrial society is the embodiment of "organic society": an increasingly coherent, integrated society-as-organism in which functions are increasingly well defined and parts increasingly interdependent. In this systematic whole, communication is the basic component of organic systems of distribution and regulation. Like the vascular system, the former (made up of roads, canals, and railways) ensures the distribution of nutritive substance. The latter functions as the equivalent to the nervous system, making it possible to manage the complex relations between a dominant centre and its periphery. (Mattelart and Mattelart 1998, pp. 8–9)

In Spencer's early reactionary philosophy—which emerged not coincidentally just after a massive wave of revolts and revolutions in 1848 (Rapport 2009)—the existing social order is akin to a spontaneously generated natural order: the top 1 percent is many hundreds of times wealthier than those in the bottom 1 percent (or even the bottom 30 percent in the United States of the present) simply because they are the thoughtful, fearless innovators who ultimately make that order work. On the flipside in this biologized theory of meritocracy are those who experience lives of servitude, sickness, and early death due their poverty, people who are probably the least fit of our species. In this philosophy, the deaths of those at the bottom are for the best. Spencer called on the thinking of the French biologist Jean-Baptiste Lamarck (1744–1829), who claimed that behavioral traits could be inherited, to suggest that criminals and those with other mental or behavioral abnormalities should be sterilized or institutionalized to prevent their passing these traits to the next generation. The more recent alt-right reliance on terms like "libtard" connect to the now well-known eugenic consequences of this notion of an organic society, leading to some of the history's most heinous crimes against humanity. Of course, some members of the so-called alt-right clearly either disbelieve or revere the Holocaust, so even the notion of it as a crime may be in dispute.

Lamarkism is now purportedly in disrepute, yet Charles Murray and other peddlers of Lamark's intellectual cousins in nineteenth-century race science continue to be influential, not only on the right (the Heritage Foundation recently deployed one of Murray's students to argue for the severe restriction of immigration by claiming that most immigrants suffered from poor IQs, a trait that would be passed on to their children, leading them to be expensive burdens on society) but also in other dominant cultural venues, such as National Public Radio. In 2012, the latter hosted an online, *Buzzfeed*-style quiz asking its listeners and readers "Do You Live in a Bubble?"—a theme Steve Bannon and others have harped on in Donald Trump's victory lap and the middle-left has partially adopted as an explicans for his success. The bubble in question related to Murray's 2012 book, *Coming Apart: The State of White America, 1960–2010.* The quiz asked questions including "Have you or your spouse ever bought a pickup truck?" and "During the 2009–2010 television season, how many of the following series did you watch regularly: *American Idol, Undercover Boss, The Big Bang Theory, Grey's Anatomy, Lost, Desperate Housewives, Two and a Half Men*, etc.?" Answers to the latter question indicated the drift of Murray's argument in *Coming Apart*, or at least one component of it.

Murray contends that the major divide in the United States is between what he calls a new "narrow elite" and the rest of the country, especially in terms of the "new and distinctive culture among a highly influential segment of American society" (2013, p. 29). Jumping off from the equally sketchy pop-sociology presented by his conservative colleague David Brooks in the book *Bobos in Paradise* (2001), he argues that this narrow elite was previously forced to endure the same popular culture as everyone else—drinking Jack Daniels, wearing clothes off the rack, and watching *Ozzie and Harriet*. Like all cultural portrayals of the time, "It was taken for granted that television programs were supposed to validate the standards that were commonly accepted as part of 'the American way of life'—a phrase that was still in common use in 1963" (Murray 2013, pp. 11–12). In short, the way you can determine whether you are part of the bubble created by this "narrow elite" or belong to the "broader elite" is by noting whether you have had to endure the latest Chuck Lorre production or have had better things to do with your time: "Much of that viewing in mainstream America consists of material that is invisible to most of the new upper class—game shows, soap operas, music videos, home shopping, and hit series that members of the new upper class have never watched even once" (ibid., p. 44). This shearing of the everyday culture of the elite and the pedestrian is purportedly the root of many of our political conflicts (especially if, like Murray, by "our" you mean white people of all classes).

He does not explain the what or why of the particular content or practices of this new upper-class culture, but he says it has come into being because more intelligent people (defined by high IQs, which he argues are correlated with higher education and higher income) are intermarrying (elite colleges serve as their primary mating grounds), living with other people with high IQs, and developing a taste bubble to distinguish themselves from the rabble. Murray wants to criticize this bubble and the inequality that it causes, illustrates, and reinforces. But he falls back on pseudoscientific notions of the United States as an IQ meritocracy, where economic and social privileges are legitimately passed on from one generation to another due to the intermarrying of highly educated, highly intelligent, wealthy people. This conception is tenuously joined with his market-oriented explanation of cultural products: if there is now an elite culture, it must be that there is an elite niche market to buy it.

While Murray's Lamarkian assertion of inherited traits (including IQ and helicopter parenting) is a holdover from his earlier work, what is more interesting for our purposes is the assumption that this elite culture is simply an outgrowth of the groups' coalescing. As he puts it, "Put people with greater educational and cognitive similarity together, and you have the makings of greater cultural similarity as well" (Murray 2013, p. 73). But the transition he is discussing should actually create the opposite: the ability of Harvard or Yale to attract the most elite talent from across the country—or even the world—suggests the potential for more cultural diversity (depending on what we mean by that term). But instead, out of these underground networks of genetically similar elites supposedly sprouts a common culture that, whatever its content, is emblematic of the inherent values and concerns of that elite. Indeed, the difference today is not so much in the ways in which culture emerges from this common ground—1950s TV, after all, was part and product of a common culture—than the fact that there is a divide in the body politic.

Murray is far from the ideal cultural theorist, but the role of culture in his explanation of the contemporary hegemonic crisis is exemplary for our purposes, both for the questions he asks (and does not) and the assumptions embedded in his reasoning. He is concerned that the relationship between the organic society and its culture has fissured. Some of this concern is infused with his reactionary notions about race as a kind of genetic bond similar to the honey fungus; class inequality, however, has severed this racial unity. The underlying rhizomes are not of the same genetic stock, and therefore they are no longer producing the fruiting bodies of culture. But, as with many accounts of culture, his description of culture as a widespread practice or media product flips this metaphor on its head. Is culture the common "way of life," the everyday colloquial practices of the average individual? Or is it the mediated representations of those practices? And what is the order of determinations? Does the common everyday culture produce the media representations? Or do those media representations suggest, validate, legitimize, stigmatize, and ultimately produce and reproduce the practices of the everyday? If the organic society is an allegorical honey fungus, this would mean that the cultural mushrooms precede and determine the direction of the rhizomatic growth beneath; or, to return to Saussure, it would mean that the speech act precedes and even produces the structure of the langue.

In effect, then, although Murray is as far away from a Marxist as one can be in the current ideological climate, his rendering of the process through which the culture of the "narrow elite" is produced and then imposed on the rest of the country—through this group's control of the means of cultural production—is almost identical to that discussed in Karl Marx and Friedrich Engels's *The German Ideology* (2011). Their contentions about the division of cultural labor and the relationship between the economic base and the ideological superstructure are infused in Murray's mechanistic rendering of the process whereby the elite developed its own culture. On the other hand, his frustration with this elite is that its members also produce a separate culture of which they are (evidently) not consumers: owners of massive chain restaurants and Budweiser, Hollywood movie producers, and Oprah Winfrey are all members of this narrow elite that shapes the cultural environment for the majority, yet they do not partake in the culture they produce. So, to invoke Stuart Hall's "Two Paradigms" (1980a) of cultural studies, we have culturalism for the rich and structuralism for the poor.

If Murray were to extend this concept to a critique of the larger political economic system, he might be on to something. But instead, he longs for a different moment—a moment when the organic society and its culture existed in unison, for all [white] Americans. Murray's nostalgia for the TV and culture of the 1950s is a perfect illustration of the assumed "value consensus" that Hall says motivated early media and cultural studies. In his article "The Rediscovery of 'Ideology': Return of the Repressed in Media Studies," Hall points first to the dominant paradigm in sociology, a more rigorous iteration of the organic society: Talcott Parsons's structural functionalist "social system." In this system,

> values played an absolutely pivotal role; for around them the integrative mechanisms which held the social order together were organized. Yet what these values were—their content and structure—or how they were produced, or how, in a highly differentiated and dynamic modern industrial capitalist society, an inclusive consensus on "the core value system" had spontaneously arisen, were questions that were not and could not be explained. (1982, p. 60)

The key word here is "spontaneously." The notion of the organic society relies on the assurance that either no coercion is involved—no one forces the values on anyone else—or the hierarchies and values that exist are the self-evident common sense that has developed over the course of history: the result of a process, but a process that is now over.

The content of this culture, these values, is irrelevant because it is assumed, after the fact, to be the result of an achieved consensus. In Murray's telling, abortion, drug use, and crime were stigmatized and stay-at-home mothers and working dads were valorized because these were the statistical norm of the everyday lives of average Americans. And if the Hollywood Production Code dictated these values for all films produced in the United States, that was because the media that emerged from this culture was, to quote Hall again,

> held to be largely reflective or expressive of an achieved consensus. The finding that, after all, the media were not very influential was predicated on the belief that, in its wider cultural sense, the media largely reinforced those values and norms which had already achieved a wide consensual foundation. Since the consensus was a "good thing," those reinforcing effects of the media were given a benign and positive reading. (1982, p. 61)

The media studies work of Hall and other early cultural studies scholars began by questioning these two assumptions—that the dominant culture was the result of a broad consensus and that the media culture was merely a reinforcing reflection of that consensus. Their "rediscovery of ideology" was facilitated first by the sociology of deviance, especially the work of Howard Becker (1997). Murray claims that in "1963, people drank like fish and smoked like chimneys, but illegal drugs were rare and exotic" (2013 p. 14). Becker contends that this was not the result of consensus but an indication of "the power of the alcohol-takers to define the cannabis-smokers as deviant" (Hall 1982, p. 62). This "hierarchy of credibility" gave certain groups "the power to define the rules of the game to which everyone was required to ascribe" (ibid.). And with these rules in place, Louis Althusser's explanation for the mechanisms of "the reproduction of the relations of production" became all the more relevant: the ideological apparatus of the media and culture served to reinforce the rules that were ultimately enforced by the repressive apparatus of the police and prisons.

Culture, then, was a site for the mutual constitution of meaning and power. From one direction, the world must be made to mean, and, in Hall's words, "in order for one meaning [of the same event] to be regularly produced, it had to win a kind of credibility, legitimacy or taken-for-grantedness for itself. That involved marginalizing, down-grading or de-legitimating alternative constructions" (1982, p. 67). Power tries to fix meanings by making it impossible (or inadvisable) to imagine an alternative meaning. This struggle over the meaning of events is most transparent when it is the least reified. In the United States, we regularly see this semiotic struggle after mass shootings, such as those in Newtown, Connecticut, or in San Bernardino, California. In the current U.S. context, the meaning of each of these tragedies is different, depending on which hegemonic bloc you subscribe to. For gun-control advocates, both are further examples of the problems caused by easy-to-acquire firearms. For those resistant to gun control, Newtown's killer played violent video games and fell through the cracks of our feeble mental health system, and the San Bernardino couple were associated with "radical

Islamic terrorism," a string of signifiers so powerful that Trump claims that only brave politicians will articulate them.

And, as Trump knows all too well, by fixing meanings in a certain way, it legitimizes power and/or generates value. For instance, the Newtown, Connecticut, "truther" movement (led by, among other people, Trump supporter Alex Jones) argues that the event itself was staged—no children were killed, no shooting occurred—by the Barack Obama administration in an elaborate plot to generate public demand for stricter gun laws. Followers of the 9/11 "truther" movement share similar beliefs. Jones gained a number of his followers through his participation in that movement, producing and self-publishing two documentaries (Loose Change [2005] and Loose Change 9/11: An American Coup [2009]) outlining the case for 9/11's being an "inside job." Jones has accrued a great deal of cultural power—which Trump found helpful during his campaign—and a small fortune of value: in 2013, it was estimated that Jones's various media and merchandising ventures were grossing more than $10 million per year. Likewise, not only have the conspiracy theories around Newtown and other mass-shooting events been a boon for right-wing politicians; the anxiety over the dominant narrative leading to stronger gun-control laws has consistently led to increased gun sales, an index that declined precipitously with the election of Trump, who was seen as a loyal defender of the Second Amendment.

I come back to value later. The point for now is that I would like to revisit the founding cultural studies interest in the relationship between meaning and power, particularly in relation to law and the state. As Hall has said of theory in general, this chapter is a detour on the way to something more important. The battle over intellectual property rights (IPR)—and property rights in general—is being fought on the grounds of something called "culture." Cultural studies scholars should be able to bring a certain level of expertise to this debate, which requires a coherent conceptualization of culture and its relation to law and the state. Unfortunately, cultural studies scholars have largely abandoned that goal in place of a focus on rhizomes, dynamic processes, subjective agency, and complexity.

Murray's recent book is notable in that he is a scholar whom most in cultural studies would chide for his retrograde politics. Yet lurking beneath these politics is a theory of culture that is similar to that of many contemporary cultural studies scholars, especially those who have adopted the concept of culture to criticize the expansion of IPR. In the balanced copyright position (exemplified by Lawrence Lessig), culture is characterized as an endlessly dynamic process, growing organically out of a cultural environment. It is less clear, however, what the status of this dynamic was in the previous era—that is, before digitization and globalization—and what the role of the formal structures of law and functional pressures of economics were before being upset by the Internet and other new media technologies. Like Murray, many proponents of these versions of culture ignore the previous rounds of primitive accumulation that have sorted the properties—and their attendant meaning, power, and value—into increasingly unequal hierarchies of owners and workers. Taking these rounds into account throws into relief the claims of what Lessig refers to as "our tradition of free culture."

As I argue in the introduction, John Locke and his discussion of value provide the pivot between property and intellectual property (IP). Critics of maximalist IPR unintentionally articulate the first level of this correlation in their conceptualization of "culture." Culture for them, like labor for Locke, is a dynamic energy that inevitably helps propel civilization further. However, unlike Locke, they do not recognize the inherent limits placed on the dynamism of culture within the reified culture of property they inhabit. As I explore in Chapter 3, the neoliberal Law and Economics tradition of the Chicago School represents what we might call the "achieved consensus" for Lessig. Thus, although he talks about a dynamic culture on one level, at a deeper level, these questions are already decided; to paraphrase Hall, cultural consensus must be assumed for the neoliberal model of the state to be seen as noncoercive. The critique of property—and IP—culture, and the state must take place on this deeper level. But to produce this critique, we must renew the field of cultural studies and its understanding of law, culture, and determination.

I propose thinking of culture in (at least) three levels and considering an array of forces operating through and between these levels that ultimately determine the behavior if not the beliefs of the subjects of that culture. This cultural efficacy will operate in different ways in each context. Our understanding of it will need to be based on careful, conjunctural analysis. But ultimately, we must be able to argue for some understanding of what Raymond Williams calls "the real order of determinations." Writing in *Towards 2000*, Williams observes:

> The cultural analysis developed within and beyond Marxism in the last sixty years has rejected the idea of specialist "areas" of society, each served by its specialist "discipline." It is a central achievement of this analysis that it has developed forms of attention to a whole social order without any dogmatic assignment of priority to this or that determining force. [While this kind of analysis] shows interactions, interconnections, and even underlying structural forms [we also

> need to establish, with some certainty] the real order of determination between different kinds of activity [and levels of efficacy]. That there always is such an order of determination cannot be doubted, from the historical evidence, though that it is not always the same order is equally clear. This is the necessary, theoretical base for the recognition of genuinely different social orders. [. . .] For it is only by continuing to attend to a whole lived social order, and at the same time identifying the primary determining forces within it, that this kind of general humanist analysis can significantly contribute to thinking about the future. (1983, p. 15)

Determination, coercion, and other synonyms for an asymmetrical if not autocratic application of power were primary topics of discussion for early cultural studies scholars. But insofar as the work on deviance illustrated that the supposed consensus of the dominant culture was a coercive imposition of a certain class (or other power bloc), the presence of deviants (or what Althusser calls "Bad Subjects" [2001, p. 181]) also pointed to the gaps and lacunae in that hegemonic system. Thus, the continued possibilities for dynamism and agency, even in a context of hegemonic determination, became one of the hallmarks of the field.

As I discuss at length in my previous book (Johnson Andrews 2016), the emergence of dynamic, distributed, demotic institutions and practices of meaning making—especially in participatory and social media—is undoubtedly one of the most important features of our contemporary conjuncture, particularly in the way it has the potential to undermine existing institutions of power, knowledge, and value. These institutions and practices are clearly the inspiration for many of the critics of IPR—along with the cultural studies work on fan fiction, active audiences, and so on that has preceded the technological infrastructure and informed the work of Lessig directly. However, like Murray, these scholars muddle what I call the levels of culture and overlook the forces of determination in favor of idyllic organic metaphors. Some of this confusion is due to a flimsy understanding of the force of law and the relationship between law and culture, particularly in the U.S. context.

In his legal scholarship, Lessig is clearly aware of the ways in which culture and law work together, particularly in the neoliberal context. In his law review article calling for a "New Chicago School," Lessig (1998) outlines the ways in which different "regulators" affect each other. The "Old Chicago School" saw only two options: the law or the market. Lessig argues that there are a variety of other ways in which to indirectly determine actions, one of which is what legal scholars call "norms" but that we could easily call "culture." Basically, the Old Chicago School assumes that the "internalization of objective constraints," à la the market, are a fact of nature; as Lessig puts it, "Any entity that did not internalize objective constraints will, over time, fail" (ibid., p. 680). This assumption is not true in practice: the pure market of the Old Chicago School exists only in theory. Instead, Lessig argues, "Internalization, or subjective effect, is a variable to be explored, not a condition to be assumed" (ibid.). In their early work, cultural studies scholars were concerned with the mechanisms through which this subjective effect was created and enforced, particularly in a society that was nominally democratic yet "committed at the same time by the concentration of economic capital and political power to the massively unequal distribution of wealth and authority" (Hall 1982, p. 63). But now Lessig and many in the field of cultural studies are more concerned with highlighting the dynamic rather than the determined.

To see law and the state as a determining force or level is not just a theoretical possibility but an assumption intrinsic to the Western model of the state. This model has form and content. The form is that, in terms of its formal legal power, it has potentially complete control over all the practices and norms within its sovereign territory. This sovereignty is hobbled on the one side by the democratic check on state power, but the sovereign and the democratic checks are constrained on the other by Chantal Mouffe's democratic paradox: the demos cannot vote to undermine the value or sanctity of private property. The dynamic vitality of the democratic franchise is displaced from the political to the economic; labor (or the labor the wealthy are able to purchase from those with nothing else to sell) becomes the foundation of property, liberty, and ultimately the state. Market freedom is the only expression of consent; state regulation is the only form of coercion.

Culture is then essential to the neoliberal order if we also mean something like ideology. The "we" interpellated by the state apparatuses must believe that the state is legitimate if the laws are to continue to guide our practices. And in this sense, as James Martel puts it, "Ideology doesn't need to be 'real' in the sense that it completely obfuscates and controls subordinate people. It simply needs to help organize and perpetuate a particular form of status quo, something that it does very well" (2017, loc. 423.). And as Perry Anderson (1976) highlights in his close reading of Antonio Gramsci, the repressive apparatuses are always ready to enforce the most vital concerns of the dominant social property relations—simultaneously ensuring obedience to those ideologies and being legitimated by them.

Although the content of the liberal democratic state appears variegated and diverse, beneath this apparently open process is a closure, the application of a model. This model of the state is based on an assertion of "natural law" and, consequently, a denial of the cultural assumptions implicit to its functioning and its political legitimacy. Therefore, to understand this model as a model, we have to be able to conceptualize its cultural assumptions as cultural. Over time, this model has become the reified culture of property that is central to the Western capitalist project. While this model remains impurely applied by the standards of the maximalist position, insofar as it exists, it has been forced on a significant portion of the population through a long series of struggles. Its continued expansion into other social formations yields similar struggles. This chapter, therefore, prepares the way for recognizing that the law and the state can be used to impose a model of culture on a certain society. This recognition sets the stage for the next chapter, which looks at the concrete process of instantiating the Lockean understanding of labor, value, property, and the state on the population of Early Modern England and Ireland. As I argue there, property and IP are forged in the same crucible with the liberal concept of culture and the modern capitalist state. As we begin pulling on one of these threads, the entire fabric is liable to come unraveled.

Property and the Process of Cultural Production

In his recent "very short introduction" to IP, Siva Vaidhyanathan says, "The copyright wars of the first decade of the twenty-first century yielded a global 'Free Culture' movement, with law professor Lawrence Lessig as its intellectual leader" (2017, xviii). But while Vaidhyanathan's earlier work (2004) on these wars describes them as a clash between "freedom and control," the pitched battles therein take place on a common ground.

IPR absolutists, such as Richard Epstein (2001, 2006b), argue that property rights—whether in so-called creative products or in general—are the foundation of the process of economic growth and social development; making these rights less clear will cripple this mechanism. Without incentives in property provided to producers, the innovation that we understand as basic to the "progress" of this capitalist order will no longer continue. This argument accords with the dominant discourse of property rights, its myth of the isolated artist/inventor whose labor should be rewarded, and the supposed widespread social benefits that rewarding monopoly property rights create. These elegant arguments ring hollow when made by corporate owners of pharmaceutical or electronics patents: many of their innovations were developed directly or indirectly with public funds, and they often subvert the disclosure laws about their inventions, thus violating their main condition for being granted the patent in the first place (Perelman 2002). Property rights maximalists argue that people do not naturally engage in these cultural processes but are motivated only by some sort of commercial return; taking away protections will reduce the total number of participants. This assertion turns the Lockean argument on its head—Locke says that people naturally engage in this labor, and we then naturally give them property for their improvement and naturally expect the state to protect their claim to this value.

When this simultaneously ethical and utilitarian line of argument is projected onto the global scale, IPR appear to be one of the most important tools of economic development. Thus, not only is it more just to have developing countries honor the IPR of multinational corporations; it is in the countries' best interest, as doing so will lead to domestic sources of growth. Keith Maskus, an economic adviser to the World Bank and the World Intellectual Property Organization (WIPO), claims that "economic analysis [. . .] supports the view that stronger IPRs have considerable promise for expanding flows of trade in technical inputs, FDI [foreign direct investment], and licensing. These in turn could expand the direct and indirect transfer of technology to developing nations." (2000, p. 236). He cautions that "such gains may not be uniformly available to all developing countries" (ibid.) but does not equivocate on his recommendation that IPR be strengthened universally—as they have been through the Trade-Related Aspects of Intellectual Property Rights (TRIPS) rider—largely on arguments like those of Maskus.

From the perspective of what I call the balanced position, the key fault of the maximalists is their assertion that IP is no different than any other property and that IPR should be protected and honored with equal vigilance. The maximalists are wrong, say those of the balanced persuasion: "culture" works differently. Works of legal scholarship, including Jessica Litman's "Copyright as Myth" (1991), Rosemary Coombe's *The Cultural Life of Intellectual Properties* (1998), and Lessig's books on this issue (2001, 2004, 2006, 2008)—as well as the latter's open-source copyright organization, Creative Commons—use the term "culture" to describe an organic process that creates a certain set of products (which, incidentally, are also called "culture"—more on this later). As Litman's "Creative Reading" (2007), among others, demonstrates, this position is analogous and in some cases directly articulated to poststructuralist considerations of authorship, audience studies understandings of the co-production of meaning, and cultural studies ethnographies on subcultural appropriations and resistant readings. The conclusion of these "culturalist" disciplinary inquiries into the process of producing and consuming cultural objects seemingly settled the debates about the political or economic determination of the cultural by showing the contingent, creative, collective process of elaborating and appropriating meaning from mass cultural products.

Inspired by these insights and the more visible processes of meaning making they see around them, critics operating from this balanced position implicitly see the emergent status quo of cultural exchange as a space of rich, participatory cultural expression that, for various, unexamined reasons, finds most of its raw materials in the realm of mass or popular culture. The latter, in a coincidence of history they do not explore, are also the cultural products that are most likely to be locked down by the tightening of IPR—copyright, trademarks, patents, and publicity rights of celebrities. When the use of these products/raw materials of culture is limited via onerous legal frameworks and exclusive rights, the social process of their valorization is subverted, and the future potential of this vibrant cultural production is threatened. Since these same cultural processes are what pass for the free and open discourse of the public sphere, limiting them via IPR is usually posited as having some political effects—limiting freedom of speech alongside the consequences for creativity in general.

In criticizing maximalist IPR laws, Lessig laments them as "a radical shift away from our tradition of free culture," speculating that they are "yet another example of a political system captured by a few powerful interests" (2004, p. 12). Yet Lessig does not seem all that animated by the previous forms of control enacted in the interest of mass media corporations. Instead, in *Remix*, his last book on IP, he describes the twentieth century as "a time of happy competition" among media distribution technologies (Lessig 2008, p. 30). The only change, it seems, is that there are now new technologies that allow consumers to take a more active role in this process.

Coombe (1998)—who is more aware, earlier on, of cultural studies work on audiences and subcultures—considers the value created around a trademark by consumers and also touches on the social process of value production in general. It is true that marketing firms work diligently to attempt to produce the value secured by trademark protections—and are paid much better than manual laborers for their attempts. But when so many marketing campaigns fall flat, it does seem like a factor is not being accounted for in the production of this value. Coombe draws on the art critic Hal Foster's idea of *Recodings*, especially to the way that "subcultural practice [. . .] recodes cultural signs" (Foster 1985, p. 170) rather than either truly resist the dominant culture or be limited by its legal structures. This line of inquiry is important, particularly if we share in Foster's goal as a critic: "to separate these practices critically and to connect them discursively in order to call them into crisis (which is after all what criticism means) so as to transform them" (ibid., p. 2). If Coombe were to consider the homology between the immaterial social production of value and the wider material production process that Marx describes, it might generate even more creative tension, if not crisis. At the moment, the sense that property is essentially different in these two forms overshadows the similarities in the social division of labor that make both "productive" and valuable.

Advocates of a balanced copyright see in this social process of cultural production the necessity and justice of a deep public domain—or, as Lessig's organization calls it, a Creative Commons. This emphasis points to one connotation of the title of this book: if there is a value to an IP, it is one that is produced within this complex cultural "flow." If the production of this value is made through a cultural process, and this cultural process itself relies on a certain kind of freedom and openness, then stronger IPR not only represent an ethically spurious appropriation of a social process of collective labors; these rights also threaten to undermine the very source of this value and to lock down culture (and the process of "improvement" and accumulation) at large. Indeed, Lessig makes this argument in his 2008 book *Remix*, wherein he looks at the ways in which the "sharing economy" made visible through digital technology can be good for the "commercial economy." Michael Heller says this dynamic is disconcerting even in real property: his argument is encapsulated in the title of his 2008 book, *The Gridlock Economy: How Too Much Ownership Wrecks Markets, Stops Innovation, and Costs Lives*. Working in the tradition of such legal theorists as Carol Rose (1994) and such economists as Elinor Ostrom (2015), Heller emphasizes the importance of the commons more generally and the variety of human institutions developed to deal with the production and distribution of resources and economic value. In contrast, Lessig is always clear that a boundary should be drawn between IP and other kinds of private ownership of productive property: culture—which is conceptualized as a separate sphere of activity from the rest of social and economic life—is different, and assigning property rights to it should be done only with the greatest of care.

In privileging this conception, Coombe and Lessig consider culture on a constrained continuum: the current configuration is mostly ideal and acceptably processual, but altering it threatens to shift culture into a kind of reified, corporate-controlled feudalism. In some moments, they offer glimpses of a more dialectical understanding of the long-standing political and economic determinations on culture, but these are mostly strategic accommodations, unintegrated into the conception itself. For instance, Coombe acknowledges the material circumstances of contemporary culture in terms of the postmodern condition (referencing the materialist explications of the latter by Fredric

Jameson [1984] and David Harvey [1990]), but she continually reiterates her intention to write "against culture" as something that can be discussed as a "noun," instead focusing on culture as "activities of expressive struggle rather than symbolic context, involving conflictual signifying practices rather than integrated systems of meaning" (1999, p. 24).

This conception leaves fundamental questions about policy, power, and the primitive accumulation of culture unanswered. It basically adopts a hegemonic understanding of culture as an abstract concept and as a concrete object. Because this inherently processual conception of culture is synonymous with creativity, innovation, democracy, and meaning, there is a slippage between it and the neoliberal understanding of "free" markets as the primary site for producing these quasi-public goods—and the contract of property as the primary means of protecting markets. In this sense, this organic field of cultural production is immanently limited by its own neoliberal enclosure.

Far from culture being an unencumbered space for the play of difference, more than a few things remain unquestionable: although it does some violence to the term, they are analytically denotative. By this I mean that they appear to be common sense: the supposed mutual benefits that we all get from private property in general and minimal regulation in the market have become hegemonic ideologies determining the dominant culture—likewise, "improvement" *qua* profit and growth as a defense of ownership and the denial of class power. These ideologies of property and profit structure our ideas and actions—either because we accept them or because we are forced to negotiate with them to make arguments in the dominant discourse. Lessig and many critics of IPR make their arguments from within this discourse; the evidence they accumulate for their case should lead them to fundamentally challenge the neoliberal culture of property. Instead, they describe culture in neoliberal terms.

Not only is this culture, an open-ended, progressive, spontaneous force, a presently achieved ideal; its validation through the democratic process is projected into the past. The property-friendly culture we have is the "best that has been thought and said" (Arnold 2009, p. 5), but instead of its being decided upon by crusty elites, it was previously selected by some earlier process of the demos' filtering out all the merely good and better options. Although the precise ideological articulation of this conception varies, its most potent form is a conservative insistence that further changes in the present will actually undermine future advances. This last point has been a mainstay of natural law proponents of property rights in general, whom John Stuart Mill calls "those important classes in European society to whose real or supposed interests democracy is adverse" (2002, pp. 3–4).

The title of this book has another possible connotation: that IPR are the product of a certain culture, one that, as I argue, is committed to a Lockean notion of "improvement" that emphasizes the necessity of exclusive, individual rights to all kinds of property (virtual, real, and in-between) and its profitable employment. In making a distinction between real and intellectual property, balanced copyright critics effectively yield this ideological ground to the maximalists. Yet this ground is precisely where the struggle should be taking place. When balanced IPR scholars situate these processes largely in relation to the "convergence culture" of new media technology, the dynamic they illustrate in terms of the culture draws directly on those culturalist scholars. However, because they place a backstop on illustrating this dynamic—on the sanctity of private property in the tangible—they must then project this dynamic backward. This requirement means implicitly validating the belief that the status quo is the result of this *ideal* of culture in action and is threatened by the adulteration of closure by these new legal frameworks. But where do these legal frameworks fit in the conception of culture? What role did they play in determining or directing the previous "processes" of culture? How widespread were the practices and theories the law determined as "right" before they were projected onto the society in question? What was the process of culture in relation to helping form this law? And, perhaps most importantly, why should we accept a law that allows all of this collectively produced value to be expropriated by a small handful of powerful owners?

Cultural Studies and the Culture Concept

To facilitate the more fundamental critique of maximalist IP and the neoliberal culture of property from which it derives, cultural studies scholars need to renew their ability to describe the effective inside to culture, despite the fact that we can, retroactively see a variety of movements—a diversity or complexity of cultures—leading into, out of, and even within the status quo. Insofar as a cultural inside exists, the state seems to be a key institution in making this inside stick, despite the current tensions or struggles around certain practices. In the case of the United States, the dominant ideology speaks of entrepreneurship, private property, the free market, and agentless transformation of the social fabric in a more progressive direction. This ideology also assumes that we have come to the most progressive social fabric possible—particularly in relation to other societies. All of these ideas are, more or less, enforced and constituted by the state (and, in the case of social transformations, are only really guaranteed when they become state policy), regardless of how anti-state these ideologies may be.

The culturalist framing of "culture as a process" in which people are continually active has been the dominant reflex of cultural studies scholars in the past two decades. Largely in reaction to what were seen as overly deterministic, structuralist arguments, they have become increasingly focused on seeing the production of meaning *qua* culture in terms of the mercurial interactions of individuals and the variegated experience of identity and the self. In his book *Inside Culture: Re-imagining the Method of Cultural Studies*, Nick Couldry surveys possible methodologies for understanding culture and settles on using Elspeth Probyn's *Sexing the Self* (1993) to help him in "*thinking* the social through the self" (2000, p. 114; emphasis original). Such scholars as Couldry accept some level of intervention on the part of social institutions and structures in terms of the limiting of options, but they ultimately deny a determining relationship between, for instance, the base of political, economic, and social relations and the "culture."

While Couldry's argument is somewhat more nuanced than my brief exposition of it allows, it generally lands where I have placed it, and this position represents a general tendency within cultural studies. Couldry admirably takes the time to read some of the early texts of the field, which allows him to return to a time when the purpose of cultural studies was more focused on illuminating "structural determination" or what I call cultural efficacy and trying to explain how a dominant ideology is able to take root, even amid the mercurial processes of subcultural appropriation and transformation. Couldry's vision of cultural studies methods is clearly meant to give more weight to the processual, culturalist paradigm in the field. However, he positions himself as reimagining the field in relation to Williams, one of the more balanced and nuanced scholars working in the tradition.

Williams himself characterizes culture as "a process" in his descriptions of it in *Keywords* and *Marxism and Literature*. In the former, he notes that this processual definition is coeval with the word "agriculture," an origin we reflect on further in the following chapter. However, especially in the latter text, Williams is keen to understand the way hegemony is maintained through struggle and transformation. In *Marxism and Literature*, he outlines the residual, dominant, and emergent, and he mentions the related concepts of alternative and oppositional culture, which he more thoroughly elaborates in his *Sociology of Culture*. Couldry objects to these concepts because he finds that they all presuppose a closed system, an evolution (or regression) of culture within a certain set of historically and geographically defined social relations:

> The strength and clarity of Williams' vision derives in part from a closure: a closure around a particular historical ideal of community.

> This leaves, on the face of it, very little room for questioning more fundamentally the value of cultural "closure" itself. In the transformed context of the late twentieth century, there are powerful arguments for avoiding closure. (2000, p. 30)

Couldry's criticism appears valid—particularly after our balanced copyright advocates have so thoroughly trashed the notion cultural closure. But like theirs, his critique is based in an ideal of what culture should look like rather than what appears as an effective closure at a certain level of analysis. In short, Couldry is using a hypothetical ideal—a value of what culture *ought to* look like—and criticizing Williams for failing to hew to this ideal when trying to describe culture as it *is*.

Couldry then enumerates the many difficulties of applying Williams's model to the present day; chief among them is that the "massive increase in inter-cultural flows of people, images, information and goods [. . .] makes the idea of cultures separated by hermetically sealed borders impossible to sustain." This global reality in turn undermines "the idea that culture is necessarily tied to place" (2000, p. 95). Assuming that there is some novelty in the level of exchange and mobility taken as essential to the process of globalization, these are, again, valid points. But how can there be "inter-cultural flows" without cultures' being closed on some analytical level? If there is no closure, they are just cultural flows, in which case there is nothing unique about the moment he describes other than the scale on which it operates.

Instead of examining the larger, effective, dominant culture that constitutes the inside of a culture, Couldry focuses on the individual self and the co-determination of the system or structure in which the self is enmeshed via complex feedback loops with chaotic, unpredictable consequences. He draws upon Ulf Hannerz, whose book *Cultural Complexity* has become a mainstay of recent critics in the field. In the words of Hannerz, who describes this as the "flow" of culture:

> I find the flow metaphor useful—for one thing, because it captures one of the paradoxes of culture. When you see a river from afar, it may look like a blue (or green or brown) line across the landscape, something of awesome permanence. But at the same time, "you cannot step into the same river twice," for it is always moving, and only in this way does it achieve durability. The same way with culture—even as you perceive structure, it is entirely dependent on ongoing process. (1992, p. 4)

Following from this, Hannerz says that culture is complex, which he insists is a "sober insistence" in place of "characterization(s) of the cultures in question in terms of some single essence" (1992, p. 4).

This is an admirable ideal for how we could think of culture. It fits well within the range of what Williams would have thought about culture at its best, but he was very careful to consider the inflection given to this characterization, realizing that the use of this definition itself was political. For him, the fact of this closure in the local community was enhanced by precisely the interpenetration of the more capitalist-oriented culture from outside (Williams 1958, p. 25). In his essay "The Idea of a Common Culture," Williams concludes with the following:

> In any society towards which we are likely to move, there will, first of all, be such considerable complexity that nobody will in that sense "possess cultural properly" in the same way; people invariably will have different aspects of the culture, will choose that rather than this, concentrate on this and neglect that. When this is an act of choice, it is completely desirable; when it is an act of someone else's choice as to what is made available and what is neglected, then of course one objects. But it is not only that the society will be more complex: that people will not and cannot share it in an even and uniform way. It is also that the idea of a common culture is in no sense the idea of a simply consenting, and certainly not of a merely conforming, society. One returns, once more, to the original emphasis of a common determination of meaning by all the people, acting sometimes as individuals, sometimes as groups, in a process which has no particular end, and which can never be supposed at any time to have finally realized itself, to have become complete. (1989, p. 37)

Williams points to the tension between choices we can make and choices determined by other forces. E. P. Thompson also highlights the ways in which a perceived closure of culture often acts as a resource for resisting and productively channeling change on the part of the members of a community. Only from a perspective that sees Western, capitalist culture as natural and adequately democratic does the resistance to its contours and determinations appear reactionary. Describing Early Modern English plebeian revolts, Thompson says:

> The conservative culture of the plebs as often as not resists, in the name of custom, those economic rationalizations and innovations

> (such as enclosure, work-discipline, unregulated "free" markets in grain) which rulers, dealers, or employers seek to impose. Innovation is more evident at the top of society than below, but since this innovation is not some normless and neutral technological/sociological process ("modernization," "rationalization") but is the innovation of capitalist process, it is most often experienced by the plebs in the form of exploitation, or the expropriation of customary use-rights, or the violent disruption of valued patterns of work and leisure. (1991, loc. 274)

These customary cultures are a resource for channeling resistance to a culture imposed from above. The former may appear "closed" and the latter more "open," but only if we assume wage labor and capital to be the ultimate expression of progress and the enlightenment.

Theodor Adorno highlights the tensions in the concept of culture, largely because he sees the progressive potential and the political closure as locked in a dialectic of process and administration, complexity and closure, dynamism and determination. On the one hand, in his more pessimistic view of contemporary society, Adorno states that "whoever speaks of culture speaks of administration as well." In this, he sees the paradox organizing "culture" toward particular ends:

> Organizations of convenience in an antagonistic society must necessarily pursue particular ends; they do this at the expense of the interests of other groups. Therefore obduracy and reification necessarily result. If such organizations continue to occupy a subordinate position within which they were totally open and honest toward their membership and its direct desires, they would be incapable of any action. The more firmly integrated they are, the greater is their prospect for asserting themselves in relation to others. The advantage of totalitarian "monolithic" nations over liberalist nations in power politics which can be internationally observed today is also applicable to the structure of organizations with a smaller format. Their external effectivity is a function of their inner homogeneity, which in turn is dependent upon the so-called totality gaining primacy over individual interests, so that the organization is forced into independence by self-preservation: at the same time this establishment of independence leads to alienation from its purposes and from the people of whom it is composed. Finally—in order to be able to pursue its goals appropriately—it enters into a contradiction with them. (2001, p. 110)

This alienation, of course, would not apply to the "organization men" who were put in charge of policing these definitions. They would eventually internalize the logic and see no contradiction: since they were in charge of policing the authentic, it would be impossible for them to be inauthentic themselves.

On the other hand, like Hannerz, Adorno thought the complexity of culture was important—but more as an ideal leading people to demand transformation than as a necessarily dynamic organic process. As Adorno says elsewhere:

> Culture, in the true sense, did not simply accommodate itself to human beings; but it always simultaneously raised a protest against the petrified relations under which they lived, thereby honoring them. Insofar as culture becomes wholly assimilated to and integrated in those petrified relations, human beings are once more debased. (2001, p. 100)

Although this ideal of culture is taken from another essay, it lies as a tension with the essay on "Culture and Administration," such that at moments the "culture" he refers to in the article is not the debased, petrified version of administered culture but the "vital" protest culture that he sees as always already possible.

Culture—at least at some level—is supposed to inspire people living in those petrified relations to take action to change those petrified relations and to continue to work at making them closer to the ideal. As Williams says earlier in his essay:

> In talking of a common culture, then, one was saying first that culture was the way of life of a people, as well as the vital and indispensable contributions of specially gifted and identifiable persons, and one was using the idea of the *common* element of the culture—its community—as a way of criticizing that divided and fragmented culture we actually have. (1989, p. 35; emphasis original)

This was, perhaps, a tall order, but it is the reason that midcentury cultural critics were focused on culture.

Between these two modes of culture should run a tension, a dialectic between what is and what could be: the petrified relations of administration versus a protest against them. This tension might be a merely negative dialectic, with no absolute sense of what comes next, but nevertheless the phantom of an ideal should at least haunt the discussion. The role of the cultural critic is not necessarily to elaborate the ideal but to help construct a method of considering the culture itself, as a whole, to identify and undermine the process of naturalization, the process of reification, that made these relations and the culture that they represented seem like a historical inevitability, honoring their fellow humans with the encouragement of continued development. Before one can present a revolt against petrified conditions, one must have some sense of what those conditions consist of—and what about them could and should be changed. This awareness requires identifying how *cultural efficacy* is constituted and specifying what components of that efficacy are the result of the kind of culture Adorno terms "administrative."

Hannerz asserts that the cohesion at a distance—the "cultural inside" of Couldry's study—is an illusion: there is no cohesion, only the anarchy of atomized individuals interacting. This template leads Couldry, at the extreme, to suggest that the individual is the best site for the study of culture. But like Murray, in the end, neither he nor Hannerz is able to present a method for discerning why a culture would ever appear to be a coherent system—much less how it might function and continue to be reproduced in many of the same terms, despite all the apparent changes. Once again, the metaphor of the organic development of culture leaves us unable to describe why one culture develops in one place over another, how this culture relates to the forces determining it (and vice versa), and how to effectively transform it.

Hannerz is discussing a form of reification: to ask why those vital rivers appear as sclerotic lines is to undermine their reification. Hannerz is earnest in his invocation of Heraclitus's maxim: indeed, we may never step in the same river twice, but the flowing water is contained between the banks. To recognize that the apparently complex processes are also determined by the banks of that river is to reinstate the dialectic of culture. Hannerz and other contemporary scholars who invoke culture rest comfortably on their undialectical conclusion rather than attempt to discern what causes this reification—or how it can be evaluated, criticized, undermined—and how this inaction is related to their prized "culture as a process." In doing so, they increase the possibility that this process will continue: to stick with the metaphor, they overlook the enormous dams being built upstream that will permanently alter the landscape. Instead, they file this lack of awareness under "change" and disregard the questions it begs. Were the rivers we step in today similarly altered? Was this alteration really of the same mode of cultural change as the ideal suggests?

In my opinion, discovering and analyzing this determination is the main goal of cultural studies. The primary method for undermining reification is not merely to take people into the apparently buzzing bumbling world of street-level culture and chide them for imagining it was somehow a cohesive, integrated whole: it is to help figure out why it appears and often functions according to rules and norms that make this totality appear natural and inalterable, like the course of a river on a map. To quote James Boyle, describing legal culture in a properly dialectical fashion, to undermine this reification is to "lay out the normative topography, the geography of assumptions within which issues are framed, possibilities foreclosed, and so on" (1996, p. 15). I see this first step as vital to investigating the cultural production of IPR: ultimately, the culture we talk about in this conversation exists and transpires on (at least) three different levels. Specifying these levels will help us understand the relationship between them—and the law, the market, and the state.

What We Talk about When We Talk about Culture

To start with a tentative definition, culture is the meaningful product of complex interrelationships between social norms, shared meanings, policies, policing, and practice. This interrelationship, although it is mobile and may shift over time, has a history, and, insofar as the culture is effective, it is effective in the confines of a certain space. Thus, part of what I am arguing is for the specificity of a culture in a certain time and place. The purpose of this argument is to be able to discuss, on the one hand, the efficacy of a culture and the interrelationship of culture and law and, on the other, the role of the state in imposing a certain cultural understanding.

My conception begins with the analytical separation of different levels of culture, which we can then discuss in terms of their dynamic, legitimating, and determining interrelationships, particularly in relation to the law. The levels I am suggesting are partially derivative of the modes and levels of culture Williams outlines in his chapter on cultural analysis in *The Long Revolution* (2001). As discussed in Williams's work, separating culture into contingent, mutually constituting levels overcomes the unhelpful collapse of this hierarchy under the simple designation of "culture." For instance, Murray's description of our new divergent culture simultaneously includes the everyday interrelationship of the upper classes and the products they enjoy. More importantly, in the balanced copyright movement, aspects I designate as C1 or C2 are discussed simply as "culture," which creates a difficulty in discussing how different levels act on one another (or not).

The framework I adopt to describe the levels of a cultural inside is building on Hannerz's description, but it is also related to what Harvey (2006) says would be a key concept were Williams to update his *Keywords* today: space. It may be common sense to notice that cultures appear more complex at the ground level than from afar, but it is equally true that moving quickly from one cultural space to another creates a disorientation that can only lead to the conclusion that the norms, practices, and beliefs of those two spaces differ. But equally specious is the notion that this difference is essential, as opposed to being the sedimentary result of previous struggles over meaning, power, and value. I explore the variables of time and space more fully below.

For now, I suggest three different levels: *Culture 1* (C1), *Culture 2* (C2), and *Culture 3* (C3). C1 is the on-the-ground, microlevel, anthropological version of culture. It is the referent of Michel de Certeau's *The Practice of Everyday Life* (1998), at once an atomized, creative, and dynamic process of transformation and a widespread, patterned set of common customs and practices. As Hall says in relation to ideology—a synonym for culture in this conceptualization—it is the "the practical as well as the theoretical knowledges which enable people to 'figure out' society, and within whose categories and discourses we 'live out' and 'experience' our objective positioning in social relations" (1986, p. 28). From this level, culture can appear to be a dynamic energy field blooming with collective social action or a sclerotic force of traditional order and informal social norms. It is here that the power of the social order clashes most objectively with the practice of deviance described by Hall. It is at this level of culture that the contradictions of the concept itself are most apparent, because they are more and less reified than at any other level. Diversity is apparent within and between local, regional, and national spaces, but as Adorno points out in terms of "administration," denying diversity within communities and highlighting it between them is politically expedient. Otherwise quotidian practices, such as wearing a headscarf, weaving cloth, or chewing coca leaves, can come to have political significance far beyond everyday patterns in use. These banal practices are often seized on as indicative of the collective power of a culture; as James C. Scott (1990, 2012) discusses in his work, everyday acts of resistance may be the most common ways in which people push back against the perceived imposition of culture from outside. Mahatma Gandhi's campaigns calling on Indians (and especially Indian women) to spin their own cloth and to make their own salt were premised on the notion that autonomy at the ground level would destabilize the entire commodity-centered political economy of the British Empire. However, these resistant practices, bearing the connotation of authenticity, can then be used for the purpose of administering a political movement in cultural terms, keeping what Scott (1979) calls "the revolution in the revolution" from getting out of hand. Therefore, even at this level, a dialectic exists between the processual development of common local practices and the enclosure of tradition or administered culture from the top level.

In our contemporary parlance—as in the discourse of culture deployed by those in cultural studies and balanced critics of absolutist IPR—there is a great deal of slippage between culture at this C1 level and the practices of folk music, craft making, and other forms of skillful, expressive production that effectively mediate communal experience. In most large societies, these practices have been replaced by the commodified culture maintained, if not monopolized, by massive transnational corporate conglomerates: branded merchandise, recorded music and film, and broadcast media of all kinds are primary examples of *Culture 2* (C2). C2 is at once the flow of (mass) meanings across space and the archive of materials held to be meaningful over time. Spatially, the need for mediation would occur, as in Benedict Anderson's *Imagined Communities*, "in all communities larger than primordial villages of face to face contact" (2006, p. 6). But this considers only the social, political mediation; even in premodern villages, the narration of the natural world—for the purposes of explanation, instruction, and even mere entertainment—takes place at an epistemological distance. The efficacy of the "deep horizontal comradeship" this distance implies cannot be denied: refusing to at least negotiate with it has significant political implications. As Anderson says, "Communities are to be distinguished not by their falsity/genuineness, but by the style in which they are imagined" (ibid.). The more widespread the community imagined—and hence the more likely the dominant representations subsume ever-more-distinctive local practices and particularities—the more mythical it becomes and the more its boundaries become defined not by what is common to the group but by what supposedly separates its members from the Other—even if the Other can be found in their midst.

The technological aspect of C2—which is central to even Anderson's conception, wherein nationalism as a practice is facilitated by the rise of the newspapers, novels, and official state languages of "print-capitalism"—has long been the focus of communication and media studies and is as important as the social psychological aspect: on the one hand, as Marshall McLuhan argues, media act as an extension of our human capacities; on the other, this extension implicates the hegemonic discourse as being the most likely content of widely shared materials, as in Hall's "Encoding/Decoding" (1980b) thesis. In short, the social power of mediated information is contingent on the interindividual, socio-ideological territory of commonly held meanings and the widespread ability to negotiate them cognitively. Hall says the most common position of the viewer in relation to this media is one of negotiation, which allows for a key moment of agency and, as Chapter 4 argues, labor on the part of the negotiator.

C2 is difficult to describe as a level common to all cultures. For media producers and consumers, C2 encompasses a basic social process of making meaning, of creatively appropriating the ambient resources, of deeply experiencing a song, a story, or an image in a pleasurable way. The degree to which this process is mediated by discs and distant signals or folk songs and stories of village elders varies significantly between societies—and even between individuals within these societies; in Régis Debray's (2000) terms, it may inspire only the "interest and curiosity" that sustains communication or the "transformation if not conversion" required by what he calls proper transmission of a transhistorical truth. *Transmission*—really another term for "cultural efficacy"—would require the alteration of practices at the C1 level as well as beliefs about them at the C2, although this depends on how much the C2 level of mediation is supposed to make the potentially malleable processes of C1 look more like administrated models imposed from above, or vice versa. At the same time, contrary to structural functionalist assumptions, the performance of practices at C1, the individual conformity to local patterns of "customs in common," is not necessarily evidence of a commonly held C2 narrative or evidence that the subject performing the practice believes something about it: it can also be evidence that the narrative (and the practice it narrates) in question must be negotiated—and that failure to do so will result in a coercive punishment. The media reaction to outbreaks of looting in U.S. cities during moments of social breakdown—hurricanes, protests, and so forth—illustrates the shallowness of many people's actual belief in the sanctity of property.

Thus, *Culture 3* (C3) rears its head. For the purposes of this analysis, C3 is a metacultural model of society. It is the fundamental legitimating narratives—and what Nicos Poulantzas (1978) calls its "institutional materiality"—that outline and enforce the appropriate practices for all the rest of society. It is a quintessential example of what Adorno means when he says, "Whoever speaks of culture speaks of administration as well" (2001, p. 107). For the purposes of this book, it is most closely associated with the Anglo-American form of the law, the state, and the dominant relations of power and production. On this topic, Coombe, ever cautioning against the use of "culture as a noun," makes this observation:

> For the past two decades, critical anthropologists have been renouncing "culture"—recognizing the origins of the concept in forms of colonial governance, acknowledging its complicity with orientalism, and showing how many, if not most, constructions of tradition and cultural identity were reifications that served and continue to serve the interests of settler and colonial elites. Less remarked upon, but no less

> important, is the emergence of a reified and stable concept of "law" in the same processes of colonial subjugation. Allying themselves with the inexorable and universal forces of science, progress and rationality, colonial rulers developed a concept of law that was the antithesis of culture, coded as superstition, irrationality, timeless stasis and organic closed systems. Peter Fitzpatrick suggests that these mythic, cultural worlds were constructed as the mute ground that enabled a European "we" to possess "law." In other words, this colonially generated image of non-European "cultures" establishes the racial foundation for law's modern identity. (1999, p. 265)

Therefore, discussing this level as cultural challenges the notion that the law, the state, and the economy are objects less suitable for a critical, cultural investigation than other branches of the social sciences. Challenging this epistemological limitation is especially crucial to undermining the hegemony of the reified culture of property as advocates of the latter fervently deny its political and cultural construction.

In theory, C3 is the macrolevel objectification of the dominant culture—one of the primary objects of cultural studies—which may or may not be mediated through C2 and which may or may not be effective at the level of C1. Like the principles of the U.S. Declaration of Independence or the U.S. Constitution, it may be a theory about the relationship between citizens, the state, and the economy but which is often untrue in practice; or it may be a narrative connecting the law to religion that would otherwise be seen as a mediating form of C2 culture but which has risen to the status of an organizing apparatus of scientific, administrative knowledge: it claims a special form of authority above and beyond any others. The functional or formal hegemony of C3 does not mean that every practice and every other mediation has to conform exactly to it—just that none can be seen to oppose or otherwise threaten the effective rule of this culture. C3 is the threshold that is supposed to limit culture at the other levels. In the present work, balanced copyright critics oppose C3 as a new, maximalist model of cultural administration, which Lessig calls "the culture of regulating culture" (2008, p. 33).

In short, when effective, culture at the C3 level provides "a dominant cultural principle upon which depend[s] the cohesion and integrity of the politically constituted social whole" (E. Wood 1991, p. 89). At this level, a dominant cultural narrative legitimates the political execution of formal social control and denies the fact of functional power. This is especially the case in nominally democratic capitalist countries, where the single law of the land must be based on some sort of social contract, and the power resulting from economic inequalities is denied by appealing to the supposed freedom of the market.

Ellen Meiksins Wood (1991) says this "pristine culture of capitalism" is primarily characterized by a sense that the political is separated from the economic and that the economic is an independently functioning realm of social life, separate from any political control. By "pristine," she refers to the ruling model of the Early Modern English state, which she says relied on "purely 'economic' modes of appropriation" (ibid., loc. 531). But to do so, they had to use the state apparatus to instantiate a culture where political freedom was contingent on economic unfreedom. It is pure in the sense that the theory of liberalism—exemplified through Locke's defense of property—depicts the coercive force of the market as an independent "natural" force when it is actually constituted through the political. In effect, therefore, *the only way in which the political can be separated from the economic is through the cultural*—through enforcing practices and legitimating beliefs that adhere to this subjective orientation, normalizing these practices through mass representations, and ideologically masking the unequal access to legal and economic resources under the universal banner of "freedom." The following chapter looks more closely at the development of the "pristine culture of capitalism"—its ideological and repressive state apparatuses—in its Early Modern context.

Discussing this level of culture in the abstract is difficult because it only exists *qua* culture when it is concretely effective, at least to some degree, throughout the cultural hierarchy—that is, from C3 down to C2 and C1. In conditions where it is obviously imposed from the top, the structure clearly determines the levels beneath it in one way or another. In a supposedly more organic situation, it can be seen as a macroreflection of the patterns found farther down the hierarchy. Either way, I argue that there exists some form of structural determination—a cultural efficacy—and that a key force of this determination is the *culture* of the law, the state, and the economy, which is then reinforced and legitimated by C2.

The culture of the law, the state, and the (macro)economy should also be understood as having two distinctive components, each of which has a culturally specific characteristic. Most obviously, the *content* of these components is cultural and includes the specificities of what and how the laws regulate, the method for generating and enforcing laws through the state and in relation to civil society, and the forms of connection and coercion that can be effected through the supposedly independent realm of the economy. But less apparently, the formal *structure* of the law is also cultural. In the case of the Western ideology of the law, the structure assumes that all the communities occupying the territory of a state operate under the singular "rule of law" governed by the central authority. In turn, this assumption means that all the areas of the country demarcated and recognized by the international community as the space of the sovereign state are the property of the sovereign state, with all the rights and responsibilities that adhere to this ownership. This form of the state derives from a cultural assumption about territorial jurisdiction that claims that, however the law is made by that state, the central state is the supreme authority. If C2 is the narrative through which the state gains its legitimacy as the nation, C3 is the formal structure of law through which the territory of the state is inscribed by what Naeem Inayatullah and David Blaney call "the magic of straight lines" (2004, p. 168).

This Realist fiction of the state is particularly important in precisely the circumstances under which it is often claimed to have less salience: those of the condition of economic globalization. Despite the dominant rhetoric, the state is absolutely necessary for creating the supposedly spontaneous interaction of private property rights in the free market. The dominant cultural logic of the state form determines the landscape of whatever cultural processes occur.

In societies where the "rule of law" adheres, the policies that determine practices are legitimated through the state in the form of laws. According this ideal, these laws are decided on democratically or are, at the very least, not doctrine handed down from a supreme leader whose authority is based on some metaphysical being rather than the will of his [*sic*] property-holding subjects. In this context, a law is considered just because it is supposedly something that most of its subjects agree is good, permitting the most meaningful and sustaining cultural practices and prohibiting the most detrimental—distinctions defined by the people who engage in those meaningful practices. This situation may not always be the case, and it is an empirical question whether it is or not. But it is true that, from an external perspective, according to the dominant culture of international relations, the law and the state are held to be the highest agents of determining cultural meaning and social practice, regardless of the democratic participation involved or the legitimacy of the policies on the ground.

In short, *within this conceptualization, the argument that C3 can determine C1 through C2 follows from the cultural assumption that it should determine these things*, at least within the boundaries of liberal democracy. And in a liberal democracy, the legitimacy of C3 is derived from the assertion that it is not an imposition: C3 is simply what seeps up from C1 through C2 in the Whiggish percolator of progress. Thus the ideology of capitalism as the pinnacle of "culture as a process."

Of course, the power of the cultural imperatives to functionally—rather than formally—define social practice at any level depends on the particulars of the concrete conjuncture. It does not necessarily follow from the structure that every practice at C1 is determined by C2 and C3 or that every dictate handed down from C3 necessarily finds its effective expression at the levels below. Part of the purpose of this construction is to provide a baseline by which we can investigate the important deviations and interactions between the levels and to think about them and the forces of determination.

Different political, social, and cultural theorists give particular weight to any one of these levels, narrowly arguing for the principle efficacy of one level or another. For instance, in *The Protestant Ethic and the Spirit of Capitalism* (2001), Max Weber sees a version of C2 as so fully determining of the practices at C1 that the purported success of U.S. capitalism can be explained by a close examination of the texts of Calvinism, Methodism, and so forth. Therefore, *the theory of how these different levels interact is itself a product of a specific cultural moment and a particular ideological framework*. In my case, I argue that a dearth of attention has been paid of late to the law and the state, to the functional force of the economy that the neoliberal state empowers in a particular way, and to the issue of structure in general. This neglect is especially evident in the discussion of culture from the balanced copyright position. It, like many contemporary cultural studies scholars, relies on a characterization of "culture as a process" that ignores the functional—neoliberal—closure at the C3 level.

This conceptualization of culture is intended to aid critics in seeing this imposition in its totality. It helps demonstrate the distinction between the content and force vectors in one culture rather than another and the "empty idea of liberty" that the hegemonic narrative of Western capitalism puts forward at the expense of all others.

This understanding allows for—even necessitates—agency in the descending levels of culture. Without the process of embedding C3 into the mediating- and ground-level cultures, it would not have any cultural efficacy. These processes are akin to the creative work of appropriation that culturalist scholars have long pointed to as evidence of the existence of resistant readers. This labor of appropriation is necessary for the instantiation of cultural value, just as it is for the production and reproduction of economic value.

While the levels of C1, C2, and C3 help us analytically describe the space of the cultural efficacy of a certain regime, the levels do not describe the efficacy itself. If these layers are understood as horizontal, parallel dimensions, organized in a spatial hierarchy, *cultural efficacy* is the vertical crystallization whereby the specific aspect of each dimension is articulated with the dimension below and/or above it. It may be temporary (i.e., conjunctural) or more fundamental, but even finding this coagulation of culture does not explain why or how the efficacy exists: it simply helps us note that this structuring element is regarded as somehow reified by subjects whose actions mutually constitute that efficacy. Moreover, many practices and theories may lie outside this vertical column of cultural efficacy, but insofar as they are not a threat to this efficacy itself, they are simply marginal or, as Hall and Becker call them, "deviant."

By the same token, as in that early cultural studies work, the troubling presence of deviance should alert us to the ideological essence of the culture being imposed. In his final contributions to the copyright debate, Lessig declares the widespread practice of piracy to be a dangerous precedent in criminality and warns that the continued ability of the average person to regularly break the law threatens to undermine the force of the law itself. The pragmatic solution he presents is to find a way for the determining glove of the law to be better fitted to the obviously dynamic invisible hand of culture—in this case, a dynamic interaction between C1 and C2 that is made possible by new technologies—without stifling the profit motive at the root of property relations more generally.

Lessig's inquiry begins from the question of what "moral platform" should be imposed in relation to copyright that will shape the behavior of the coming generation and retain the more general cultural efficacy of the law. He says that "we should always be thinking about how to moderate regulation in light of the likelihood that the target of regulation will comply. It does no one any good to regulate in ways that we know people will not obey" (2008, p. xx). His libertarian warning to IPR maximalists is that "developing the habit of mind, especially in youth, of avoiding laws because they are seen to be wrong, or silly, or unjust, develops a practice of thinking that could bleed beyond the original source" (ibid., p. 283). In other words, the lack of maximalist IPR's cultural efficacy at the C1 level—at the level of basic practices—threatens to destabilize the more fundamental efficacy of the cultural assumption in "the rule of law." This "rule of law" is especially vulnerable at the moment because, for libertarianism to work, subjects must be disciplined via a political apparatus that denies it is political—that is, it is beyond the capacity of those subjects to alter the apparatus in their favor. The only source of legitimation is through the cultural aspect of these apparatuses. Yet this circumstance creates a culture that is always already determined and, therefore, hardly "free."

Lessig's commitment to the "bigger problem" of "Reforming Us" follows from his long-stated concern, explored more fully in Chapter 3, with shifting the balance of social control to making "culture serve power" rather than simply hoping the law alone will restrict culture. Moments arise when key anchors are shorn from their moorings, when a crisis of economic production and accumulation coincides with a crisis of political legitimacy: these times produce an opening for discussion about those anchors themselves, about rearranging the limits and harnessing the pressures in a novel, more productive, or generally beneficial way. Lessig recognizes that the current conjuncture threatens to be such a crisis, but he also recognizes that the understanding of law that maximalists hold is fragile and, if pushed by a strong social movement, would take little force to break it.

Toward a Critical Cultural Studies of Law, Culture, and Property

The Law and Economics tradition from which Lessig emerged was generated in reaction to what Barbara Fried calls "The First Law and Economics Movement" and its descendants in the Critical Legal Studies movement of the 1980s. The central insight of the former is the dialectic between formal (*de jure*) and functional (*de facto*) power. These definitions are derived from the early-twentieth-century U.S. legal realist Robert Hale, who argued for the necessary constitutional distinction between formal versus functional liberty (cf. B. Fried 1998). If, following Wood above, the political is separated from the economic, then the formal liberty that we all have as citizens is undermined by the lack of functional liberty. Or, as Hale says from the other direction, coercion not only was effected through the formal, public state; it was also effected through the functional coercion of inequalities in economic power.

Within the analytical hierarchy above, this caveat says that the law (as C3) is used to determine the processes of culture in the various levels. It has the potential to solidify certain practices, creating a "status-quo neutrality" (Sunstein 1993, p. 3) and, to return to the most important element of this study, reifying certain policies and practices as natural and prepolitical. Yet formal, legal measures are only one dimension of power used to determine this cultural efficacy. They couple with functional power that exists within the social formation working through and beyond the formal guarantees of the state. In the words of Poulantzas, "relations of power, *go far beyond the state*" (1978, p. 36; emphasis original).

This power dynamic would seem to contradict the notion of the law's or the state's determining culture, again leaning more in the direction of a Foucauldian understanding of micropolitical struggles (Foucault 1980). However, responding to this "seemingly libertarian" conception, Poulantzas asserts that "the State plays a constitutive role not only in the relations of production and the powers which they realize, but also in the totality of power relations at every level of society" (1978, p. 45). Still, he cautions against "statist" conceptions: "It is struggles which make up the primary field of power relations and which invariably have primacy over the state" (ibid.). In other words, the formal guarantees of the law, insofar as they help constitute relations of power and solidify the terms of the struggles, play a determinate role, even if there is a surplus of functional power beyond these formal guarantees. This ultimately is Hale's argument: the formal law of the state does not necessarily coerce people into, for instance, the wage relationship, but by guaranteeing property relationships in a certain way, it ensures the inequality of economic resources can be used as a functionally coercive force. It is, effectively, "law making by unofficial minorities" (Hale 1920).

In contrast, Lessig is concerned that the challenges posed to the legitimacy of current copyright law will undermine all formal power—that is, the law—*precisely because the state lacks the functional power to enforce formal IP protection*. This mismatch between formal and functional power is a new development brought on by changes in the institutional arrangements around media production and distribution technologies and emergent cultural practices. For many years, the economic expense of the technology required for production and distribution of mass media culture gave large U.S. corporations *functional* control over the inflows of C2 at national and, arguably, international levels; although these corporations were guaranteed by *formal* rights to the content that flowed through their networks, these rights were secondary to their virtual monopoly over the process of distribution. Alterations to the technical environment have undermined this monopoly and the corporations' functional control, making formal rights more important in preventing alternative methods of distribution. Thus, the formal changes—the implementation of ever-more-extensive private property rights to control intangible materials—are meant to cement what had been an informal, but functional, determination of the national and international division of cultural labor and its proceeds. Lessig recognizes this change, but he sees the former situation—as a "natural" product of the technology rather than an economic monopoly sanctioned by the state.

I discuss IPR and the division of labor further in Chapter 4. For now, I want to highlight the assertion that power lies beyond formal rights or laws. Following the early work of Michel Foucault, I find that many cultural studies scholars see power mainly in terms of the power of the state or other social institutions. The economic is considered only in relation to the state and society; the relative freedom of the economic in advanced capitalist countries is seen as evidence that this social formation has a different kind of efficacy. When nominally Marxist or structuralist arguments are considered from this perspective, they are filtered through this relational prism such that the conclusions they reach appear overly deterministic or, to paraphrase Foucault, more fitting for the nineteenth century. This perspective has resulted in a well-developed sense of the power of social institutions not formally integrated with the political apparatus of the state—and thus a useful understanding of functional, relational power. While this understanding could, theoretically, be applied to a variety of aspects of social life, it is rarely considered in terms of the economy as a source of social power. Yet the functional power of capital is quite important, especially in predominantly capitalist societies, where the *de facto* disciplinary power of the economy is constituted through the formal *de jure* guarantees of the state.

The ideologies of neoliberal capitalism make it easy to overlook the functional power of the economy: the state is sclerotic, corrupt, and inefficient, while the economy is characterized as possessing the same dynamic, mercurial, and even democratic quality that is usually attributed to the cultural by "culturalist" scholars. The "free market" is supposedly the solitary space of "culture as a process." Without an alternative space of noneconomic interaction—a space of civil society—it is difficult to imagine the "free market" as a disciplinary mechanism on par with the state. Therefore, the perspectives that validate "culture as a process" more readily recognize the functional power of symbolic or cultural capital than of financial capital. The latter wields far more functional power than is usually admitted in the determination of the cultural, particularly in contemporary Western societies. The functional power of capital is not separate from the formal "political" power of the state, which guarantees its functional capabilities against any form of expropriation. These functional capabilities are clearly significant—more so than the functional control over the ambient media culture by a handful of corporate conglomerates.

The reified culture of property at the center of this book amplifies and exnominates the functional economic power granted to the holders of property in the means of social production through the formal, legal protection of property. My focus on the *power of productive property* is informed by a broader critique, most cogently developed by Robert Hale and his early-twentieth-century colleagues. For this group, the power that the coalition—or class—of citizens wielded through their ownership of productive property was extremely important. As Barbara Fried summarizes:

> Hale, along with a number of other Realists, argued that the so-called private power exerted by private parties to a bargain was in fact public power delegated by the state through its laws of property and contract. Such laws granted individual owners [. . .] the right to withhold property entirely and the privilege to waive that right on condition that others meet the demanded price, and these laws were ultimately backed up by state force. (1998, p. 65)

Hale's characterization of the function of economic power, ensured by the state, bolsters the notion that C3 can determine the cultural formation throughout the descending levels without depriving agents at those levels of agency. The efficacy of C3 functions predominantly through the supposedly informal vector of the economy, yet the latter is sanctified through the formal channel of the law. The functional potential of the economic may be more powerful, but it rides on the rails of the law. This seems especially true when there appears to be no regulation at all. As the following chapters outline, however, this appearance is an example of ideology *par excellence*—as the imaginary relationship of individuals to their real conditions of existence.

From the critical, cultural studies scholars' perspective—and that of the Frankfurt School before them—the question should be how and why nominally democratic polities and ostensibly pluralist societies would largely acquiesce to what Karl Polanyi discusses as the fascist direction of the corporatist welfare state. The ease with which postwar capitalism was able to stifle the internal strife of the interwar years could not be explained by the interaction of C1 and C3 alone. It was not simply the top-down imposition of a new cultural climate—there had to be some psycho-socio-cultural mediation between these levels to make this new culture effective. Indeed, the process of using all three levels to impose new ways of life was being perfected by the early, administrative communications researchers whom Adorno rejected.

Midcentury media and cultural studies scholars considered the C2 level of mediated communication and creative expression as a primary ground on which to set up a struggle against the cultural efficacy of this model. Althusser's separation of the ideological state apparatus as an autonomous space of social agency and cultural production was one version of the cultural Marxism that infused diverse movements, many of which were striving to show, by prefigurative, performative example, a new way of living at the C1 level: the situationists' return to the authenticity of directly lived reality, the autonomists of the "Hot Autumn," the rising Third World, and the outbursts of 1968 in Northern/Western cultures. Insofar as they targeted the mediated level of efficacy, they seemed to confirm this hypothesis. But although these movements targeted a certain level of culture, they never meant to change only this level.

Likewise, the origin of copyright—explored in the following chapter—was indeed meant to stifle freedom of expression, but the speech copyright stifled was speech for and about something. It emerged from movements' demanding an alteration to the terms of the newly universalizing state—either to narrowing its jurisdiction or altering the content of its law. The true site of this struggle was the social property relationship legitimated by law and protected by the unitary, territorial state. The current critics of IPR, however, largely allow for both of the above to remain beyond reproach. Here lies the central contradiction that most mainstream critics of IP are unable to solve: the paradox between liberalism and democracy, explored most fully in Chapter 3.

The culture of pure capitalism necessitates a single state, with sovereign jurisdiction over an ever-expanding space. The legitimacy of this jurisdiction supposedly hinges on the fact that it is there to secure political freedom: the state is there to protect everyone, equally, from the state. However, it is also legitimated by its protection of property, which is distributed unequally. The supposed formal, political freedom is therefore undermined by a functional economic unfreedom; at the same time, the dynamic freedom of economic production, of the social production of value, is ultimately determined by these same juridical laws. The democratic force of politics is, therefore, limited by the liberal restrictions on the political, an arrangement that is legitimated from C3 to C1 by C2.

This conception and these dialectics are fleshed out more fully in the articulation of the arguments of the book. The overall point to take away is that the conceptualization helps differentiate levels of culture such that we can see how it is possible to view culture as, simultaneously, a process, a commodified product, and an administered structure. The purpose for outlining this conceptualization is to make feasible a discussion of what I call "the reified culture of property." The following chapter looks at the origins of this reified culture in Early Modern England and the writings of Sir Francis Bacon and Locke. The process through which their cultural ideal was imposed on the population is a good example of one technique by which culture at the C3 level is able to achieve cultural efficacy throughout the cultural hierarchy—namely, by destroying all the competing practices at the C1 level, invalidating any competing narratives at the C2 level, and instantiating the dominant narrative of "improvement" as the solitary justifying narrative of the newly hewn unitary state. The degree of naked coercion displayed in its implementation seems starkly removed from the process of implementing IPR on a global scale. But, as this book aims to show, the implementation of the deeper culture of property is the real context of the latter. Thus, we must return to the source of both before coming back to the present implementation of IPR.

2

Property, Primitive Accumulation, and the Liberal State

The legitimacy of the contemporary neoliberal state rests on a reified culture of property that asserts a certain understanding of value in relation to labor, coercion, and the state: any value derived from productive property should flow back to the legal owner, even if that value is objectively the result of a much broader process of social production. Paradoxically, it also claims that the owner's right to that property is based on the fact that it has value. This value is assumed to be the result of an "improvement" to the property through the owner's labors; therefore, the owner has a right to the value and the property. This circular argument forms the foundation of the liberal defense of the state—a defense that its supporters claim is natural rather than political. The legitimate liberal state defends only this form of economic freedom, an exception to the popular rule that cannot be altered through democratic challenges. John Locke presents the earliest and most coherent version of this defense, but, as this chapter argues, he represented an emergent "structure of feeling" within certain sectors of the English ruling classes.

Yet Locke and his fellow members of the emergent capitalist classes reaped the benefit of a vigorously active, absolutist state, whose control over the population, its means of communication (i.e., the printing press), the political economic processes of enclosure, primitive accumulation, and "improvement" led to what Christopher Hill (1982) terms "a century of revolution." Locke's liberal ideology of private property and the state was invented to simultaneously fend off absolutism and the challenges of the displaced population who resisted the imposition of capitalist social relations. This chapter places Locke's ideas in this context to further contextualize the neoliberal apologists of the Law and Economics movement (discussed in the following chapter) and their influence on the debate over intellectual property rights (IPR).

The relation of this reified culture of property to the contemporary debate about IPR is twofold. On the one hand, this precise reified culture provides the underpinning of the absolutist IPR offensive. As Rosemary Coombe argues in her book *The Cultural Life of Intellectual Properties* (1998), most advocates for absolutist IPR make arguments that are rooted in a Lockean understanding of property as he presents it in the *Second Treatise of Government*. Herein, Locke argues that "whatsoever he removes out of the State that Nature hath provided and left it in, he hath mixed his *Labour* with, and joined to it something that is his own, and thereby makes it his *Property*" (1988, p. 288; emphasis original). Coombe discusses this stance particularly in reference to trademark law, which, in the past few decades, has been transformed from something that companies are required to protect to give customers some modicum of quality assurance into a property in and of itself. The implications of this shift are certainly interesting to chart, but in challenging the legitimacy of the Lockean notion of property only in its applicability to trademarks, copyright, or publicity rights, Coombe reifies the overall arguments about property, labor (or, as Ellen Meiksins Wood [2002] discusses it, "improvement"), and the role of the state as the cultural background from which these claims to property emerge.

On the other hand, Coombe and others challenge ways in which the production of value is conceived in this Lockean perspective: they note processes of digitization and globalization that illuminate the broader process of social production visible in relation to the objects of IPR. While these critics fail to challenge the reified culture of property, the conversation they begin opens the discussion—and the visibility—of the larger process of social production that creates value throughout the capitalist economy. In this discussion, the debate about IPR has much to teach us about the reified culture of property, even if it fails to challenge the latter in any fundamental sense.

The present chapter synthesizes several historians' accounts of the prehistory and implementation of this reified culture—at a moment when most aspects of it were up for discussion—and highlights the coeval emergence of property and intellectual property (IP). In conceptual terms, it looks at the historical origin of the framework of culture I outline in the previous chapter:

the moment when the modern, capitalist nation-state was consolidated in seventeenth-century England. This political formation allowed for a certain model of culture (C3) to be instantiated on the population—largely in terms similar to Locke's understanding of "improvement"—and to reshape English society, culture, and ecology in the direction of what is now modern capitalism. I argue that the peculiarly "pure" form of the English state, relying as it did on the notion of natural law, makes the cultural aspect of this model more important than most. However, unlike today, this culture was not reified. A fierce struggle ensued, and the population defending the commons had to be coerced into accepting this model of culture. The origins of the modern concepts of IPR can be found here, with the first use of patents and copyrights. But in this moment, copyright was largely used by the crown to secure the larger culture of property against this revolt. Locke penned his defense of the liberal state in the context of trying to stave off further threats to this emergent culture of property. His success in this endeavor can be measured by its continued reification to this day.

As I have argued throughout this book, the debate about IPR is really more about the history of property rights and what the present debate can tell us about the reified culture of property. The present chapter looks at the historical development of this reified culture of property and extracts several key points in relation to the political forms and cultural ideologies that make this reified culture effective in the current day. First I look at the development of the basic conception of a national law, administered by the state. This system seems like a natural phenomenon in contemporary, Western societies, but in the early seventeenth century, it was virtually nonexistent, with various authorities of the rising state, the receding clergy of the Roman empire, private merchant lawyers, and the judges of local feudal courts locked in what legal scholars Michael Tigar and Madeline Levy call a "jurisdictional covetousness" over which court had a right to govern which populations, territories, and transactions (2000, pp. 47–48).

Looking at this state consolidation may seem arcane to readers overly focused on the narrow topic of IPR, but it is especially relevant to the contemporary discussion of IPR on a global scale. As Keith A. Maskus points out, "The TRIPS [Trade-Related Aspects of Intellectual Property Rights] agreement is important beyond its strengthening of IPRs. It is the first multilateral trade accord that aims at achieving partial harmonization in an extensive area of business regulation. Undoubtedly, it forms the vanguard of efforts to establish deep integration of domestic regulatory policies among countries" (2000, p. 2). In the Early Modern era, the merchant class was the most animated about the need for a centralized law, as the parcelized and overlapping authorities made it difficult to complete transactions between even relatively nearby spaces. One result of the centralization of this era was to project merchant law upward into the central state to ease commerce for the merchant class. Maskus employs the euphemism of "harmonization" in his account, but what he really means is that a single law would govern all transactions involving IPR—but also all transactions that could possibly be subjected to its logic—making it easier for the transnational capitalist class to conduct its affairs. Maskus sees TRIPS as a vanguard to be replicated in future accords, but it is really just a continuation of the process that began several hundred years ago with the consolidation of a single "law of the land" within the Early Modern English polity. A. Samuel Oddi (1996) refers to harmonization as "a polite form of economic imperialism," underscoring the ways in which harmonization advocates justify the imposition of Western IPR standards via "natural law" defenses of patent ownership. If contemporary transnational treaty harmonization continues the state consolidation that began in the seventeenth century, that is also the moment when the cultural content of capital-friendly "natural law" was secured after a revolutionary struggle.

Like the TRIPS process of harmonization in IPR, this Early Modern state consolidation proceeded in stages, with the discourse of natural law appropriated by various political movements promoting different visions of what the future of English society might look like. In terms of the conceptualization of culture I discuss in the previous chapter, these competing theories were mediations existing at the C2 level that hoped to gain purchase within the political institutions. These institutions were increasingly articulated to the empty signifier of "natural law" at the C3 level. Thus the political struggle over the articulation of the meaning of "natural law" was also a struggle between concrete proponents of radically different social formations—between democratic freedom in the commons or the slavery of capitalist property relations. In the end, the movements for a social and democratic "leveling" lost out to proponents of what became the Lockean defense of property—enshrined in the Great Restoration of 1688, which also brought Locke and his fellow ex-patriots back to the homeland. In the end, this "natural law" was really a justification of the status quo that Locke had (anonymously) assisted in creating, employing the ideas of improvement that were central to the culture of property reshaping England according to this model.

While this polity is ostensibly rooted in the traditions of liberalism and democracy, it ultimately rests on the former, which permanently forms a backstop to the latter. Liberalism in this formulation refers to the economic freedom in the market, which was the first demand of Locke and his fellow agricultural capitalists at the forefront of that movement. But this economic freedom inevitably produces—and helps amplify—massive inequalities of wealth. If the only charge of the state is to defend property absolutely, this charge effectively means that the state only functions as an apparatus of repression for all but the richest in society. Even though the concept limits liberty and democracy to the protection of property, the elite ideologists of classical liberalism hope to convince the property-less majority that they really are free, a key illustration of Chantal Mouffe's "democratic paradox," which I discuss in the following chapter. A perfect illustration of this paradox in relation to IPR is in the original implementation of copyright in the Early Modern English state. In his book *Authors and Owners: The Invention of Copyright*, Mark Rose describes the rationale behind the English state's copyright contract with the Stationers Company: "The primary interest of the state in granting this monopoly was not, however, the securing of stationers' property rights but the establishment of a more effective system for governmental surveillance of the press" (1995, p. 12). As it had been for centuries, religion was the hegemonic mediating culture of the time, and the most popular publishing of the time was religious in nature. The printing press—born with Johannes Gutenberg's publication of the Bible—soon led (or at least helped lead) to the Protestant Reformation and, shortly after, the separation of the Church of England from the rest of the Roman Catholic Empire. Within England, throughout the end of the sixteenth century and the beginning of the seventeenth, competing movements guided by conflicting religious interpretations vied for hegemony. Even Locke, who famously encouraged religious toleration, saw no contradiction in "suppressing an opinion manifestly (or covertly) aiming at disturbing public order (say, a revolutionary pamphlet)" (Lærke 2009, p. 5). Included in his list of forbiddable religions was Catholicism, atheism, and some Protestant sects, all of which "represented serious threats to the stability of the State" (ibid.).

The English state introduced copyright to stifle competing narratives of religion, especially those articulating natural law along more democratic lines. These competing narratives and the movements they represented and inspired are a perfect example of what critics of maximalist IPR describe as "culture as a process": they were creative appropriations of contemporary (religious) culture that produced competing interpretations (C2) of legitimate practices (C1) and regimes of governance (C3). The use of copyright to stifle this "free speech" was not merely in the interest of supporting the authority of the absolutist state; it was also a blatant attempt to undermine the possibility that citizens or counterhegemonic movements could use this process of cultural appropriation to challenge the legitimacy of the emergent culture of property at the C3 level. The process of implementing a culture of "improvement" in English society produced a chaotic interplay of these movements and ideas. This process of implementation, these competing discourses of property and natural law, and the echoes of both in the contemporary discourses around IPR form the main subject of this chapter.

The final subject of this chapter is intercalated between these. It is the account of what it takes to make a society "natural" according to the liberal orthodoxy of the reified culture of property. As this chapter outlines, the peculiar natural law presumption of liberalism is that the property and rights that it secures *against* the state are said to *precede* it: the English state, as a liberal apparatus, is disavowed as such within the ideology of liberalism, despite the state's essential role in forcefully constructing the material, legal, and ultimately punitive infrastructure for that ideology to flourish. And a casual glance at the historical record clearly reveals a very active state, working in the interests of one class over another.

It is one thing to contend that natural law precedes the state and thus the state must be overthrown to resume ancient liberties. But when doing this requires the revolutionaries to fight with *other* revolutionaries about what those ancient liberties are, calling the cultural, political content of that state "natural" is highly suspect. Insofar as liberal capitalist democracy became the hegemonic culture of late-seventeenth-century England, it was due to the forceful, political repression of any competing ideologies. This chapter not only calls into question this assertion of natural law but also highlights recent historical accounts documenting the longevity and coerciveness of the project to impose the model I discuss throughout this book as the "reified culture of property."

Central to Locke's defense of private property and to the liberal state is the notion of "improvement." By improving, or increasing the value or profitability, of the property, one justifies one's ownership. The flipside of this hypothetical scenario justifies dispossession: if one does not improve the land according to the dominant definition of improvement, it is not valid as property. The ideology of improvement originates more than a century before Locke was writing, and in that time, the new central state, far from being ancillary to this ideology, helped instantiate it. As Marcus Rediker and Peter Linebaugh discuss, the early seventeenth-century English state forced laborers to build ports for commerce, drain swamps, enclose land, and chop down forests for the various agricultural projects of early English capitalism. This endeavor was a massive, state-directed project of improvement, the rewards of which were then, after the fact, claimed as a natural right by the newly landed classes lucky enough to assert ownership. It puts the lie to the minimal state involvement in the economy that liberalism claims as one of its central dogmas.

This chapter gives a brief account of some of these efforts as a way of underlining the interpenetration of the political and economic spheres. The purpose of this discussion in relation to the larger project is to highlight the involvement of the state in the order that liberalism claims is natural. This involvement is replicated in the monopoly rights and government aid given to the culture industry conglomerates who now claim IPR over our collective cultural commons. Recognizing what Karl Marx calls the "primitive accumulation" of productive property and the state aid given to accumulators is an important historical challenge to the reified culture of property.

Far from a "natural" process of individual improvement, primitive accumulation is a historical, political project that instantiates this culture of property and creates a population who has nothing to sell but its labor—or, as Michael Perelman (2000) articulates it, the elimination of this population's ability to provide for itself. The Early Modern English state projects improved the environment for a proto-capitalist future while simultaneously eliminating the commons that supported autonomous populations who were able to subsist without working for the enclosing landlords.

While the ideology of capitalism did not yet exist per se, the capitalist relationship between meaning, power, and value was already immanent. These mutually constituting threads wound around each other, helping manifest built space, a legal order, and an ideal subject of the nascent capitalist society, which C. B. Macpherson (1962) calls "possessive individualism." The effect, if not the stated goal, of these endeavors was to eliminate the spaces "beyond the pale": to minimize the areas where the power of the central state did not reach and the means through which people were able to exist outside the range of its administration. It was simultaneously an effort to eliminate divergent practices and "idle" citizens who were not laboring according to the new cultural mandates of improvement. Poor laws, workhouses, and threats of prison and "transportation" to the colonies were all used to discipline these subsisting populations into submission to the state and the emergent hegemonic order. The history of eliminating the commons, beginning at least in the seventeenth century and continuing today, is also a history of eliminating divergent definitions of natural law and instantiating the new culture of improvement that we now understand as the reified culture of property. The processes documented in this chapter provide the prehistory of liberalism (or neoliberalism as we understand it today). Insofar as contemporary critics of IPR focus on the loss of a strictly cultural process of production, they do little to challenge the reification of this culture at large or its inertia toward absolutist intellectual property defended by the equivalent of an absolutist international regime.

"Nobody Puts Baby in the Corner—That's Where We Keep the Serfs!"

In 2005, the American Film Institute (AFI)—an organization created in 1967 to "preserve America's fast-disappearing film heritage" (AFI, 2005)—asked a jury of fifteen hundred filmmakers, artists, critics, historians, and others in the "creative community" to score a ballot of "the 100 top film quotes of all time." The project was part of the AFI's continuing effort to remind people of the roles that movies play in our lives and the ways in which viewers use movie quotations in their daily lives, such that "circulating through popular culture, [the quotes] become part of the national lexicon and evoke the memory of a treasured film, thus ensuring and enlivening its historical legacy" (ibid.). At the top of the list were lines from *Casablanca* ("Here's looking at you"), *The Godfather* ("offer he can't refuse"), and *The Wizard of Oz* ("Toto, I have a feeling we're not in Kansas anymore"), with the top honors, predictably, going to Clark Gable for his final utterance of "Frankly, my dear, I don't give a damn" in *Gone with the Wind*.

Near the bottom of the list (#98) is Patrick Swayze's now-famous line from the 1987 movie *Dirty Dancing*: "Nobody puts Baby in the corner!" Although he utters it to defend the right of a teen girl to perform in a dance review at an upstate New York summer resort, the moment appears as a solemn, heroic intervention, on par with fighting off the invading Russians, which was what Swayze and his *Dirty Dancing* partner, Jennifer Grey, had done in their previous film together (*Red Dawn*). As IPR critic Coombe might argue (and the AFI would likely agree), while the filmmakers obviously produced a movie that has inspired this interest, it is the interaction of the film in the cultural circuit that has solidified its place in our common consciousness. And who among us has not said that line—or at least heard it said—in some other colloquial setting? To be honest, I think I had only heard it repeated in conversation: when I reviewed that film for this chapter, I clearly had no memory of the original scene.

In short, people obviously refer to something more than just the scene itself when using this phrase. In her work on trademark, legal scholar Rochelle Dreyfuss (1990) finds a similar dynamic at work. In Coombe's account, Dreyfuss separates the "signaling function" of the trademark from its "expressive capacity," which explains the "expressive genericity" in "the marketplace of ideas" in ways beyond the original intent (Coombe 1998, p. 67). In semiotic terms, because there is always a gap between signifier and signified—between the trademark and what it means culturally—there is a lot of room for new meanings to take root. Yet according to trademark law, the owner has a monopoly on the rents created by that trademark as well as control over its "expressive genericity": they have the power to define what can legally be said using—and, in some cases, about—a trademark or its owner. And even where they are not formally granted this power, the functional economic clout of the most powerful trademark holders guarantees that the law often operates as though they have been.

Trademark's legal function is supposed to be an indication to a diffuse consumer base as to who is responsible for the creation of a product. While diverse origins are given to this idea, in U.S. history, Naomi Klein (2002) and others trace it to the late nineteenth century, when, on the one hand, commodity consumption was becoming widespread and, because of emergent railway infrastructure, these commodities ceased to be mainly provided by local companies or individuals with whom consumers had a direct relationship. Creating trust and establishing responsibility for the product was central to the political and legal construction of trademark. Since interlopers using a similar mark could undermine consumers' ability to make decisions based on their relationship with the sole legal owner of that mark, it was a form of privatized quality control in an era when, outside the market and the mercantilist and then the imperialist state, few other regulators existed.

In short, the "signaling function" of trademark was supposed to give people information about, to use Locke's terminology, whose labor was behind the commodity in question (Dreyfuss 1990, p. 399). In the contemporary international division of labor, the "labor" of production is more fetishized—in Marx's usage, not Sigmund Freud's—by the use of trademarks, where the labor of materially producing the commodity is left to invisible others a world away, sutured by the IPR that ensures the majority of the value flows back to the corporate owner. Through this "signaling function," the trademark "owner" is protected from other producers' using the same mark or name to sell similar items. Owners are periodically required to formally prove that a cultural association exists between their exclusive marks and the products or services in question. They are also required to demonstrate their efforts to prevent the marks themselves from becoming generic—for example, such products as Kleenex, Xerox, or Google, for which the mark has become the general term for the kind of product sold and thus no longer exclusively refers to a particular product produced by a particular company. Protecting this cultural association as a legal right is primarily intended to serve the consumers, but, with the expansion of the "expressive capacity" of trademarks, the boundaries of ownership and the production of value are blurred. The ubiquity of trademarks in our everyday lives has led to their use to mean much more than their owners' intended or their signaling function in the marketplace.

Dreyfuss is concerned with the First Amendment implications of letting trademark owners control every appropriation of their "ideograms," a concern that Coombe shares. Coombe looks at appropriations of diverse trademarks—by local culture jamming organizations, among others—and notes the ways in which IPR protection stifles freedom of speech, asserting that cultural studies scholars of the structuralist and culturalist paradigms are unable to address the "logic of the commodity when applied to cultural forms": "Intellectual Property laws enable such commodification and create conditions for a dialectical cultural politics shaped by the relationship between those who claim proprietary interests and those who seek to appropriate such signifiers [e.g., trademarks] for new agendas" (1998, p. 134).

In *Copyrights and Copywrongs*, Siva Vaidhyanathan asserts that it is precisely because of these First Amendment concerns that Locke would not approve of having his "theories of real property misapplied to copyright," as he was "one of the strongest critics of both censorship and monopoly power" (2001, p. 199n12). Locke's fear of censorship and monopoly power is more ambivalent in his other writings. He believed in religious toleration, except, of course, for those Catholics and atheists, whose works he thought should be actively censored. But his most memorable statement on the "liberty of the press" was as a book connoisseur: he found the pirated volumes of Europe far preferable to those sanctioned by the crown, which might be why he chose to publish his *Two Treatises of Government* illicitly, anonymously, and abroad (Locke 1997).

But as with many products of meaning, power, and value that circulate in the popular culture, Locke's articulation of property rights was quickly incorporated into the dominant culture; his arguments justify virtually every kind of primitive accumulation, so long as it is in the interest of capitalist "improvement." More important for this chapter, since Locke says this absolute protection of property is required because the state should reflect our legitimate support of improvement, ownership now implies improvement. Other authors have discussed this stance in terms of the ideology of meritocracy (Littler 2017), but both ideologies rest on the liberal capitalist assumption that if someone owns something, he or she must have worked for it.

To return to the legacy of that fictional drama in the New York summer resort, in August 2007, news reports began circulating that Lionsgate Pictures, which holds the rights to *Dirty Dancing*, had issued a lawsuit and an order to cease and desist to fifteen companies that had been using the line

"Nobody puts Baby in the corner!" on clothes and other commodities. Citing the AFI list as evidence, the suit claimed that the quote was "well known and associated with the *Dirty Dancing* motion picture and the Mark." Despite the fact that Lionsgate had no trademark on file for the line, the lawsuit claimed that these companies owed damages and restitution to the "Plaintiff [who] markets and sells merchandise with the movie trademarks through approved licensees as part of the *Dirty Dancing* line of approved merchandise" (*Lionsgate Entertainment Inc. v. Carter's Inc. et al.* 2007).

Contrary to Lionsgate's claim, it is at best ambiguous that it was owed a licensing fee. The studio had not trademarked the line itself at the time of the lawsuit, and a phrase of this length could not be reasonably copyrighted. Lionsgate simply claimed that because it held the copyright to the larger work and a trademark in the name of the film, it should be able to own any expressions related to these properties. If the companies in question were not being threatened by a lengthy, expensive lawsuit—and a jury trial—it would have made sense for them to claim they were making legal use of the phrase: there was no trademark infringement since Lionsgate had no registered trademark in it. However, the case eventually settled out of court, apparently because one of the merchants agreed to enter into a licensing agreement with Lionsgate.

While paying the licensing fees was a reasonable way to avoid a costly lawsuit, the resulting agreement effectively consecrated Lionsgate's legal claim as valid. As James Gibson (2007) argues, "risk averse" licensing actually helps solidify claims of property rights holders. On the one hand, entering a licensing agreement with a trademark or copyright owner gives that owner a great deal more latitude over what can be said with or through it. Since U.S. law is unclear on when the use of copyrighted or trademarked material falls under fair use, Gibson says the common practice—particularly in clearing distribution rights for movies—among risk management lawyers is to license even uses that would probably not have necessitated the license. It is often worth the relatively small, yet still substantial, fees and corporate terms compared with the potentially immense legal costs of getting sued. Over time, the market for these previously unnecessary licenses can be used in the courts to help accrue new rights to the owners of IPR. The mechanisms through which this process happens are the licensing market (for copyright) and consumer surveys (in trademark), both of which are inordinately influenced by market-based understandings of value and the dominant culture of property, where, again, all value produced using a property should flow back to the owner.

The early news coverage of Lionsgate's suit reveals the depth of the culture of property in the Anglo-Saxon sphere of influence that no mere misapplication of Locke can explain. Lionsgate is described as follows: "the studio responsible for the timeless classic *Dirty Dancing*" (Warcutter 2007), "the studio behind 1980s cult hit *Dirty Dancing*" (*The Guardian* 2007), and "the makers of iconic movie *Dirty Dancing*" (WENN 2007). But Lionsgate was not even a twinkle in its executives' eyes in 1987 when the film was made by Vestron Pictures, a production spin-off of distributor Vestron Video. Lionsgate acquired the rights to *Dirty Dancing* when it acquired Artisan Entertainment in 2003, which used to be, among other names, Live Entertainment, which acquired Vestron's catalog when the company went bankrupt in 1993. In other words, Lionsgate was not, as various news reports asserted, the "studio behind," nor was it "responsible" for "making" or "producing" *Dirty Dancing*. Only one news post by the movie review website *Rotten Tomatoes* correctly describes Lionsgate as "the studio that owns the film's rights" (Giles 2007). In other words, the Lockean argument than labor justifies ownership is refracted into an assumption that, if the property is owned, then the owner must have created its value.

This example is indicative of a deeper reflex. It shows the force of the Lockean notion of property—and the inflection that it and the liberal tradition have been given over the past three centuries. Coombe and Dreyfuss criticize the idea that if something has value, then that value should go back to the owner. But the more fundamental assumption about property—and not just IP—is that, if it is legally owned by someone, it is not all that important how they got it. This interpretation is also a misapprehension of Locke's central questions, which had more to do with the nature of power and obligation and, most importantly, the correct structure of the state. As this chapter argues, these misapprehensions of Lionsgate's role in the production of that value actually shows a very common assumption of Locke and of theories of property and the state in general. This misapprehension is fundamental to the liberal tradition; it is an interpretation that uses history and tradition to justify its legitimacy but depends on asking none of the difficult questions about the history of the material social relations themselves—an interpretation, in short, that none of the critics of IPR is wont to question because it so deeply structures the policies of the neoliberal capitalist state and its hegemonic cultural ideologies.

Returning to the early seventeenth century and the struggle over the coercive imposition of these ideas gives significant insight into the current push for stronger IPR. It shows that, although the specific articulations may change, the role of the liberal state in defending property before democracy remains the same. As Tigar and Levy note in their book *Law and the Rise of Capitalism*:

> The eighteenth-century bourgeois notion of the laissez-faire state as a neutral arbiter was nowhere in evidence in [sixteenth- and seventeenth-century] Tudor England; the state was concededly an instrument, shared by the crown and its powerful allies, to smash resistance to a new system of social relations. The later legal ideology of property as a natural right was an ideology for those who already owned land or were in the process of acquiring it in the normal course of trade [or the nascent state-aided imperialism]; it was another way of saying that whoever had managed to capture a portion of the earth in the previous hundred years' troubles ought to be able to keep it. (2000, p. 192)

Tigar and Levy are right to find a contradiction in the state coercion used to instantiate the social relations that modern liberalism sees as "natural." The doctrine of "natural law" insists that the property relations protected by the state predate the state. Using the political state apparatus to reshape a population, its culture, and its social property relations should be heretical to a consistent version of liberalism; yet because the absolutism is in the service of capitalist private property, it is absolved. More surprising than this inconsistency is the astounding fact that each generation of citizens residing in the nominally liberal West needs to be reminded that "the moralization of the means of violence has been the task of liberal and progressive intellectuals since they first competed with clerics for moral authority" (Seymour 2008, p. 218).

While the expansion of IPR has certainly not been accompanied by the same degree of physical violence, the "legal ideology of property as a natural right" has performed a similar function in the current era. As I discuss in *Hegemony, Mass Media and Cultural Studies* (Johnson Andrews 2016), mention in the introduction here, and explore further in Chapter 4, the monopoly of most U.S./European media conglomerates was originally not in the content that they distributed but in the distribution system itself. It was relatively difficult to start and profitably maintain a competitive media distribution company—which was the most important state-granted monopoly to even the biggest production companies, particularly in broadcast media, which required government licenses to operate. IPR made certain that only the legitimate "owner" of the media would be able to distribute content with the kind of profit margins enjoyed by the major global media conglomerates.

This circumstance was less true in the era of videocassettes than it was during the studio system. The original production company of *Dirty Dancing* was a subsidiary of Vestron Video, which made most of its money by redistributing older or even new independent films. When Vestron went bankrupt, Live Entertainment, another video distribution company, acquired the catalog of copyrights more than any real property. But even then, IPR were the valuable insurance it needed to guarantee a return on its investment in distribution infrastructure. Digital technology was supposed to facilitate this return, but it has also undermined it in that distribution is now easier than ever. IPR was supposed to help these incumbent owners retain their monopoly and prevent the devalorization of this sunk capital: an explicit goal of the U.S. Congressional support for the Digital Millennium Copyright Act (DMCA) was to help the culture industries of yore transition to the content industries of the information age. In other words, increased IPR on a global scale, like private property rights in the seventeenth century, "was another way of saying that whoever had managed to capture a portion of the earth in the previous hundred years' troubles ought to be able to keep it" (Tigar and Levy 2000, p. 192).

The purpose of going back to the seventeenth century is to outline the early articulation of this culture of property as well as to see the social struggles that produced it and the parallels to those over IPR today. The model of economic development Locke supported was based on agriculture, thus making land—real property—the most important asset. But even Locke realized that the only way this asset could be "improved" was if laborers worked the land for its owner, who then appropriated the value of said labor. Dispossessing cottagers served a twofold purpose in the imposition of this model. Primitive accumulation is the consolidation of resources and the political use of that asymmetrical material position to compel laborers into a wage-relationship: this was, in the end, what property meant in Locke's time. In our own era, with the hegemonic, postindustrial, informational economic model, the objects covered by IPR serve the same socioeconomic function. Focusing too closely on the objects themselves, drawing distinctions between them and that which came before, ignores the basic similarity in the political economic purpose these property rights serve.

This similarity of purpose makes it all the more important to embed property and IPR in the history of the use of the state to impose and enforce models of socioeconomic development. This chapter shifts the stakes of the present struggle over IP to the role of "models" as metacultural ideals (what the previous chapter refers to as "C3") and the relation of these models to the agency of the populations subjected to them. Looking at the Early Modern processes that coercively instantiated the capitalist-oriented understanding of property, value, and the state is essential to recognizing the nature of the more contemporary struggle.

On the other hand, as Walter Benjamin says, "Every image of the past that is not recognized by the present as one of its own concerns threatens to disappear irretrievably" (1969, p. 255), which is another way of saying that history is almost always the history of the present. As I have explored elsewhere (Johnson Andrews 2017), contemporary critics of maximalist IPR are familiar with the era of enclosure, but often only in a metaphorical sense. Christopher May (2000) asks whether IPR are the "New Enclosures"; James Boyle describes IPR as "the second enclosure movement" in a 2003 article that carefully compares IPR to the seventeenth-century enclosures and followed this up with a 2008 book subtitled "Enclosing the Commons of the Mind" (Boyle 2003, 2008); and Peter Drahos and John Braithwaite (2003) discuss the expansion of these rules on the international level through TRIPS as a form of feudalism. Lawrence Lessig invokes this moment in his "creative commons" organization. Many others are keenly aware of the parallels between our moment and the enclosure movements of yore.

However, this past is often read through the lens of the more general reified culture of property. Benjamin also says, "The past can be seized only as an image which flashes up at an instant when it can be recognized and is never seen again" (1969, p. 255). The framework through which critics of the maximalist vision of copyright have "recognized" this history almost guarantees the misrecognition of the stakes of the struggle. These scholars recognize that something can be learned from looking at this earlier moment. They invoke the specter of feudalism, of the enclosure of the common as a similar occurrence, but its effects are seen as immutable. This view is clearest in the distinction that all insist needs to be made between what Lessig (following conventional economic discourse) calls "rivalrous" and "nonrivalrous" resources (2001, p. 21). The definitions themselves inherently imply the model of what Macpherson (1962) calls "possessive market society." As Lessig puts it, a resource is nonrivalrous when "your consumption [of it] does not rival my own." For example, "no matter how many times you read a poem, there's as much left over as there was when you started." (2001, p. 22). In contrast, in the commons in rivalrous resources, Lessig cites the standard "The Tragedy of the Commons" article by Garrett Hardin (1968). Hardin says the commons without property and enclosure result in a Hobbesian struggle over resources between what Macpherson calls self-interested, possessive individuals. The result: "freedom in a commons brings ruin to all" (Lessig 2001, pp. 21–22).

In addition to denying the fact that commons actually exist in rivalrous resources—which Lessig barely acknowledges—Hardin's perspective presumes the state apparatus and the cultural disposition of a modern capitalist order. In short, Hardin (and Lessig) presume a reified culture of property that, before the seventeenth century, did not exist. Lessig may be making a strategic accommodation in leaving this culture of property unquestioned, but my suspicion is that he is unable to see the more fundamental similarity in the way that value is created and appropriated in both. Because of this misrecognition, he assumes that the previous enclosures in real property are beyond question. Here, Hardin's own defense of enclosure seems apt:

> Every new enclosure of the commons involves the infringement of somebody's personal liberty. Infringements made in the distant past are accepted because no contemporary complains of a loss. It is the newly proposed infringements that we vigorously oppose; cries of "rights" and "freedom" fill the air. (1968, p. 1248)

To be clear, I agree with the project of the balanced copyright movement. I think Lessig, especially, is right to vigorously impose these new infringements. However, the basis from which he works implies the acceptance of infringements made in the distant past. The use he and others make of the history of property, this "image which flashes up at an instant" (Benjamin 1969, p. 255), does not do justice to the complexity of that—or our own—moment.

This chapter is an attempt to prevent this misrecognition and the historical oblivion that Benjamin says it portends. This erasure is a common component of the liberal defense of property, as is the pattern of state-aided primitive accumulation that preceded it. The definition of primitive accumulation, again, is not just that it moves common resources behind fences; it also forces the population that relied on the use of that common into a working relationship with the newly minted owners. Insofar as this system represented freedom, it was the freedom to work for the landlords. By focusing on the problem of IPR in isolation from the problem of the reified culture of property in general, critics of IPR tacitly agree that the rest of this bill of goods is accurately described on the label: "Freedom," "Liberty," or (at least) "Economic Growth." Therefore, I begin by looking at these fundamental questions of law and culture in relation to property and the culture of improvement central to the liberal state. Then I examine how Locke's own understanding of "improvement" was tied up in the struggle to impose it on the Early Modern English population. Religious ideology and pirate publishing were key to that struggle, making the early imposition of IP a tool for stifling dissent against the imposition of property rights in general.

Imposing the Culture of Improvement

If we were to look at a map of the legitimacy of power, of the clarity of law at this point in Western European history, it would be a confusing jumble akin to what Naeem Inayatullah and David Blaney term "Multiple and Overlapping Sovereignties." They discuss this concept in opposition to "'the empire of uniformity' imposed through the reign of straight lines" (Inayatullah and Blaney 2004, p. 187). They are speaking of international boundaries, but the Early Modern divisions within European states were just as problematic. No such empire of uniformity existed, which was a problem, especially for some within the English polity. The "jurisdictional covetousness of the ecclesiastical, seigniorial and royal courts" described by legal scholars Tigar and Levy (2000, p. 47) was accompanied and interspersed by spaces beyond the pale.

The meaning of the phrase "beyond the pale" is significant. According to the *Oxford English Dictionary*, the earliest connotation of "pale" is of "a stake, fence, or boundary" ("Pale" 2007). At roughly the same time (circa 1400 C.E.), it meant a staff that was used for fighting and, simultaneously, a post soldiers used "to represent an opponent during fighting practice." The three connotations together—the pale as a boundary, a weapon, and a representation of the Other—resonate with the pattern of feudal law: it is a space in which the political is much more at play, suturing the indeterminacies of the body politic with the threat of violence. The ideology of Catholicism provided some common ground, but its tenuous hold was contested and arbitrary, particularly in England, where it was recently substituted with a local Protestant interpretation. As in Theodor Adorno's understanding of culture as administration, internal cohesion was constituted in opposition to external religious dominions. Thus, the supposed contrast—made by Montesquieu among others—between the laws of Islamic countries encircling Western Europe and, slightly later, of Catholic (or "Roman") laws in the rest of Europe contradicted that of England (P. Anderson 1979, pp. 398–400). To speak of a space "beyond the pale" in this environment was largely aspirational: there was barely a pale to go beyond.

This fact was apparent to the different authorities vying for absolute jurisdiction over populations and territories as well as those populations themselves. As Perry Anderson puts it, "Although the feudal class tried on occasion to enforce the rule *nulle terre sans seigneur* ["no land without a master"], in practice this was never achieved in any feudal social formation: communal lands—pastures, meadows and forest—and scattered allods always remained a significant sector of peasant autonomy and resistance" (1996, p. 148). No land without a master also meant no person without a master: citizens with a legitimate space of freedom from direct political authority within the feudal order were *sans seigneur*. This status was especially important in the towns. The presence of these spaces—common spaces where free people could provide for themselves—was essential to the struggle that ensued over the ideology of natural law as well as the material practices of Early Modern capitalism. But unless someone was trying to move from one place to another (an activity that would have been prohibited for many in the order) or making a transaction between these jurisdictions, the "parcelized sovereignty" of the feudal order would not be all that apparent, nor would the actual absence of a supreme authority in all things temporal.

By the early seventeenth century, the two dominant English meanings of the phrase "beyond the pale" were more indicative of the predominance of the modern state. By this point, it referred first to a district or territory outside "determined bounds" or not "subject to a particular jurisdiction." By projecting an outside to the law's jurisdiction, it assumed the existence of an inside where the law was effective, and a more absolute form of government administered it. The use of this phrase in relation to the area of Ireland not subject to English jurisdiction—the area "beyond the pale"—was indicative of its imperial connotation and the desire to incorporate the people and spaces that remained outside the pale of the law. It was a return to the imperial roots of the Roman notion of natural law in the form of *jus gentium*: a law for all peoples. At the same time, the reemergence of natural law as the justification for ecclesiastical and royal law owed as much to the bourgeois lawyers working for the crown and the church as it did the ideas and practices carried across time and space from the East by traders and crusaders: as Tigar and Levy point out, these were sometimes the same people, as some of the earliest traders (and international financiers) were the Knights Templar (2000, p. 68).

"Natural law" was in this sense transcendent, expanding beyond politics and history, unlimited by space, time, or so-called bad subjects (Althusser 2001, p. 181). As Louis Althusser says of natural law theories, "The end of history [is] inscribed in its origins" (2007, p. 26). The aspect of the law that becomes more evident in this later understanding of "beyond the pale" is its extension inward—or, at the very least, in its governance of individual performance of the practices that provide evidence of this inner characteristic. Following the axiom "kneel, pray, and you will believe" may not produce the desired result, but from the outside, all the kneeling and praying (C1) can give the illusion of belief (C2). The projection of this process from C3 downward, central to the modern ideology of the law, is the process Althusser (2001) discusses in terms of "interpellation" of subjects in ideology.

Althusser's use of Christianity as his primary example of ideology is a convenient anachronism. As Alain Supiot argues, religion is the perfect model by which to think about how the modern state and the law function:

> We should not forget that the meaning of the word "religion" has changed into its opposite with the secularization of society. There is religion and Religion. Whereas previously Religion constituted the dogmatic foundation of society, nowadays [religion] is a question of individual freedom; a public affair has become a private one, which is why discussing religion today is unfailingly a source of misunderstanding. In medieval Europe, Religion was not a private matter and so has no existence in the sense of the word today. [. . .] The fact that Christianity no longer has any constitutional position in certain Western countries in no way implies that the latter are not founded on dogma. States, no less than people, continue to be sustained by indemonstrable certainties, beliefs that are not the result of free choice because they are part and parcel of one's identity. (2007, p. xiii–xiv)

As Carl Schmitt puts it in *Political Theology* (2006), "All significant concepts of the modern theory of the state are secularized theological concepts." In light of the importance of what he calls "the exception" to the constitution of state authority, the other meaning of "beyond the pale" comes to the fore (ibid., loc. 916). It refers to not only what is outside the physical bounds of the newly defined territorial sovereignty but also what is "outside the limits of acceptable behaviour; unacceptable or improper" ("Pale" 2007). In this definition, the state hopes to describe, in straight lines, not only the limits of its territory but also the paths people take to cross it—and maybe even what they wear while they do it.

The actions of the central state in this modern iteration are not merely intended to exert control over the territory; they are also designed to enculturate the state's subjects to the same set of norms. In his account of the prehistory of IPR, May finds the need for this central state to be a function in the wider expanse of trade. He says that, as the "scope and extent of the change expands [. . . ,] exchange becomes impersonal" (2000, p. 19). This impersonality makes it more necessary to have formal rules drawn up. As the practice of transnational trade projects authority upward into a universal state, it also reveals the need to make the rules adhering *internal* to an exchange applicable to individuals who are technically external to the exchange. In other words, it means making the rules of that which had previously governed only transactions in the market (or on the capitalist plantation) the rules of the total society. We see this transition in relation to the current expansion of liberal conceptions of IPR and the criminalization of piracy. On the other hand, the rules must not only threaten repression but also encourage belief. As May says, "If enforcement was entirely dependent on active policing and force, the advantages of complex economic exchange would be unlikely to arise" (ibid., p. 20). Thus, the rules themselves must become so reified and so natural that people police themselves through informal social norms, which helps mutually constitute the authority of the state policies and the actors officially charged with enforcing them. Ideological efficacy makes it necessary to have culture serve power. As May summarizes, "This leads to efforts to produce a legitimized and socially embedded set of norms and principles which will in most cases ensure behaviour accords with the formal rules without being policed" (ibid., pp. 19–20). Or, as we might put it here, take a set of theories and behaviors that previously existed as one set of theories at C2 and one set of norms developed through behaviors, practices, and social interactions at C1 and project them upward into a universal set of behavioral guidelines that should discipline all actors throughout the social field.

In the period between 1200 and 1500, the church funded universities for the study and promulgation of canon law as "natural law." It saw the economic advantages of trade, even as it saw the detrimental social consequences. It sought to bring commerce into its system of morals. In this context, with the help of the nascent class of bourgeois lawyers, it "translated Roman 'natural reason' into 'natural law' and set up God rather than the common consent of humanity as the arbiter of that law" (Tigar and Levy 2000, p. 49). Still, the patchwork of jurisdictions created problems for merchants, and distance from Rome made the church's power more and less effective. In England, the much earlier alliance of merchants and the king, the weakness of the Roman order to begin with, the international political and economic situations, and the reverberations of Martin Luther's ninety-nine theses created an opportunity to eliminate the ties of religion to Rome. There were perfectly logical political and economic reasons for the split with Rome, but ideologically, it opened Pandora's box.

The split between England and Rome made the king the supreme governor of the Church of England. The split was not supposed to do away with religion altogether; it was intended to meld the two major, competing internal judicial institutions and eliminate the (foreign) ecclesiastical court's meddling in temporal matters. Religion was supposed to continue as the basis for the monarch's temporal powers. As Wood (2002) contends, the English state was more centralized in general than any other in Europe at the time, and the split helped seal (formally, at least) that domestic centralization from external jurisdiction. The appropriation of church lands—including many areas of commons—had the effect of enlarging the gentry, and the rising cost of wool in international markets created pressure to continue the trend of enclosures, to the point where Sir Thomas More, in *Utopia* (1516), spoke of men being eaten by sheep. The Tudor state, accustomed to suppressing rebels, having done it several times during the split with Rome, was well prepared to use force to introduce a new culture.

Wood argues that England was also unique in Europe in the culture it chose to impose—and the emphasis it gave to the meaning of "liberalism":

> The characteristic ideology that set England apart from other European cultures was above all the ideology of "improvement": not the Enlightenment idea of the improvement of *humanity* but the improvement of *property*, the ethic—and indeed the science—of profit, the commitment to increasing the productivity of labour, the production of exchange value, and the practice of enclosure and dispossession. (2002, p. 189; emphasis original)

The contradiction that left-oriented critics have highlighted since Marx (1973) criticized the "Robinsonades" of classical political economy is that this ideal of the capitalist subject is no more natural than the Enlightenment notion of freedom and democracy. The liberal utopia requires institutions, laws, and ultimately police and prisons to bring its ideal vision of humanity into being.

The subject posited in the English case has been discussed in a variety of ways, but one of its more substantial descriptions is given by Macpherson in *The Political Theory of Possessive Individualism* (1962). He provides a close reading of several major political theorists, especially Thomas Hobbes and Locke, which uncovers what he argues are the historical, cultural assumptions behind their arguments. Much of the theoretical value—at the time and since then—of these philosophers has to do with their claims to be making universal pronouncements on the nature of human interaction. On the contrary, Macpherson argues, their observations about the state, civil society, private property, and value have a history, although they appeal to ideas of natural law. More importantly, they are an active creation and the result of the very society they purport to describe as natural. Hobbes, for instance, claims that the state, the "Leviathan" of *Leviathan*, is necessary because, as he is often quoted, if it were not for the state to mediate between people, life would be "nasty, brutish, and short." Hobbes, like Freud in *Civilization and Its Discontents*, argues from what he claims is psychological human nature:

if humans were to live in a "state of nature," they would be so innately competitive that they would be willing to kill or be killed, ruthlessly and without end, unless some strong force in the form of the state mitigated this behavior.

Macpherson argues that even Hobbes admits that this acquisitiveness is not something that drives every individual; some people are perfectly content with what they have. Hobbes's understanding of humankind is therefore based on his observations of the emergent values and assumptions of "possessive market society," which "requires the assumption of a model of society which permits and requires the continual invasion of every man by every other [and in which] even the innately moderate man in society must seek more power simply to protect his present level" (Macpherson 1962, pp. 41–42). In a "possessive market society," an "exchange of commodities through the price-making mechanism of the market permeates the relations between individuals, for in this market all possessions, including men's energies, are commodities" (ibid., p. 55). This state of affairs "requires a compulsive framework of law. At the very least, life and property must be secured, [and] contracts must be defined and enforced" (ibid., pp. 56–57).

Therefore, Macpherson argues, Hobbes's understanding of the state of nature is what he terms a logical not a historical hypothesis: it is not based on a precivilized man in a state of nature but is a "logical hypothesis reached by setting aside completely the historically acquired characteristics of men":

> His state of nature is a statement of the behaviour to which men as they now are, men who live in civilized societies and have the desires of civilized men, would be led if all law and contract enforcement [. . .] were removed. To get the state of nature, Hobbes sets aside law, but not the socially acquired behaviour and desires of men. (1962, p. 22)

In this way, Macpherson argues, Hobbes's psychological postulates about human nature are socially constructed, generalized from observations made in his own society. Macpherson refutes this transhistorical human nature at the foundation of Hobbes's argument by highlighting its historic specificity. In this chapter, I flesh out Macpherson's refutation by surveying the role of the state in helping manifest the possessive market society and the subject of value (A. Smith 2007) that inhabits it.

Sir Frances Bacon, an early philosopher of scientific reason and the method of natural history, was one of the forerunners of the seventeenth-century advocates of agricultural improvement. Bacon died before the English Civil War broke out (and hence before the Interregnum and Restoration, when the improvers had their heyday), but he participated in laying the groundwork for it—ideologically, politically, and, ultimately, materially. The imposition of the market mentality, of this understanding of property, of the social division of labor, was not easy to effect, nor, as Linebaugh and Rediker (2000, ch. 2) point out, was the infrastructure needed to advance it already present. They—and Hill (1972, ch. 3)—agree that these were actually mutually dependent ends.

The sixteenth-century enclosures (for the purposes of wool farming) helped create a large number of "masterless men," peasants who had been "freed" of their feudal obligations. This process was accelerated in the early part of the seventeenth century by endeavors that were meant to simultaneously build the capitalist infrastructure and interpellate the subjects to inhabit it. The enclosure of commons, the draining of fens, and disafforestation not only created new spaces for capital investment *qua* improvement; they removed the people who lived in those spaces, leading to "the obliteration of the communing habitus" (Linebaugh and Rediker 2000, p. 43). But at the same time, this building project, in Neal Wood's terms, "[gave] permanent employment to such people, putting an end to their vagrancy" (1984, p. 65). In other words, on one level, it was a disciplinary project, in Foucauldian terms—although, like the "discipline" that Foucault finds exemplary in Jeremy Bentham's work, it was discipline for a purpose, namely laying the physical and ideological groundwork for a fundamental change in social organization.

At the same time, the increased use of punishment against these outliers helped strengthen the image of the state as a powerful institution above the long-standing authorities at the village or manor level. Whether this purpose was clearly foreseen—whether the goal of capitalism per se was something already understood by the ruling classes of the day—is somewhat beside the point. These processes had their own advantages. It was useful to eliminate the communing *habitus* and disrupt the ability of these "masterless men" to subsist outside the emerging paradigm of wage labor. Their continued existence was a threat to that order: "Disafforestation and enclosure could thus be regarded as a national duty, a kindness to the idle poor, as well as of more immediate benefit to the rich encloser" (Hill 1972, p. 51). The pale of the law increasingly suggested that some behaviors and subjects within the polity were also "beyond the pale."

Of course, peasants did not willingly accept this suggestion: the specter haunting England at the time was less that the lower classes would join and rise up—although that was feared as well—than that they would writhe around uncontrollably, confounding these efforts to build a new and "improved" society. Linebaugh and Rediker find many references in this period to the character of Greek mythology they use as the title of their book: *The Many-Headed Hydra* (2000). They cite Sir Walter Raleigh, the former landlord in colonial Ireland and the author of the first English attempt at colonizing America, as making one of the first references to this creature in his *History of the World*, which he wrote while imprisoned for his part in a plot to execute King James I: "In it [he] mentioned Hercules and 'the serpent Hydra, which had nine heads whereof one being cut off, two grew in place.' Raleigh, of course, identified with Hercules, and he used the hydra to symbolize the growing disorders of capitalism" (Linebaugh and Rediker 2000, pp. 36–37). This metaphor "suffused English ruling-class culture in the seventeenth century," and it increasingly saw the lower classes—particularly those that threatened rebellion with anti-enclosure riots—as "unnatural" and, in the words of Bacon, "monstrous" (ibid.). Citing a little-read treatise of Bacon's called *An Advertisement Touching a Holy War* (1859), they outline the internal enemies that were "adequate to his proposed jihad":

> A death sentence was justified against those unavowed by God, those who had defaced natural reason and were neither nations in right nor nations in name, "but multitudes only, and swarms of people." Elsewhere in the same essay Bacon referred to "shoals" and "routs" of people. By taking his terms from natural history [. . .] and applying them to people, Bacon drew on his theory of monstrousness. These people had degenerated from the laws of nature and taken "in their body and frame of estate a monstrosity." [. . .] Bacon drew upon classical antiquity, the Bible, and recent history to provide seven examples of such "multitudes" that deserved destruction: West Indians; Canaanites; pirates; land rovers; assassins; Amazons; and Anabaptists. (Ibid., p. 39)

Like the liberal ideal of natural law and Hobbes's ahistorical hypothesis about the state of nature, Bacon's conception of what is monstrous consists of a reverse presentation of the historical sequence. Despite the harsh and complicated process of imposition, Bacon calls his preferred order "natural," an early iteration of the organic metaphors discussed in the previous chapter.

The inclusion of Anabaptists in this mix was likely a more general reference to the variety of Protestant sects cropping up—especially those who most threatened the power of the Tudor state. According to Hill, Anabaptists challenged not only the authority of the central state but also the emergent system of private property:

> Anabaptists' basic belief was that children shouldn't be baptized at birth, but that acceptance of baptism—reception into the church—should be the voluntary act of an adult. This clearly subverted the concept of a national church to which every English man and woman belonged: it envisaged instead the formation of voluntary congregations by those who believed themselves to be among the elect. An Anabaptist must logically object to the payment of tithes, the ten percent of everyone's earnings which, in theory at least, went to support the ministers of the state church. Many Anabaptists refused to swear oaths, since they objected to religious ceremony being used for secular judicial purposes; others rejected war and military service. Still more were alleged to carry egalitarianism to the extent of denying the right of private property. (1972, p. 26)

Although there are now many other ways in which to construct seditious doctrine, the dominant ideology of the day was that of Protestantism, and it was on this ground that these revolts were charted, especially right before and after the outbreak of civil war. As Anderson (1964) points out, many of the revolutionary ideas of the period were framed in terms of religion; nevertheless, they were still revolutionary, and one can see the outlines of most of the "bourgeois" ideas of freedom and democracy within these movements. Chief among them was the notion, highlighted in Linebaugh and Rediker (2000), that God was "no respecter of persons." The phrase appears throughout the protest literature of the time—especially in the works of the Levellers, including John Lilburne and Richard Overton, and the Digger Gerrard Winstanley.

The anarchist egalitarianism of the Anabaptists represented "the specter of communism"; Bacon wanted to "cut them off the face of the earth" (Linebaugh and Rediker 2000, p. 65). This meant not only "the expansion and intensification of state terror" but also the elimination of the places where these ideas could take root (ibid.). Realizing control over these spaces was a political project no less than an economic one: the targets of this "holy war" were "unnatural." What was natural was the profitable improvement of land: the latter would become the cornerstone of Locke's political doctrine.

But well before Locke took up Bacon's ideas on improvement, he had the opportunity to enjoy the state-sponsored work of reshaping nature. Looking out over his family's holdings in "the marshy lands of Somerset" (N. Wood 1984, p. 21), he would have known it had to be subjected to what Linebaugh and Rediker call "the labors of appropriation." One of these labors was the draining of the fens—or wetlands:

> An Act of Parliament in 1600 made it possible for big shareholders in the fens to suppress the common rights that stood in the way of their drainage schemes. New plans and works, requiring unprecedented concentrations of labor, proliferated. King James organized hundreds in the drainage and enclosure of parts of Somerset in the early seventeenth century, turning a communing economy of fishing, fowling, reed cutting and peat digging into a capitalist economy of sheep raising. Coastal lands were reclaimed and inland peat moors drained in the Somerset "warths." (Linebaugh and Rediker 2000, p. 44)

While Locke's specific Somerset property might not have been subjected to these state labors, the scale of the project meant that he must have known about someplace nearby that had. This process took a lot of work, as did the building of ports and systems for drawing water into London. As this moment was also the beginning of England's colonization projects in the New World, the work was transatlantic. The newly founded Virginia Company, in which Bacon was an investor, benefited greatly from the policy of "transportation"—the deportation of criminals as indentured servants in the colonies. In 1617, this policy was extended to felons, but informal banishment practices soon followed for the Irish, Gypsies, and Africans, as well as for the poor and "idle": "The minister John Donne promised in a sermon of 1622 that the Virginia Company 'shall sweep your streets, and wash your dores, from idle persons, and the children of idle persons, and imploy them: and, truly, if the whole country [of the nascent United States] were such a [prison], to force idle persons to work, it had a good use'" (Linebaugh and Rediker 2000, p. 59).

Although disciplining the labor force may not have been the ultimate objective, law enforcement was focused on teaching the emergent proletariat, with no property except their labor, of the sanctity of private property. Linebaugh and Rediker emphasize the increased use of public punishment—hangings, workhouses, prisons—much of which was focused on the poor and petty criminals. For instance, "of the 436 people hanged in Essex between 1620 and 1680, 166 were burglars, 38 were highway robbers, and 110 were thieves. In the 1630s thieves were hanged for stealing goods valued at as little as eighteen pence" (Linebaugh and Rediker 2000, p. 51). Keeping this order was one of the most public uses of the centralizing state apparatus at the time. The Star Chamber, the "royal prerogative court," and the Privy Council (both of which Bacon at one time either led or sat on) are notoriously remembered in this period for their increasingly punitive measures, especially the use of torture, to deter opposition as well as to enforce the aforementioned monopolies (Hill 1982, p. 27).

In particular, the increasingly capitalist state power continued to find the monopoly of copyright statutes a particularly important mechanism for political control. Geoffrey Robertson (2007) notes that the Leveller Lilburne's popularity was greatly increased when he stood up to the court in his trial for printing seditious literature, basically pleading the fifth by saying that he had a right to not incriminate himself. In response, "The Star Chamber ordered him whipped all the way from Fleet Street to Westminster—a sentence carried out viciously before a large crowd who cheered this courageous young man, whom they dubbed 'Freeborn John'" (ibid., p. xvii).

Here, Linebaugh and Rediker overlook the other expansion of the state in this period, which I would consider to be an early example of what Karl Polanyi calls a "double movement." The double movement is like the riot: the language of the unheard, who then disrupt the culture oppressing them. In the cases of the double movement that Polanyi explores, it is a declaration saying that "leaving the fate of soil and people to the market would be tantamount to annihilating them. Accordingly, the countermove [or double movement] consisted in checking the action of the market in respect to the factors of production, labor, and land" (2001, p. 137). Polanyi sees the resulting process as "embedding" liberalism in the society through the state. In retrospect, this view is somewhat contradictory, considering the work that the Tudor and Stuart states did to create the market economy. Although it is now seen as an obvious "improvement" by most scholars, the enclosure of land was a state-led project even before it was done for economic efficiency. As Jack Goldstone mirrors the discussion of Linebaugh and Rediker in pointing out: "The monarchy too participated in the enclosure movement, particularly enclosure of waste and fen; in fact its intense efforts to turn a greater profit from the Royal Forests and fens made the Crown probably the single largest encloser of the early seventeenth century" (1983, p. 156).

But at the same time, the monarchy deployed the Star Chamber to stifle enclosure when it suited state priorities, particularly to maintain order when a nascent "double movement" arose. Barrington Moore produces an account of this:

> Since the English peasants had won for themselves a relatively envious position under the protection of the custom of the manor, it is no wonder that they looked to the protection of custom and tradition as the dike which might defend them against the invading capitalist flood, from which they were scarcely in the position to profit. [. . .] The crown under Elizabeth and the first two Stuarts made some effort to mitigate the effects of these trends on both the peasants and the poorer

> classes in the towns. Large numbers of the peasants, cast adrift, were becoming a menace to good order, to the point where intermittent revolts occurred. One careful historian calls royal policy one of spasmodic benevolence. During the Eleven Years Tyranny, when Charles I ruled through Strafford and Laud without a Parliament, the attempt to apply benevolence may have been more vigorous. Such royal courts as the Star Chamber and the Court of Requests gave the peasant what protection he did obtain against eviction through enclosures. (1967, pp. 12–13)

Moore seems to indicate that, even if there were some official change in social property relations, much authority still yielded to local customs. Polanyi sees it in roughly these same terms, saying that, even if enclosure were promoted as an improvement, the Tudor and Stuart regimes controlled the pace of conversion:

> The "nationalization" of labor legislation through the Statute of Artificers (1563) and the Poor Law (1601) removed labor from the danger zone, and the anti-enclosure policy of the Tudors and early Stuarts was one consistent protest against the principle of the gainful use of landed property. [. . .] Change from arable land to pasture and the accompanying enclosure movement [was a] trend in economic progress. Yet, but for the consistently maintained policy of the Tudor and early Stuart statesmen, the rate of that progress might have been ruinous, and have turned the process into a degenerative instead of a constructive event. (2001, pp. 39, 73)

Of course, to come back to Linebaugh and Rediker, since the Poor Laws that Polanyi mentions decreed that "beggary was severely punished; vagrancy, in the case of repetition, was a capital offense [and] the able-bodied poor should be put to work so as to earn their keep" (2001, p. 91), they are likewise evidence that the interventionist state was essential in these formative years. The state was the largest encloser, yet it was also performing a public service by organizing labor to build infrastructure and preventing the ruffians from causing disorder.

Like those advocating for improvement, the administrators of the English state might not have had a clear vision of their preferred relationship between the market and state—or at least not as clear as the neoliberals discussed in the following chapter. But even where the state did not advocate a "pure culture of capitalism," it did so out of a desire to retain control of the country—and thus to ensure the sanctity of the increasingly productive private property. This process is what Perelman (2000), following Marx, calls the "secret history of political accumulation": the state was central to the imposition of the market economy, even if politics on the ground led to populist policies to stem the possibility that the state's newly centralized powers would be threatened by anti-enclosure riots and other social pressures. The policies around vagrancy and theft and the spectacular increase of capital punishment, banishment, and transportation to the colonies were essential to disciplining the freshly "freed" workforce, whose labor would soon serve to legitimate the owners of private productive property and the state charged with exclusively defending that property. Having looked at the process of state centralization, I now turn to the more specific content of that state in relation to natural law. This centralization followed from the period when the English Civil War began, setting off a society-wide struggle to define the reconstituted state.

The Struggle over the Properties of "Natural Law"

Ideologically and politically, the overturning (ever so briefly) of the monarchy unleashed the forces that the Stuart state had been suppressing. The radical threats—such as the Parliamentary forces aligned against the king—were diverse. The grievances of the New Model Army and the Levellers were ostensibly over the issue of equal suffrage, but a common misinterpretation of this idea at the time might give a better sense of the ambiguity of the moment—namely, that equal suffrage meant "everyone should have to suffer equally" (Hill 1972). Likewise, the signifiers of "freedom" and "liberty" had been opened up for very specific class interpretations. Making one of these "natural" was largely the stakes of the postrevolutionary struggle:

> Words are deceptive because their meanings change. When members of Parliament spoke in defense of "liberty and property" they meant something more like "privilege and property" than is conveyed by the modern sense of the word liberty. [. . .] But in the mouths of the Levellers the "liberties of Englishmen" came to mean something very different and much more modern; "freeborn John" Lilburne was to make a democratic slogan out of what had been a class distinction. (Hill 1982, p. 38)

Likewise, Hill contends, "common law" or "natural law" was often specifically enforced for that separate species of humanity, the propertied classes.

Here Hill and I are using a certain definition of class—one that Macpherson sees as "defined at least implicitly in terms of *productive* property, [and that] was an important criterion of different forms of government" (1977, p. 11; emphasis original).

The emphasis on "productive" property points to the already developed class relations such that a large number of people no longer had subsistence plots of land as cottagers or alternative means of survival through the various forms of commons that had previously existed. The effect of this situation was the consolidation of the commons and small farms into much larger holdings. These parcels were arguably more productive—a claim we evaluate in the following chapter—and were one of the first spaces of English capitalism. They provide the first meaning of "productive": relative to the earlier arrangement, they were more productive. To the laborers forced to work—or not work—on this land by the compulsion of economic necessity, this distinction of "productive" was meaningless. The laborers no longer had any way to produce for themselves, so the possible increase in yields did little to aid them directly: only by working these lands for the owners could they live. In this sense, the shift to productive property was experienced as primitive accumulation, and the defense of productive private property became a defense of slavery.

To speak of "the liberties of Englishmen" in this context was not hypothetical or utopian: it was to take the memory of what had been a regular form of life—working for one's own subsistence on the common—and ask for it to be reinstated. In this context, it is easy to see economic and political democracy as of a piece—much as Thomas Jefferson believed the yeoman farmers of the United States would more ably exercise the franchise with plots of land to call their own. In Macpherson's (1977) assessment, until the nineteenth century, most visions of democracy assumed it would take place in a classless or one-classed society. While many of the English radicals were concerned with their role in making laws, the "classless" society often had more of an appeal than its possibly political democratic character. But this articulation was carefully dissected during the English Civil War, when Moore says, "Radical threats from within the army, from the Levellers and the Diggers, [Oliver] Cromwell and his associates fended off with firmness and skill" (Moore 1967, p. 17).

The debates held in 1647 at the church in Putney between Cromwell and the members of his New Model Army over the future of the English state are often viewed as a turning point. There, Cromwell's son-in-law Henry Ireton said, "The main thing I speak for, is because I have an eye to property" (Baker 2007, p. 73). Ireton meant making property ownership—or what he called a "fixed local interest"—a condition of suffrage within the new state. As in the United States, the property restriction was long seen as a way of keeping democracy without explicitly making liberalism (i.e., the protection of productive private property rights) its limit. Those with a "fixed local interest" would be less likely to vote for anyone who would undermine property's sanctity. When the United States removed its property restriction, Marx says it would seem that "the state as a state abolishes private property [. . .] when it removes the property qualification" (1972, p. 33). As he goes on to say, the issue is not so simple, but it articulates the threat felt by Ireton and other associates of Cromwell.

If Ireton (and many others) thought that opening democracy to men without property would inevitably lead the state toward redistribution, one branch of the Levellers thought that democracy would be incidental if everyone were able to produce for themselves: "The ideal of all the Levellers was a society where all men had enough property to work on as independent producers, and where none had the kind of amount of property which would enable them to be an exploitative class" (Macpherson 1977, p. 15). Linebaugh and Rediker echo this sentiment in their discussion of the Levellers: "The fork in the road at Putney pointed to either a future with the commons and without slavery, or to one with slavery and without the commons" (2000, p. 106).

Contrary to the *ex post facto* rationalization of the capitalist order (e.g., Hardin's "The Tragedy of the Commons" [1968] mentioned at the beginning of this chapter), which asserts economic democracy is a utopian scheme, "the commons were a reality, not a pie in the sky":

> As soldiers at Putney gathered wood for their campfire, they knew that the debates had relevance to all commoners. Those in Putney, for example, enjoyed common pasture, furze, turf, underwood, and stones, as well as river resources of smelly salmon, flounder, shad, roach, dace, barbell, eel, and gudgeon. The debates had a special urgency for those affected by the decision of Charles I in 1637 to enclose 236 acres of wastelands between Hampton Court and Richmond for a hunting park. Clarendon, the royalist, noted that the attack on common rights "increased the murmur and noise of the people," which would eventually grow into a revolutionary clamor and bring down a succession of tyrants: Archbishop Laud, Lord Strafford, and King Charles I. (Linebaugh and Rediker 2000, p. 109)

Linebaugh and Rediker may overstate the significance of the popular force alone, but the fact is that, at the moment, people had a living memory of what the commons looked like. In the following chapter, I look at the economic arguments about how efficient this arrangement was at the time, but the point is that the commoning culture was alive and functional for the people involved in this undertaking.

Likewise, the previous years had given them a real sense of slavery. When the Levellers and soldiers at Putney discussed slavery, it was not related to race, a cultural concept invented a few decades later in Virginia; instead, slavery was understood as directly related to the dissolution of the commons. In other words, slavery was something that all people could experience—and that many newly freed peasants *had* experienced: the impressing of peasants into soldiers or sailors, poor laws that forced them to labor on the projects of state building, and the simple enclosure of the commons and/or the loss of freehold status on the land:

> What was at issue, then, was not a rhetorical abstraction of political propaganda, but something real, experienced, suffered and known. A rough definition of slavery at the time would include these features: it began with an act of expropriation and terror; it affected children and young people particularly; it compelled violent exploitation; and more often than not, it ended in death. The hewers and drawers, or the laboring subjects of the Atlantic economy, met this definition in an era well before race and ethnicity came to define slavery. (Linebaugh and Rediker 2000, p. 111)

The cause of slavery was therefore directly related to the changing property relation in the commons. The debate that was ostensibly about representation in the parliament was understood as a political and an economic argument.

Colonel Thomas Rainsborough was particularly sympathetic to the arguments being made in the army for universal manhood suffrage and comprehended the implications in a fairly reasonable way. He did not necessarily see the impressment of peasants into the army as a form of slavery—yet. But he saw that if the soldiers who had been fighting were not given a vote, then it was a particularly unjust result (an argument whose logic is evident in the U.S. Constitution's Twenty-Sixth Amendment, granting voting rights to Vietnam draft–era eighteen-year-old citizens). Rainsborough was convinced that subjects should not be bound by a government they did not choose and that property restrictions would empower either class: a poor man might vote for redistribution just as easily as a rich one:

> A gentleman lives in a country and has got three or four lordships, as some men have (God knows how they got them); and when Parlia-

> ment is called he must be a Parliament-man; and it may be he sees some poor men, they live near this man, he can crush them—I have known an invasion to make sure he has turned the poor men out of doors; and I would fain to know whether the potency of rich men do not this, and so keep them under the greatest tyranny that was ever wrought in the world. (Baker 2007, p. 75)

In short, restricting the franchise to the large property holders meant those with little or no property would be condemned to the loss of the commons and their effective return to slavery and serfdom.

These were the stakes as the Levellers attempted to rearticulate natural rights as the right to the commons and small proprietorship. As Macpherson says, "They found the rot had set in with exploitative private property. The small private property of the independent producer was a natural right. The large private property which enabled its owner to exploit the rest was a contradiction of natural right" (1977, p. 15). The debate was less over property as such than over whose right to property was more important. The concentration of large landholders was rightly seen as a threat to peasant proprietorship (much less commons use by cottagers and others who did not own the land they worked); thus, if parliamentary consent were limited to the former, the majority of the latter would end up serving them in much the same way they had before their feudal dues had been commuted. Thus, whether as a cause or an effect of the proposed legislative model, the goal of retaining some claim to these economic rights was as important as the proposed political rights.

In this light, Hill distinguishes "constitutional Levellers" from what he calls "physical force Levellers." The former were more concerned with issues of democratic participation and consent and were involved in the Putney debates. He says that they were "not in fundamental disagreement with the type of society that was being set up by the English Revolution. They accepted the sanctity of private property, and their desire to extend democracy was within the limits of a capitalist society" (Hill 1972, p. 123). Macpherson's interpretation (and statements made within the debates themselves) makes this distinction debatable. For either side, "extending democracy" opened the possibility to move well outside the "limits of a capitalist society." Hill claims that the moderate constitutional wing—mostly embodied by Lilburne and Sir John Wildman—was interested in reform (or, in our present terms, "balance") and, when it seemed they could have won the debate at Putney, they were undermined by the grandees of the Model Army, who "stole the [constitutional] Levellers Republican clothes" and therefore lost them the support of the peasantry (1972, pp. 122–123).

In contrast were what Hill calls the "physical force Levellers," among whom he also includes Lilburne. This wing, he says, "was less concerned with constitutional issues, more with economics, with defending the poor against the rich, the common people against great men" (1972, p. 114). This impulse pointed to a much broader concern among the population and, in particular, among the army. So, for instance, in "October 1647 soldiers were demanding that no duke, marquis or earl should have more than £2000 a year, and that the income of other classes should be proportionally restricted" (ibid., p. 115). Their defense of the poor was not limited to thoughts: "Levellers were foremost in inciting the Buckinghamshire anti-enclosure movement" (ibid., p. 117). The name "Levellers" referred to the impulse to "level" the hedges and fences that enclosed land and, to quote a Buckinghamshire pamphlet, "all men being alike privileged by birth, so all men were to enjoy the creatures alike without property one more than the other" (ibid.). In other words, social leveling was implied in the leveling of the hedges around property.

Hill asserts that "similar ideas were arising simultaneously, that is to say, in more or less sophisticated forms, in various parts of the country" (1972, p. 117). Thus, when our contemporary neoconservative Michael Barone equates all these ideas with support for the commonwealth and the Rump Parliament and claims that "these were popular causes with two generations of radical historians in the twentieth century, but not with the mass of the English people in the seventeenth," he is obviously less concerned with the specifics than with upholding a different version of history (2007, p. 14). For instance, he says that the radical Protestant doctrines of Lilburne and others were unpopular, yet he (like Locke) finds it reasonable that there the state would repress them. In 1648, when the Levellers' program was laid out and circulated among the population, it reportedly received forty thousand signatures, which in an era before Internet polling is at least significant (Baker 2007, p. 124n1). This is not to deny that, as James C. Scott has discussed at length, "even in a revolutionary movement, the popular vision of what is at issue may diverge considerably from that of its intelligentsia" (1979, p. 99). However, when reactionary revisionists claim that there was little popular support for the revolution—particularly the violent or economically radical wings of the revolution—it rings hollow, especially since they are otherwise unconcerned with the popular consent to the measures they advocate. In this case, the issue seems to be that Barone and others overlook the "revolution within the revolution" in ways that Scott might contest. Since this critique is often made against socialist revolutionaries, it seems fitting that what we find here is the more communist revolution within the capitalist one.

In any case, Hill calls this wing "the physical force Levellers" not because of their goals but because of their observation on the necessary methods. They not only advocated a different model of society but also understood that, in the words of Lilburne, "there is now no power executed in England but a power of force; a just and moral act done by a troop of horse [*sic*] being as good as law as now I can see executed by any judge in England" (Hill 1972, p. 65). Likewise,

> the Levellers thought that the state had broken down in the course of the civil war; until it was legitimately refounded a state of nature existed in which the sword was the only remaining authority. [. . .] If the Agitators had managed to capture control of the Army [before the Putney Debates], a Leveller theory of military dictatorship in the interest of democracy would certainly have emerged: the Leveller repudiation of military violence sprang from their dislike of the purposes for which this violence was used. (Ibid., p. 66)

More recently, Robertson has agreed that "the power of their ideas was to gather momentum" (2007, p. xxvi), but the loss of the army's support doomed their implementation. Therefore, the ideas and arguments lived on and presented an alternative articulation of liberty and freedom. Yet behind them also lay the question of the relationship between equality, terror, and the law. Locke, the most prominent theorist of this time in this regard, would attempt to answer it.

Solidifying Locke's Culture of Property

For many Early Modern English subjects, the commons were a lived memory. The natural law that Hobbes asserted existed outside the state was actually being imposed from within it: contrary to Macpherson's evenhanded, logical analysis, the best way to see Hobbes as consistent is to see him speaking to a certain class. Hobbes was wrong, however, in thinking that the "common person" would be so easily swayed by the reasoning he provided for the need for a Leviathan. In making this assumption, he is just one in a long line of political thinkers who believe that a *demotic* uprising would occur only if the "common person" had the "blank slate" of their consciousness, as Hobbes puts it, "scribbled over with the opinions of their Doctors" (1968, p. 379). Several centuries later, in his book *Road to Serfdom*, Friedrich von Hayek (1994) diagnoses the preponderance of interventionist states as the result of a half century or so of German propaganda rather than the ravages of the free market he praises.

This is not to say that propaganda did not play some part in this or any resistance. Hill asserts that the London Levellers had the most militant program of trying to avert the effects of the emergent property and primitive accumulation. Chief among these were the group of London printers, like Lilburne, who were also important in crafting the ideology that, in later years, would be seen as similar to the radical democracy that inspired antislavery, anticolonial, and anti–free market campaigns. These ideas, of course, did not lead to the revolt—they just helped catalyze some of the calls for agrarian reform and broader democracy that were already circulating.

Still, in the 1660s, the Restoration government—and Parliament in particular—took Hobbes's advice about tamping down on the potential for the "common people" to be led astray. The Treason Act and the King's Sole Right over the Militia Act of 1661 created a central army and reduced the possibility of a revived New Model Army. The Tenures Abolition Act of 1660 gave the government a steadier source of income by establishing excise taxes on tea, chocolate, and other commodities. Even if he had underplayed the possibility that common people would be able to think for themselves, Hobbes had also given a sense that it would be the state's duty to keep that from happening. Since religion was one of the primary ideological instruments (as Hobbes mentions, "whole Nations [can] be brought to *acquiesce* in the great Mysteries of the Christian Religion" [1968, p. 379; emphasis original]), it was also targeted. In addition to the Corporation Act of 1661, which made it mandatory for any elected official at every level of the state to take an oath to the Supremacy of the King and to the Church of England, restrictions were placed on the movement of all people (especially nonconformist preachers), the size of congregations, and people's ability to circulate petitions in the manner used by the Levellers to drum up support for Parliamentary measures. The Uniformity Act of 1662 created a common catechism and a steady stream of income for London printers, who held the exclusive patent for *The Book of Common Prayer*. And the Licensing of the Press Act of 1662 made sure that this text was one of the only religious (and hence nonseditious) titles available in London's stalls.

To see this censorship as merely about the freedom of speech, press, or religion—which is roughly how most contemporary critics of copyright do—misses the major reason for granting this patent to the Stationers Company. It was to protect the power of the king, the church, and the law, all of which had been restored with the promise of "security of property as established by Parliament" (Barone 2007, p. 15). The defense of property and class power was at the root of IP, and, although some of the articulations of both institutions have changed, much of this relationship has stayed the same. Aside from the early "labors of appropriation" discussed in this chapter, the real pressure to make this mode of society dominant seems to be generated after 1660, when the movement that produced the ideology of agricultural improvement, inspired by Bacon's idea of "natural" history and leading to Locke's philosophy of property and the state in the *Second Treatise*, really took hold (N. Wood 1984, ch. 3).

The emergent paradigm was that, instead of the state's owning all the land and allowing the landholding classes of the feudal order to squeeze rent out of the peasants who worked on it, the state would protect the private property of the landowners against the newly dispossessed peasants—some of whom were astute enough to understand that this shift meant the end of their way of life, the end of their ability to produce independently. Leaving aside the possibility that they could take advantage of the vistas opening in the growing English Empire (by becoming servants for an indefinite time, they could possibly take possession of some bit of the "commons" abroad), commoners understood that this stance ultimately meant slavery for them—or what they referred to as slavery. The state, as they understood it, was not the opposite of a state of nature; it was the instrument of its nasty, brutish imposition. It secured the order by which wealthier people could continually invade the territory on which they subsisted, secure it by violence—legal or physical—and retain it as their own.

Since that time, each of these ideological and political frameworks has experienced reversals and retrenchments, but what we witness today is much more akin to this original moment than the critics of IPR, who look back to it benignly, like to admit. Although religion is increasingly invested with a similar role in political rhetoric, the "dogmatic resources" being drawn on are more in the area of economics (which we consider in the following chapter). That the dominant capitalist class of today looks to Locke on this matter makes much sense, but, again, it tells us more about how we should read the current moment critically than about how the emergent culture of maximalist IPR is misusing the residual notions of the early eighteenth century.

Locke's *Second Treatise of Government* was likely written in the early 1680s during the exclusion crisis, during which Locke had taken sides with the excluders rather than James II (and was possibly also involved in the Rye House Plot to have the heir to the throne killed), and at roughly the same time as Robert Filmer's *Patriarcha* was published. Locke is normally seen as being engaged in a debate with Hobbes, with the former dismissing the notion of an absolute power that Hobbes thought necessary and introducing the outlines of a constitutional monarchy. Insofar as Locke was inspired by

James Harrington's demand that there be a separation of powers, this view is accurate. But according to Peter Laslett (1988) and David McNally (1989), Locke's real debate was with Filmer. While informed by Locke's economic philosophy, the *Second Treatise* was meant to be a political doctrine that would refute Filmer, who argued that the divine right of kings was the only means for private property to exist. For if, according to the Bible, God gave everyone the earth in common, only one of his "patriarchs" on earth could legitimate its ownership. In a democracy, without an absolute patriarch, private property would only be justified with a plebiscite for every expropriation from the commons. Alternatively, if the king could be said to govern only by consent, then land should be taken out of the common only by consent. In other words, Filmer reopened the conflict of the English Civil War and challenged the idea of "natural law" that had been introduced. More importantly, he challenged the emerging constitutional monarchy and the class power it guaranteed, particularly for the continued enclosure of land.

While Locke allows for a parliamentary form of government (thus supposedly laying the grounds for democracy in the United States), the main distinction with Filmer is that Locke founds his notion of political obligation on a labor theory of property. The ownership of property, in turn, he founds on the notion of improvement. Locke was part of a group of people advocating that land be "improved," which meant, at the time, enclosed and transferred to the private ownership of an improving landlord. Although he admits that people might hold some places in common by contract, he argues that any land that was not so held should be converted. In short, Locke makes his ideology of improvement not only a policy program for the intensification of agriculture but the very foundation of the state. On the other hand, it means that anyone who was not using land in this way would be wasting it and should legally be dispossessed.

Locke never claimed authorship of his *Treatises*. They were published anonymously, and their authorship was heavily debated at the time. The implication of the second treatise at the moment—and ever since—has been to remove the current property distribution from history. The past history was erased, and the future history was determined, or, as Georg Lukács says, "There is history, but there is no longer any" (1971, p. 48). The people who owned land were presumed to have acquired this land through their labor. On the other hand, the people who were not using land for the purposes of private, capitalist improvement could legitimately be dispossessed since they were wasting it. This ideology is clearly related to the expansion of the liberal state through the British Empire and the continuing consolidation of large agrarian holdings within the confines of the newly hewn United Kingdom.

For many years, scholars in the political economy of media, such as Janet Wasko (2001), have pointed out that the "synergy" strategy of major media conglomerates, such as Disney, has been to use channels they already own to promote other portions of their businesses. So ABC, which is a Disney property, is a venue that Disney can use to highlight other Disney products—theme parks, movies, and so on. This synergy cuts down on the transaction costs: if you want a bunch of free advertising, buy a TV station.

Disney is also well known among critics of maximalist IPR, with its persistent lobbying to extend copyright—now for more than half a century past the death of the author (i.e., Walt Disney). By owning these properties, Disney is able to control not only all forms of speech about them but also all the (legal) revenue that they generate. Part of what makes these properties profitable is Disney's vast network of media corporations, which allows the company to exploit these properties more fully. Disney has also acquired Marvel Comics' and Lucasfilm's lucrative libraries and copyrights, an $8 billion investment that will surely pay for itself quite quickly.

But a new movement is afoot among smaller studios that lack significant infrastructure but have, through a different series of consolidations and buyouts—such as the one that Lionsgate used to acquire the rights to *Dirty Dancing*—come to own a significant chunk of our popular culture in the form of "libraries" of movies. Of course, calling these collections "libraries" is a bit of a misnomer. Somewhere, an actual, physical library of these acquired films may exist, but the most important acquisition is the *copyrights* to these films, which can be parlayed into a panoply of derivative works and licensed products.

Lionsgate Studios acquired the distribution rights for the 1987 film *Dirty Dancing* when it purchased Artisan Entertainment (and its library of seven thousand titles) in 2003 for $220 million (Waxman 2003). By 2007, when it filed a lawsuit to defend the trademark for and the *idea* that one could trademark the phrase "Nobody puts Baby in the corner," it had released the twentieth-anniversary DVD of *Dirty Dancing*, sponsored musical renditions of the film in Toronto and New York, allowed a much-panned TV remake, and commissioned a video game premised on the film. In 2015, the studio reported gross revenues of more than US$2.2 billion and a net income of $180 million, almost equal to the investment it had made in Artisan a decade earlier.

Into this development step a variety of independent licensing and marketing firms. These firms have little to do with copyright per se. Instead, they seek to take those copyrighted works and make them into trademarks, thus expanding the kinds of things that the company can charge people for doing with those works. However, as with the phrase "Nobody puts Baby in the corner," this type of work is done through an expanded, anarchic social process: people repeating the phrase at parties, making jokes around it in reference to current events, possibly making their own objects with the phrase. This exponentially larger process of appropriation is what actually creates the cultural value around an object like this movie quote. However, like the Lockean notion that all value created should flow back to the owner, it assumes a certain class division, a certain division of labor.

Trademark is a thorny legal category, but in this case, the basic trend, in addition to claiming more rights, is to create a new line of goods with this trademark that, just as Disney did before, create synergy. Only this time, the synergy is developed completely after the fact. Lionsgate had nothing to do with *Dirty Dancing*, but it has approved (and probably asked for) the production of a video game and a Broadway musical based on the film. It is a fairly craven strategy in terms of exploiting our collective popular culture, but it also makes it much clearer that the very broad definition of ownership being inserted into international trade agreements is about much more than simple movie piracy.

Like the promulgation of copyright restriction in the early Tudor regime, it is basically collusion between industry and government to lock up the cultural and the technological means of production and to solidify the social hierarchy and the economic division of labor: it is just done through the political assignment of monopoly economic rights instead of the purely political feudal control. This use of the state to defend the "economic freedom" of massive property owners has become so commonplace in the Anglo-American sphere that it can effectively be discussed as "natural law" with little need to defend it on historical or even pragmatic terms. Its export to places that do not share this history is bound to create animosity and pushback, especially when it cuts into one of the key promises of the postwar era: that opening economies to Western intervention would facilitate technology transfer, thus helping development.

Intellectual property laws, as subsequent chapters argue more centrally, protect not only the owners of purely cultural products; in trade and bilateral investment agreements, they protect the current owners of technological knowledge, product design, and brand identity by ensuring that they can continue to reap the level of reward they currently enjoy, despite the fact that they must allow the use of these things to exploit the valuable labor of the developing world. Whether this situation is ethical or defensible is not the issue: this chapter outlines a historical explanation for why it would seem unquestionable and even natural. Critics of IPR should understand, however, that this class protection is the larger function of IPR in these treaties: by focusing narrowly on the issues of creative process, they miss a larger, more important pattern. In short, whatever labor was used to produce the cultural value of a film or the use value of a pair of Levis, the contracting corporation is committed to reaping the rewards of that value. And, as in the Lockean compromise with the Hobbesian Leviathan, the best way to ensure this relationship was—and still is—with a strong state apparatus.

The following chapter outlines the resurgence of this liberal understanding of property in the form of the Law and Economics movement in the United States during the late twentieth century. In part, I discuss this movement in terms of the ways in which it replaced the ideological understanding of natural law that Locke rooted in religion with a similarly ideological understanding of natural law based in a certain tradition of economics. In short, whereas the stakes of the struggle in the Lockean moment were the articulation of different interpretations of natural law, the Law and Economics movement has made its own arguments about economics into a "natural law" of human behavior and interaction. Its advocates then insist that the law itself should move out of the way and allow the pure economic logic they describe to sort out the claims of the participants within a transaction: if it does not, then it will create all sorts of perversions that economics alone would never create; conversely and simultaneously, they insist that this economic logic is so inevitable that, whatever the law does, it cannot stop the effects of its logic on the transactions. The law, in other words, is simultaneously omnipotent and impotent.

The reason to look at this movement in relation to IPR is twofold. On the one hand, it represents the modern articulation of the Lockean understanding of property and its relation to the state. The model it advocates the state to impose (and, perversely, insists already exists in reality) is that of the "purely economic" order that Wood discusses. But unlike the moment of Lockean imposition, it is able to articulate this view with a modern, scientific claim to rational productivity rather than being forced to transubstantiate political economic claims into those of religious ideology. The problem is that, while it wants to base its legitimacy on this pure logic, it has to contend with the ways in which economics is already incorporated into the modern welfare state: thus, ideologically, it has to rely on the utilitarian claims to greater productivity that, in any other environment, it would denounce as an explicit interpenetration of the political with the economic.

Lessig is central to this movement—and especially to trying to help it understand the role of culture and social norms with regard to the functioning of the legal side of the discipline. In this endeavor, Lessig forces the political constitution of the law—rather than its basis in upholding the natural laws of economics—into the open. In other words, he undermines the claims to "natural law" that are otherwise reified elements of the culture of property. He does so to help the movement more forcefully craft human behavior in the direction of pure economic logic, but his intervention allows for a discussion about what those norms should actually be.

In both cases, the logic behind the movement is essentially identical to the reified culture of property that this book argues should be the true target of the balanced critics of IPR. After all, as this chapter illustrates, according to this reified culture, the claims to ownership in productive property, whatever its material status, are basic to the capitalist order in which that property exists. Without criticizing the latter, the former will remain rational according to this dominant logic.

3

Law, Economics, and the Apolitical Culture of Capitalism

Christopher Hill uses the term "physical force Levellers" to describe the contingent of the English Civil War who believed that, even if they were given political enfranchisement, unless there was a leveling of property, they would be forced into slavery by those who could use their economic means as a power over them (1972, p. 114). In much the same way, early-twentieth-century "realist" legal scholars contended that the formal restraints of contract law were inadequate in the face of increasingly consolidated corporate ownership of productive property. In that context, "a 'legalist' consciousness that excludes 'result-oriented' jurisprudence as contrary to the rule of law also inevitably discourages the pursuit of substantive justice" (Horwitz 1977, p. 566). This contention was all the more the case in the early twentieth century, when the common reaction of the state to labor militancy was to defend the "negative liberty" of the owners of productive property, often with state troops.

The liberal break on the more radical Leveller impulse, established in part by John Locke's anonymous pamphlets collected in *Two Treatises of Government*, is a germinal iteration of what Chantal Mouffe (2000) discusses as "the democratic paradox." Mouffe finds this paradox in relation to the way that liberalism relies on and resists democracy: "What cannot be contestable in a liberal democracy is the idea that it is legitimate to establish limits to popular sovereignty in the name of liberty. Hence its paradoxical nature" (2000, p. 4). By claiming that government was subject to a democratic revolution only when it failed to uphold "the Natural Liberty" of the people, Locke strictly confines what democracy means: democracy is valid only if it continues to support the absolute protection of productive private property (1988, p. 412). The capitalist state is necessary to defend the property rights of owners—Locke says this is virtually its only reason for existing. The paradox is that a democratic government requires the consent of the governed, yet to govern, it must remain legitimate to the majority of the population. Its hegemony becomes especially precarious if the majority begins to see that property's protection mostly serves a smaller and smaller slice of the electorate.

In introducing Jürgen Habermas's tome *Between Facts and Norms*, William Rehg argues that a functional state requires that "at least some portion of a population, indeed the majority, must look at legal rules as standards that everyone ought to follow, whether because they reflect the ways of ancestors, the structure of the cosmos, or the will of God, or because they have been democratically approved or simply enacted according to established procedures" (Habermas 1998, loc. 170). The concept of legitimacy—central to Habermas's work—comes to the fore when we consider the cultural efficacy of the law and the state in any given order. The paradox of the liberal notion of the state is that it projects a politically democratic facade in front of an edifice built on economic inequality. Or, in the words of the legal historian Morton Horwitz:

> It creates formal equality—a not inconsiderable virtue—but it promotes substantive inequality by creating a consciousness that radically separates law from politics, means from ends, processes from outcomes. By promoting procedural justice it enables the shrewd, the calculating, and the wealthy to manipulate its forms to their own advantage. And it ratifies and legitimates an adversarial, competitive, and atomistic conception of human relations. (1977, p. 566)

The "First Law and Economics Movement" chronicled by Barbara Fried (1998) sought to address this problem in the United States of the early 1900s by tempering the property absolutism with pragmatism: labor rights, social safety nets, safety and health regulations—policies that U.S. president Franklin Roosevelt would call "sane radicalism" (Olmsted 2015, p. 39). A key strategy of these scholars was "the choice to co-opt traditional 'natural rights' talk to its own political ends" (B. Fried 1998, p. 22). Robert Hale, the key scholar in this earlier movement, pointedly critiqued the Lockean assumptions of the laissez-faire state, attempting to take it on its own terms. As Fried summarizes, "Hale's wholesale revision of property rights [. . .] is largely internal to the natural rights tradition that it critiques, grounded on the Lockean imperative that people have an exclusive right to that which they have created with their own labor" (ibid., p. 73).

During a time of increasing labor militancy, Hale's rearticulation of Locke's argument had significant political implications. While he was only one of many scholars working on this issue at the time, the struggle to define natural rights in an alternative fashion was as important as the Levellers' refashioning of the concept in the seventeenth century, extending all the way to President Roosevelt, who tried to articulate a Second Bill of Rights in terms of economic and social equality (Sunstein 2004). Economics rather than religion formed the most potent cultural narrative. Therefore, the reaction against these policies was staged largely on the grounds of simply applying economics to the law. In the past four decades, this neoliberal doctrine of law and economics has become the hegemonic ideology, aiding in the reconsolidation of the apolitical, liberal definition of the state as defender of the reified culture of property.

The late-twentieth-century descendants of Locke's ideology—which I discuss as the Law and Economics movement—do not shrink from its paradoxical implications, but they have a ready answer. They assert that their interpretation of the morality and utility of neoliberal economic theory and the natural law limits on "positive rights" are an accurate representation of the natural world; therefore, there should be little democratic discussion of the economic policies—all of which are seen as policies ultimately bearing on property. Bryan Caplan asserts that, since voters do not all adhere to his narrow interpretation of the virtue of markets, "weakening democracy in favor of markets could be a good thing" (2011, p. 11). Jason Brennan's *Against Democracy* (2017) argues much the same, and Hans-Hermann Hoppe (2001) goes so far as to recommend we return to a monarchy as the "lesser evil" compared to democracy. Nancy MacLean's history of James Buchanan's role at George Mason University's (GMU's) economics department (where Caplan now teaches) and elsewhere is titled *Democracy in Chains* (2017).

While some critics disagree with MacLean's account of Buchanan's support for Virginia's resistance to desegregation, few take issue with her main thesis about the movement that Buchanan helped advance:

> Their cause, they say, is liberty. But by that they mean the insulation of private property rights from the reach of government—and the takeover of what was long public (schools, prisons, western lands, and much more) by corporations, a system that would radically reduce the freedom of the many. In a nutshell, they aim to hollow out democratic

resistance. And by its own lights, the cause is nearing success. (2017, pp. 28–29)

Buchanan is less central to this movement than MacLean proposes, but he was an economist present at the Mont Pelerin society meetings of the 1940s, he trained at the University of Chicago, and he served as a leader at the college that has since received the most money from the Koch brothers (from 2011 to 2014 alone, GMU received more than $48 million in Koch family monies [Barakat 2016]). In this sense, Buchanan is a good stand-in for the transformation of neoliberal hegemony over the past seventy years.

This chapter examines the moral and utilitarian arguments of the contemporary Law and Economics movement, which has taken it upon itself to revive the Lockean understanding of the liberal state (or, as Milton Friedman called it, the neoliberal, because it returned to the values of classical liberalism. It fits into the historical lineage started in the previous chapter, with Henry Ireton at Putney, his eye to property. In addition to this linear historical connection, however, the Law and Economics movement is also performing a similar political role to Locke's ideology of property in the late seventeenth century. In the face of a variety of movements bent on articulating their own understanding of this liberty, property, and natural law, Locke helped solidify natural law as articulated in the liberal capitalist conception of law and the state: the state would defend property, and any attempt to adjust property distribution should be met with a revolution. The contemporary Law and Economics movement, as the present chapter illustrates, has been similarly motivated to rearticulate the proper relationship between law, economics, and the state, trying to resist a similar set of leveling impulses and reclaim the mantle of liberty from midcentury liberals and the emergent civil rights movement.

The Law and Economics movement is especially crucial to understanding Lawrence Lessig's position as a preeminent voice in the battle for some form of "balanced copyright." But before choosing this stance, he was focused on creating what he termed a "New Chicago School" within the Law and Economics movement. The "Old Chicago School" he problematizes is known as one of the earliest fonts of the contemporary Law and Economics tradition. As an insurgent within the Chicago School of Law, Lessig (1995, 1996, 1998) called for a more explicit understanding of how the legal basis of the dominant economic system was inherently underpinned by an unexamined (or at least underexamined) set of cultural and social norms. Lessig's evaluation did not question the *validity* of the cultural and social norms posited by the Old Chicago School but instead hypothesized that using social and cultural norms to regulate social behavior could be an extra-legal tool for policy makers.

In other words, the cultural efficacy of the system does not function as the Law and Economics movement postulates. To take the framework we have developed for talking about law and cultural efficacy, insofar as its postulates are correct, it is either because other forms of efficacy—present in the practices of C1, beliefs of C2, and institutions of C3—help (and have historically helped) generate the predicted behaviors. As explored in the previous chapter, where one "discovers" the ideal subject of "possessive market society," it is often because state institutions have, at some previous moment, reformed C1 practices, censored C2 media, and instituted repressive C3 laws to force people to operate in ways that are more like the economic postulates of the Law and Economics movement. These postulates are, at best, a helpful index of human behavior in cultures where this efficacy adheres—similar to C. B. Macpherson's assessment of Thomas Hobbes discussed in the previous chapter. However, at worst, they are ways of modeling the state according to what Richard Epstein calls an "economic imperialism" (1997, p. 1168) forcibly coercing individuals into acting according to the postulates when necessary.

In calling for this "New Chicago School," Lessig opts for a middle ground, invoking Michel Foucault's analysis of similar, nineteenth-century projects to "make culture serve power" (1998, p. 691). While he does so in the context of the potential downside, it is clear that he also intends the reference to the disciplinary practices of the nineteenth century—so often the subject of cultural studies ire—as a model of what might be called stateless social regulation. But far from seeing this model as a problem, he sees it as admirably making explicit what many liberal theorists simply assume—namely, that the supposedly essential characteristics of the so-called state of nature had to be thoroughly inculcated through a variety of regulatory and repressive means.

Thus, while he critiques the Law and Economics movement, he basically accepts its understanding of what our culture should look like. His main concern is how to more effectively get there. Here, he represents the "democratic paradox" from the opposite direction: if it is evident that there is not a general cultural understanding of "liberty" and "property" along liberal lines, how can these be imposed on a society without the antidemocratic authoritarianism that liberalism was supposed to contest? A recent answer, given by Cass Sunstein, his former Chicago School of Law colleague, and Richard Thaler is that "libertarian paternalism is not an oxymoron" (2003). The article (expanded into their popular book *Nudge* [2008]) takes libertarianism (i.e., the absence of a paternalistic state) as an unquestioned paradigm, and hence the title well represents the paradox at hand—that is, how do we make people act more like they are *supposed* to act, or how do we *make* people act more like libertarians presume them to think and act without using the coercive state that libertarians claim to oppose?

Viewing Lessig's later arguments about copyright in terms of a "free culture" against this backdrop brings the real foundations of his critique into relief. The distinction he makes between "the physics of piracy of the intangible [and] the physics of piracy of the tangible" (2004, p. 64) serve as the jumping off point of the next chapter, which focuses on the use of the state to secure the rights of intellectual property (IP) against intrusion or dispossession, insisting that every state commit itself to preserving the value of that property. Hence, the attempt by owners of IP to secure maximalist rights is not a deviation from the historical practice of liberalism but represents some of its most cherished goals.

In his work on copyright, Lessig tries to produce a rigorous critique of existing conditions of property relations, but the conditions he finds unimpeachable are the true source of the injustice he perceives. The supposed democratic content of the "free culture" interactions within that state are significant, but they cannot be read at face value. The necessary continuation of a class-divided democracy is especially evident in the very distinction Lessig tries to make between tangible and intangible property, a partition that mirrors the global division of labor and its distributional consequences. This observation leads into the next chapter, which considers Lessig and other intellectual property rights (IPR) critics' discussions of the social production of value: under the reified culture of capitalism, this value is appropriated through the social division of labor.

While it is beyond the scope of this work to trace fully the articulation of the democratic paradox throughout the history of Anglo-American modernity, this brief overview of some of its most germinal thinkers should help situate the archaic resources that the latest Law and Economics tradition relies on—as well as the "so-called primitive accumulation" that the field overlooks in its historical accounts, a process that extends from the end of the previous chapter to the present day. The primary goal of this chapter is to outline the cultural assumptions and political goals that remain implicit in the arguments of adherents to the neoliberal ideology of the Law and Economics movement, despite their claims to scientific and ethical objectivity. The Law and Economics movement was founded on a certain set of cultural assumptions, which must be taken for granted from the outset. Lessig does not contest the logic or rationality of these assumptions: he just pragmatically recommends that social norms must be implanted rather than expected to be natural.

I begin by covering the more recent history leading up to the current Law and Economics movement and the battle over what these norms and assumptions could and should be. I then address these cultural assumptions and the economic theory behind them. I argue that this theory—embodied by Friedrich von Hayek and Ludwig von Mises—includes a tacit agreement that they should be coercively implanted, and then I turn to a close analysis of Ronald Coase and D. McCloskey. I then return to Lessig and the reason his challenge of maximalist IPR fails—precisely because it fails to challenge the reified culture of property on which the Law and Economics movement was founded.

From Locke and *Lochner* to the *West Coast Hotel* and Back: A Short Prehistory of Law and Economics

As with Locke, proponents of the contemporary Law and Economics tradition maintain the democratic paradox inherent in liberalism. They justify their ideology as simultaneously ethical or deontological and utilitarian. On the one hand, their property-protecting liberalism is said to be deontologically, morally superior—stealing property is theft!—and should be followed as strictly as possible no matter the social or ecological consequences. This pure theoretical view, which haunts most Law and Economics movement analyses, is also the clearest reproduction of the reified culture of property, as seen in Locke. Here, as discussed in the previous chapter, the liberal state is removed from politics: no matter what democratic demands may emerge, no legitimate state action can be used to alter the status quo of social property relations. On the other hand, even in the Lockean understanding, the consequences of this deontological stance are inevitably posed as more efficient and hence superior from a version of the utilitarian perspective. Thus, the ethical stance is doubly legitimate, as it is also economically superior.

This utilitarian Locke, a student of Sir Francis Bacon, sees enclosing and improving property as not just a political right to be defended against government intervention but a general social good—using, in this case, the application of science to the improvement of yields. Tucked into section 37 of the chapter "On Property" in the third edition of his *Second Treatise of Government*, Locke introduces a unique defense of private property that economic liberals have stressed ever since:

> He who appropriates land to himself by his labour, does not lessen but increases the common stock of mankind. For the provisions serving

> to the support of human life, produced by one acre of inclosed and cultivated land, are (to speak much within compasse) ten times more, than those which are yielded by an acre of Land, of an equal richness, lyeing waste in common. And therefore, he that incloses Land and has a greater plenty of conveniences of life from ten acres, than he could have from an hundred left to Nature, may truly be said, to give ninety acres to Mankind. (1988, p. 294)

Or, as Macpherson paraphrases, "Private appropriation in this way, actually increases the amount that is left over for others" (1962, p. 212). In other words, in addition to the political defense, Locke proposes that his *economic* model is more productive. Within the Law and Economics movement, and the general U.S. discourse on property rights, this orthodoxy reigns: private ownership provides incentives for the "improvement" of real property and IP, producing more output than would exist otherwise—for instance, in a social commons.

But even this utilitarianism is haunted by a version of the democratic paradox. As Macpherson points out, it "assumes, of course, that the increase in the whole product will be distributed to the benefit, or at least not to the loss, of those left without enough land" (1962, p. 212). Thus, this arrangement is therefore more useful (and therefore more moral) only if the increased yields are somehow distributed somewhat equitably. Unfortunately, that would be a form of socialism, a concept that was yet to be invented, but that it is safe to assume Locke would not have looked on kindly as a solution. The only limitation he allows is that we have a right to only the amount of land that we were able to improve. If we, for instance, produced—or accumulated—more than we needed, that would be wasteful because it would rot. But since money makes it possible to trade that extra yield for hard currency, there is effectively no longer a limit on what the capitalist owner can accumulate. And, insofar as we all agree to use money, we are also agreeing to the unequal distribution of wealth.

Locke shores up this defense by giving a different response to the so-called sufficiency argument: there is enough land out there for everyone to improve; if people were upset by the "natural laws" guiding someone's claim to property, they could just take a walk and find a new place to improve. For some insight into what this journey might entail, he claims that, in the beginning, "All the world was *America*" (Locke 1988, p. 301; emphasis original), by which he means that, in the beginning all land was open, unenclosed, and, more importantly, unimproved. Since then, the land had entered private hands because those people had made improvements on it.

We will return to the mutual constitution of the utilitarian and deontological justification of neoliberalism. For the moment, it is worth noting a different dimension of the ideal liberal subject that emerges between them and its specific articulation in the U.S. context. Setting aside the very material effects of Locke's statement ("All the world was *America*") in terms of its justification of the expropriation and destruction of Native American cultures, the most contradictory element of the neoliberal embrace of Locke's ideology of enclosure and improvement in the U.S. context is that it ultimately undermines one of the enduring images of its ideal citizen: the yeoman farmer.

Lessig draws on this figure in *Remix* (2008), especially in relation to the cultural sensibilities created by amateur artists, to which I return in the following chapter. For now, I want to highlight what Lessig says that Thomas Jefferson appreciated about this figure:

> Jefferson believed that the ethic of a yeoman farmer—one practiced in the discipline of creating according to an economy of discipline, as any farmer on the edge of civilization in eighteenth-century America would—was critical to democratic self-governance. Yeoman self-sufficiency was thus not a virtue because it was an efficient way to make food. Yeoman self-sufficiency was a virtue because of what it did to the self, and in turn, what it did to democratic society, the union of many individual selves. (2008, p. 27)

In its material fundamentals, yeoman self-sufficiency is akin to the supposedly inefficient commons and other allodial plots of land; these were best enclosed by the "improvement," according to Locke. But the liberty that property provided was political, economic, and cultural.

The eighteenth- and nineteenth-century United States was one of the few places where—at least for free (white) laborers—this yeoman ideal adhered. For much of the nineteenth century, there was a property requirement for voting, but the democratic ethos and self-sufficiency of property was as important as the franchise it bestowed. As among the more radical Levellers of the English Civil War, property was not just a signifier of social status; it represented freedom from wage slavery and the political interference of the wealthy. C. Wright Mills estimates that in the mid-nineteenth-century United States, "perhaps four-fifths of the free people who worked owned property" (2002, loc. 348). This property did more than grant them the right to participate in elections:

> Small property meant security insofar as the market mechanism worked and slump and boom balanced each other into new and greater harmonies. The wide spread of rural property was especially important because small owners had one security that no other kind of holding could offer—the security, even if at low levels, of the shuttle between the market chance and subsistence. (Ibid., loc. 369)

Mills asserts, "Liberalism's ideal was set forth for the domain of small property." He quotes Noah Webster, writing around the time when Jefferson was singing the praises of the yeoman, who declared, "An equality of property, with the necessity of alienation constantly operating to destroy combinations of powerful families, is the very soul of a Republic. While this continues, the people will inevitably possess both power and freedom; when this is lost, power departs, liberty expires, and a commonwealth will inevitably assume some other form" (Mills 2002, loc. 375).

Webster wrote this in 1787, more than a century after Locke and his improvers had established the need for enclosures and the efficiency gains of large farms. In England at the time, the Parliamentary enclosures that McCloskey analyzes, discussed below, were in full swing. And while Webster appears to share something like Locke's understanding of liberty, his articulation of it is almost inverted: like the Levellers at Putney, he is concerned not with improvement or efficiency but with the concentrated property holders—"the combinations of powerful families"—and the power these combinations would yield over those with less property, or no property at all (cited in Mills 2002, loc. 375).

A century after Webster wrote this, his fears were being realized with the increasing concentration of land, wealth, and power. As chronicled by many historians, this era was the age of what Alan Trachtenberg calls *The Incorporation of America* (2007). In this environment, the power of property became, in the words of Mills, a class power rather than an individual power. And a law and a state protecting property became a class state. In the absence of small property and self-provision for the majority, the political implications were immediately evident. As Jefferson Cowie puts it:

> What did citizenship mean when corporate directors, hundreds if not thousands of miles distant, made decisions that might devastate one community even as they bestowed temporary blessings on another? While protection from corruption and declension could only come from a strong, independent, republican citizenry, the decades had not been good to that ideal. (2016, loc. 577)

This "incorporation" continued the long march of capitalist primitive accumulation, first in land and property and then, as we explore in the next chapter, of the tacit knowledge and "intellectual property" of the craftsman forced into factories and deskilled by scientific management.

In the early twentieth century, the first Law and Economics movement rose to challenge this state of affairs on ethical grounds. It developed into a more coherent doctrine of realist jurisprudence, which observed that formal equalities in law are undermined by inequalities like those of concentrated property—or, indeed, the control of the property workers needed to produce value. This doctrine in effect created a utilitarian argument for some rebalancing of the political and economic scales. Hale and his associates in this earlier era were not making a strong Marxist argument that "maldistribution of wealth was an inevitable by-product of capitalism"; instead, they believed that the notion of positive liberty "required the state to redistribute wealth to ensure to each citizen the minimum necessary for economic and moral autonomy" (B. Fried 1998, p. 43). In short, it was an attempt to restore the kind of liberty that Jefferson had praised in the yeoman, but in an era when fewer people possessed property.

At roughly the same time, as Mark Blyth (2002) shows, welfare economists, such as Arthur Pigou and John Maynard Keynes, were arguing for the economic utility of state intervention. The effect of these interventions, directly or indirectly, was meant to stem the power of property owners, which was already being challenged by a forceful and popular labor movement and the specter of unprecedented Soviet productivity—all of which was exacerbated by the onset of the Great Depression. But these economists also provided a utilitarian argument for countercyclical government spending and regulatory support for workers' social wages. Here, the property that became most important to the utilitarian and moral arguments was the only property that most citizens possessed: their labor power.

For the thirty years before the Great Depression, the struggle between labor and capital had raged relentlessly, with the law and the state siding almost exclusively with capital and large property owners. In the pivotal case *Lochner v. New York*, the Supreme Court effectively made it unconstitutional for a state to regulate economic arrangements. The 1905 ruling instituted a broad reading of the due-process clause of the Fourteenth Amendment, which claimed that it included "freedom of contract." In other words, the state could not intervene in the supposedly rational, noncoerced contract made between employer and employee without "due process" of law—that is, it was depriving one or both of them of "life, liberty, or property." The Fourteenth Amendment allowed the federal government to overrule state laws in this regard, most importantly in the national outlawing of slavery, but the *Lochner* reading of it effectively reinstated slavery for many workers, white and black.

The current Law and Economics movement is largely motivated by a desire to return to the legal framework of what is known as the *Lochner* era. In the version told by neoliberal legal scholars, such as David Bernstein, the *Lochner*-era Supreme Court should be lauded for its consistent record of ruling against attempts by states to interfere with "the liberty of contract" through what he calls "class legislation" (2006, p. 1488). Bernstein sees no inconsistency in the fact that the opposite of legislation favoring workers and the destitute is not some neutral, class-free legislation but legislation that favors the interests of capital.

In the case in question, the liberty of contract looked like this: the bakers' union in New York supported legislation to limit the working day to ten hours, with a maximum of sixty hours per week. This guideline was informal at first; employers who agreed to this limit tended to value their workers and be committed to their businesses and consumers in a more socially beneficial way. The thinking behind the original policy regulated hours as an index for preventing a range of other workplace hazards. Inspectors had found that some of the most highly unsanitary conditions in which bread was baked—roaches, rats, and other signs of potential pestilence—often correlated with hiring the cheapest workers and forcing them to work twelve or sixteen hours a day, such that most bakers simply slept on site. Those business owners who would turn a blind eye to the desperate conditions of their laborers were also likely to look the other way on a few rats, so long as no one found out. So insisting on this limit on the working day and week would likely help uphold the health regulations that were also part of what became the New York Bakeshop Act of 1895. But its effects were short-lived: by 1905, the Supreme Court had ruled the act unconstitutional.

Bernstein celebrates *Lochner*, asserting that the market was creating a better environment for most workers and that state legislation was unnecessary. He counterposes "the market" with the results of workers organizing for their rights: they are not the state, but they are a form of spontaneously organized reaction to the market—almost exactly what Karl Polanyi describes as a double movement, and likely the real reason there was any improvement in those working conditions. Yet Bernstein objects to them in principle: unions, like the state, interfere with the "freedom of contract," especially in a closed shop. Instead, the market alone helped improve wages, hours, and working conditions for the bakers; therefore, the law extending these labor standards to all bakeries was unnecessary—and, he asserts, racially motivated. However, he also observes that the bakeries that did not have these standards—some of them with cockroaches so thick on the walls that the bakers dared not go to sleep—were the ones without unions. He admits that the Bakeshop Act might have improved those standards for all workers—and observes that *Lochner* likely made it difficult for unions to improve standards informally in the future. Yet all the while, Bernstein remains steadfast in claiming that the market had the most effect on the improvement of standards for the bulk of workers, simultaneously vilifying and eulogizing the factor that likely did the most to improve those standards (2006, pp. 1492–1505).

For Bernstein to say that *Lochner* accords with his understanding of "liberty" highlights one of the key premises of the movement he is part of—and the way it differs from Webster's view of the concept. For Bernstein, all transactions measured by the market are inherently voluntary—that is, free from coercion. Coercion, in the liberal tradition, can come from only the state; if an actor's decision is forced by the market or an economic power unsupported by the state, then it is not coercion but a force of nature. Hale criticized this notion, saying, "Under any coherent definition of coercion, the sphere of private, 'voluntary' market relations was indistinguishable from direct exercises of public power" (B. Fried 1998, p. 36).

The *Lochner*-era court set a series of precedents that reinforced the assertion that economic transactions were inherently the result of a voluntary contract. While "liberty" in contracts would seem to be separate from property rights, in the case of an economy that produced more for exchange rather than use, "rights of ownership were determined in the first instance by bargains between factors of production" (B. Fried 1998, p. 108). Therefore, from the liberal perspective, attempts by the state (in this case, the state of New York) to regulate working conditions not only interfered with the freedom of contract guaranteed by the due-process clauses of the Fifth and Fourteenth Amendments to the Constitution; they also interfered with property rights.

Bernstein's position, which is representative of this ideological inclination, is that if a worker's labor is his or her alienable property, and that worker agrees to work for longer than sixty hours a week, that should be his or her right. State intervention—such as laws regulating the length of the working day—interfere with the liberty of contract and, hence, the freedom of property. Hale—one of the *Lochner* contemporaries whom Bernstein ignores—objects. Following a long line of thinkers, including Marx, Hale asserts that all property is the result of political decisions and the coercive force of the state. Therefore, as Fried summarizes:

> When the government intervened in private market relations to curb the use of certain private bargaining power, it did not inject coercion

> for the first time into those relations. Rather it merely changed the relative distribution of coercive power. Whether in any given case that redistribution would increase or decrease the aggregate liberty of its citizens was therefore an empirical not an analytical question, and one that could not be answered by reference to abstract (constitutional) rights. Thus, concluded Hale, "there is no *a priori* reason for regarding planned governmental intervention in the economic sphere as inimical to economic liberty, or even to that special form of it known as free enterprise." (1998, p. 36)

Compelled by ideas like Hale's, along with those of such Progressive public intellectuals as John Dewey, combined with the Great Depression, massive social upheaval, the threat of an even more militant labor movement at home, and Communist pressure abroad, President Roosevelt forced through a number of measures to help the government—at the federal and state levels—regulate business and "protect the rights of personal freedom and of private property of all its citizens" rather than just those of the business elite (Olmsted 2015, p. 41). Chief among his actions was his threat to add additional justices to the Supreme Court if they did not rule in favor of certain New Deal legislation; this threat allegedly resulted in the Supreme Court verdict in *West Coast Hotel Co. v. Parrish*, which allowed individual states to intervene in their economic matters and effectively overturned *Lochner*.

There is much to be commended in the notion that individuals should be free to agree to any contract with any other individual. The debate at the heart of *Lochner*—whether workers should be able to agree to work twelve or sixteen or twenty hours of dangerous, unsanitary labor or whether there should be limits on the contract that no party can alter—finds an analogue in the very restrictive and counterproductive prohibition of most sex work in the United States. Melissa Gira Grant (2014) reports that sex workers themselves believe that these laws—often officially enacted to protect sex workers from the supposedly inevitable perils of their profession—make them less safe. This hypothesis—or at least a belief in it among those who perform this labor—would appear to be borne out by the fact that the legalization of sex work in Las Vegas was followed quickly by a push for unionization and self-protection in the workplace. But this model of public action is precisely what Bernstein rejects in upholding *Lochner*, which overturned a law that unionized workers had helped enact; it is "class legislation," but only because it is focused on the power of the working-class individual instead of the sacrosanct property rights of the capitalist employer. Bernstein, for instance, has no objection to the use of state force to compel workers back on the job.

In contrast, before becoming president, Roosevelt served as the governor of New York: And while *Lochner* made it harder to pass official legislation giving workers rights, Roosevelt broke with his predecessors in that he "refused to send in state troops to break strikes, opting instead to urge both sides to negotiate" (Olmsted 2015, p. 39).

The power of capital in a labor contract depends on workers' having as little leverage as possible in the negotiations—as few rights, regulations, and social wages standing between their docile production of surplus value and death. Therefore, it is no coincidence that Lochner's legacy ended in 1937, when the Supreme Court ruled on *West Coast Hotel v. Parrish* and the constitutionality of Washington State's minimum wage law—which, at the time, had been established at $14.50 per week of forty-eight working hours. Sunstein echoes Hale in arguing the move from *Lochner* to *Parrish* as effectively signaling that "the failure to impose a minimum wage is not nonintervention at all but simply another form of action" (1987, p. 880). This move simultaneously shifted the baseline of what should be considered the natural status quo and what government neutrality would look like in maintaining that status quo: "We may thus understand *Lochner* as a case that failed because it selected, as the baseline for constitutional analysis, a system that was state-created, hardly neutral, and without prepolitical status" (ibid., p. 882). We could say the same of all classical liberal—and neoliberal—defenses of property over liberty: their baseline assumes a context deeply shaped by class-oriented, state-aided primitive accumulation. By definition, this context is not a prepolitical state of nature but the result of concerted and asymmetrical political power. The court's decision in *Parrish* reads as if it were penned by Hale:

> The exploitation of a class of workers who are in an unequal position with respect to bargaining power and are thus relatively defenceless [*sic*] against the denial of a living wage is not only detrimental to their health and well being but casts a direct burden for their support upon the community. What these workers lose in wages the taxpayers are called upon to pay. (Quoted in Lessig 1995, p. 460)

This last point echoes today's campaigns for a $15 minimum wage in the United States, which often highlight the large number of low-wage service workers who qualify for and receive public assistance. *Parrish* not only changed the baseline but also recognized the fact of the power struggle at the site of production and the communal interest in resolving that struggle with some equity and fairness, concluding that "aspects of the economy previously thought independent were actually dependent." This realization, in turn, "justified the states' increased regulation" (ibid., p. 461).

(Neo)Liberalism and the Marginal Price of Coercion

The more recent Law and Economics tradition is often understood in a straightforward manner: it is a method of legal inquiry that applies the ostensibly scientific discoveries of economics to the law. Alternatively, it can also be a method of economic inquiry that investigates the economic effects of legal interventions: for instance, you should not think that a law protecting the environment is costless. For every molecule of particulate matter that a factory has to keep out of the air, its product is getting that much more expensive to produce—and hence for consumers to purchase. Richard Posner (1972), a close colleague of Lessig (who clerked for Posner briefly), and one of the movement's most venerable members, recommends the use of cost/benefit analyses in place of questions of ethics or rights in deciding what the law should say: you may say your children have a right to be protected from lead paint or asbestos, but who is going to pay for that?

Thus, this relatively innocuous sounding call for what we might term an interdisciplinary approach to legal and economic analysis most often becomes a demand to force markets to work in the place of regulations that populations most often demand of their states. While presenting arguments similar to Bernstein's, Epstein is more disciplined in his ability to hew this line: in a CATO Institute–sponsored tract, *How Progressives Rewrote the Constitution*, he claims that government regulations against child labor or limiting the working day in the United States were unnecessary because the standards themselves were improving already, just as Adam Smith had predicted: "Increases in technology and productivity redounded to the benefit of all" (2006a, p. 7). One can see the market as the sole force in creating greater wages and labor standards only if one isolates Epstein's market-centered ideology from the actual historical circumstances, particularly in the *Lochner* case, where it was not just market forces but organized labor that brought about those changes in union contracts and legislation. As Mike Davis points out, these legislative initiatives occurred following 1936–1937, a period of massive social activism and labor unrest—"a sustained offensive that was quite unequalled in American history for its tactical creativity as well as its demonstration of the power of the collective worker in modern industry" (1986, p. 60). It was, in effect, a cultural change that the legislatures, and eventually the courts, registered as constitutional. Evidence that this was a concerted, democratic effort, however, does little to change the balance of Epstein's interpretation.

The now-hegemonic Law and Economics movement, in contrast, was funded largely by corporate elites disgruntled with this new form of liberalism. Beginning (at least) with Sidney Blumenthal's *The Rise of the Counter-Establishment* (1986), many historians and political scientists have chronicled the various iterations of these movements. Blumenthal and others chart the vigilant, well-funded groups (such as the Koch Brothers' Cato Institute, founded in 1977; the Heritage Foundation, launched in 1973; and especially the John M. Olin Foundation, established in 1953, which spent most of its more than $370 million funding law and economics programs at law schools around the country) that were doing their best to work on instituting their ideology as policy. They sought to roll back what Fried calls "the progressive assault on *laissez-faire*" on a variety of fronts. First, they attempted to reinstate the political philosophy of Locke's natural law, which says that the state is illegitimate if it interferes with the liberty of private property. Second, they linked this political philosophy with a libertarian economic theory promoting the necessity and elegance of markets, a system whose utility demanded unencumbered private property to function. Over the past half century, these moral (or deontological) and utilitarian claims were intertwined in law and economics departments, think tanks, and the rhetorical assault for *laissez-faire* now generally understood as neoliberalism. The political and economic aspects of this movement are reliant on a deeply embedded culture of property, and the past few decades have seen a baroque cascade of ideological institutions constructed to defend it.

Unfortunately, this chapter cannot evaluate the entire historical development of this contemporary movement (or the movement that preceded it). In addition to contributing to the academic and intellectual ideas and institutions I explore later, Kevin Kruse argues that these corporate sponsors "advanced a new blend of conservative religion, economics, and politics that one observer aptly anointed 'Christian libertarianism'" (2015, p. 24). Lisa McGirr (2015) looks at the white, Christian suburbanites that formed the grass roots of this effort. I bracket conventional religion and look at the new dominant ideology legitimating government: economics. In 1962, Daniel Bell said, "The business community hailed [Hayek's *Road to Serfdom*] with alacrity." But its enthusiasm was more "for its catch-phrase title than for its prescriptions": "Because of the ideological use to which the book was put, it soon became apparent that Hayek could never become a convincing adversary to Keynesian thought" (Bell 1962, p. 80).

But at that time, as Kim Phillips-Fein (2010) and Kathryn Olmsted (2015) highlight, the business people entranced by Hayek's catchphrase and those like them were funding private foundations, think tanks, and academics such that less than two decades later, Hayek would influence Ronald Reagan, Margaret Thatcher, and the neoliberal revolution as a whole. Like MacLean, Mark Blyth (2002), Angus Burgin (2012), Philip Mirowski (2013), and Daniel Stedman Jones (2014) focus on the various institutions and academics that helped raise Austrian and other neoliberal economic ideologies to the status of orthodox thought. Recent work, such as David Harvey's (2005), has focused on the dynamic reversal in the dominant understanding of economics in the early 1970s (see also Duménil and Lévy 2004).

Certainly the economic aspect is important, but, as Blumenthal notes, the legal side is no less significant. Jason Stahl (2016) focuses on the rise of conservative think tanks since 1945, while Steven Teles (2012) follows the development of the conservative legal movement through funding law schools and the Federalist Society. As Blumenthal argues, the crowning achievement of the neoliberal retrenchment has been the realignment of the courts toward this Law and Economics tradition: "By naming more than half of the federal judiciary, Reagan would install on the bench the legal wing of the Counter-Establishment. In this way he would entrench [liberal] ideology in what has historically been a bulwark of conservatism" (1986, p. 10). In other words, while cultural studies scholars were increasingly dismissing the idea that the state and the economy could determine culture, legal scholars and economists—and their corporate backers—were banking on its being able to do so. As Ronald A. Klain (2017) has recently pointed out, this influence continues: despite Donald Trump's general ineffectiveness, "he is proving wildly successful in one respect: naming youthful conservative nominees to the federal bench in record-setting numbers."

As S. M. Amadae (2003) has recently argued, some of the motivation of this movement lay in designing a mathematical, scientific defense of the economic necessity of capitalism as part of the Cold War's goal of contesting Communism. From the economic side, therefore, the goal was to create a rigorous science that would "rationalize" neoliberal understandings of capitalist democracy. Any hint of a socialist mentality was to be countered with this scientific defense of the classical liberal state. Since it is pitched as a scientific method for "creating a just society within the constraints of rationality," the only method for doing this is through "the erosion of traditional worldviews" in which the market mentality does not exist. In other words, for "Rational Choice Liberalism" (Amadae's name for the combination of political and economic theories that were roped together in creating this "natural science") to be able to claim full, scientific relevance, it must perform that Baconian elimination of the spaces where it does not hold sway. In Amadae's words, "Overlooked by many economists, however, is the residual concern that even the market requires a basic level of normative consensus" (ibid., p. 289). Our supposed libertarian nature must have the guiding hand of the libertarian economist who will design libertarian institutions and incentives—much along the lines of Hobbes's and Locke's rules for the poor—which will help enculturate them properly, with the occasional bit of shock therapy when necessary to eliminate any "irrational" elements, such as so-called traditional culture or what Hayek (1989) would later call "atavistic" thinking, aka any cultural or social norm that does not fit into this selfish, utility-maximizing frame. It is a policy of destroying a society to save it.

As in Locke's time, a C2 narrative is projected upward into the structure of the state so that it can be imposed on society at large. Like the ideology of "improvement," this discourse of economics is not merely descriptive but also normative and prescriptive. For example, as one neoliberal celebrant of this tradition explains, "Whenever we speak of rational behaviour we always mean rational behavior directed primarily to selfish ends" (Amadae 2003, p. 5). Sentiments like these demonstrate that the science of economics on which the Law and Economics movement is based does not even pretend to display the full range of human social motivations: only selfish behavior is rational. The fact that some choices—for instance, those favoring interpersonal relationships, care, environmental sustainability, collective action, or "general welfare"—are ruled as impossible at the outset magnifies the narrow goals and the capitalist class faction ideologically favored by Law and Economics movement, particularly in the U.S. context. There, to synthesize Thomas Piketty (2014) and Loïc Wacquant (2009), inequality has become more extreme almost precisely in proportion to the withdrawal of the social safety net—from health care to education to wage increases and Social Security—and the expansion of the military-prison-industrial complex. The last thirty years have provided a series of test cases for this hypothesis, where the introduction of neoliberal economic policies does less for economic growth within any one country than it does for increasing inequality at a global level.

And thus the full contradiction of the liberal defense of the state comes full circle—from Locke to neoliberalism. The primary neoliberal objection to social democracy is that the state should not be involved in shifting resources or rights to promote social justice. But if its adherents were intellectually consistent, they would also have to agree that it was equally inefficient and unjust when the U.S. government effectively funneled trillions of dollars in lower-class wealth to a small number of already wealthy investors who are apparently immune to criminal law (Taibbi 2014).

As in Locke's time, the actual distribution of wealth is already the result of massive state intervention and often violent processes of primitive accumulation. But unlike in Locke's time, the contemporary Law and Economics movement originally emerged at a moment when the power of capital had been momentarily subdued through the New Deal and other policies of midcentury liberalism. As Amadae says of one of the principal architects of the neoliberal theoretical reaction, "Buchanan is forced, by both his view of traditional moral consensus and his view upholding free trade and private property, to support the status quo arrangement of society" (2003, p. 152). But by "debunking the delusion that government bureaucracy acts in the best interests of constituents," Buchanan's principal goal was to overturn the actually existing status quo, reinstating a libertarian moral consensus to "lift the veil of illusion from wide-eyed, naïve believers in socialism and welfare economics" (ibid., pp. 153–154). In other words, Buchanan was actually in favor of a radically altered status quo, which would more clearly reflect what he imagined the status quo arrangement of society should be.

This recalls Ellen Meiksins Wood's description of a "pristine culture" of capitalism from previous chapters. She describes this idea in terms of the separation of the economic from the political. The consequence of this separation in its pure form is not that the economic sphere is *actually* separated from the political. The formal policies of the state are used to make the coercive function of the market effective—and to determine the dynamic processes of culture into a framework of commodification and the social division of labor. However, the ideology of natural law envisions these policies as apolitical, and any movement or individual who attempts to change them is accused of "politicization." The pure separation of the economic from the political is therefore achieved only through the cultural: it is only when this separation has been effected completely and any alternative arrangement has been eliminated that the complete reification of this culture is possible.

As Mises, the godfather of liberal economics, laments in his book *Liberalism*, "Nowhere was this program ever completely carried out" (1985, p. 1). Mises opens his defense of his preferred political economic model with the distressed observation that "even in England, which has been called the homeland of liberalism and the model liberal country, the proponents of liberal policies never succeeded in winning all their demands" (ibid.). His defense of this order is certainly based on an idea that it is good, and even that it is natural, but more than either of these, Mises contends that it creates more wealth than comparable systems of political economy. This claim is based on a broad, historical observation that countries that ostensibly got closest to this model increased their overall wealth at a rapid pace (although he neglects to control for imperialism, slavery, and other crimes against humanity). On the other hand, he argues, "If one wants to know what liberalism is and what it aims at, one cannot simply turn to history for the information and inquire what the liberal politicians stood for and what they accomplished. For liberalism nowhere succeeded in carrying out its program as it had intended" (ibid., p. 3).

The Law and Economics tradition forms the most recent, explicit, and coherent defense of the liberalism that Mises proscribed in its purity. While it is, as Mises was, ostensibly engaged in some level of economic analysis, the economic analysis itself is a product of asserting as descriptive (rather than normative) the assumptions entailed in the pure theory of liberalism. While a larger project of comparing social interaction to legal rules might be productive, the outlines of the Law and Economics approach have hardened into reified cultural truths presumed to be the starting and ending points in analyzing social interaction in relation to law. In order, these cultural presumptions are the following:

1. All human action is purposeful, voluntary, and meant to maximize individual wealth.
2. Property is the natural, sacrosanct possession gained through purposeful action of its possessor.
3. The exchange of property among owners is a voluntary exchange among formal equals, and therefore the resultant exchange represents their rational, informed, individual assessment of how it will best, and most efficiently, meet their particular ends.
4. The market—or the "price system"—represents in aggregate these transactions. Since it presumed to be the product of these rational actors voluntarily exchanging to achieve maximum efficiency, the aggregate of these transactions is presumed to be efficient.

Following the conception of the previous chapters, these cultural assumptions must presume the efficacy of the culture they are promoting to assume that no (illegitimate) coercion is involved in imposing it. It is so deeply effective that *every* practice that is undertaken at the C1 level is presumed in one way or another to follow this economizing logic. Therefore, when reading these practices from above, as Mises does in his book *Human Action* (2000), one can simply assume that, if an action is taken (for instance, if a worker entered into a contract), it is taken in a purposeful manner and according to the belief structure associated with maximizing one's wealth. In sociology, this is closest to Talcott Parsons's (1937) structural functionalism, which was equally convinced of the structure itself being a representative of the aggregation of the beliefs of the actors in the system. Parsons, in turn, was inspired by Max Weber's (2001) speculations about the "protestant ethic" making U.S. capitalism more successful.

In practice, there is a structural folly in these premises. In the list above, proposition 1 is presumed to be the foundation of the entire structure in a direct, linear way. It exists before any of the others as a natural phenomenon. It is from the premise of the individual rational actor that the society governed by the capitalist market (proposition 4) is right and effective. As in Macpherson's critique of Hobbes, where the logical is substituted for a historical hypothesis, if proposition 1 is reliant on proposition 2 or 3 or even 4 for its motivation, then it is no longer an innate essence of human nature but a result of the structure itself. Therefore, the structure cannot be defended on the basis that it represents in aggregate the natural tendency at proposition 1—unless it is assumed that the price and property system at propositions 2, 3, and 4 are actually designed expressly to impose or reinforce proposition 1, thus reintroducing coercion into the supposed utopia of liberty.

As it happens, Mises's follower Hayek (1945), in his most-oft-quoted article on the price system, effectively advocates this last approach: the price system should be made to force everyone to act in accordance with the other premises. And by default, this discipline will need to be wrought by some higher power—like, say, a totalitarian state. This illustrates the second problem that this set of cultural presumptions suggests—namely, that they defy the liberal limits placed on the state by effectively demanding the imposition of an exclusive culture on society. The logical hypothesis that liberalism is merely the protection of negative rights is contradicted by the fact that it is really historically involved in the instantiation of a new way of life, a new individual, along the lines of what Isaiah Berlin (2002) criticizes as a form of positive liberty—but a positive liberty for property owners alone. A longer explication of Hayek's proposed system sustains this interpretation.

Hayek sets out to show the way markets, via the price system, help transmit important information that would never be accounted for in a system of central planning. In other words, it is a technical, utilitarian economic defense of the liberal (as opposed to socialist) state. For example, he discusses the ways in which the price of tin helps communicate to all the possible buyers and sellers of tin how they should adjust their practices:

> The most significant fact about this system is the economy of knowledge with which it operates, or how little the individual participants need to know in order to be able to take the right action. In abbreviated form, by a kind of symbol, only the most essential information is passed on, and passed on only to those concerned. (Hayek 1945, p. 527)

In other words, by reading only the price signal, the individual actor can accordingly adjust his action toward the "right" action, which is that of economizing and rational efficiency, creating a "rapid adaptation to changes in the particular circumstances of time and place" (Hayek 1945, p. 524). Altogether, "the whole acts as one market, not because any of its members survey the whole field, but because their limited individual fields of vision sufficiently overlap so that through many intermediaries the relevant information is communicated to all" (ibid., p. 526).

Hayek's elegant description of this system has led many to see it as analogous of the anarchistic interactions that are made possible by the Internet: projects such as Wikipedia, the free software movement often represented by Richard Stallman, representing the difference between what Eric Raymond calls "the cathedral and the bazaar" (2001). Sunstein, Lessig's colleague in the "New" Law and Economics tradition, eloquently affirms Hayek's thoughts on markets as a tool for generating knowledge in *Infotopia* (2006). Even Yochai Benkler, who is ultimately critical of something like proposition 1, incorporates many of Hayek's assertions into his work (2002, 2007). But the elegance of Hayek's description belies a hidden assumption and desire—that the price mechanism will be not only a communication system but also a disciplinary mechanism. While he is singing its praises, Hayek speculates as to why it is left to him to make these observations on the market: because "it is not the product of human design and [the] people guided by it usually do not know why they are made to do what they do" (1945, p. 527).

Hayek's vision of the natural, disembedded market makes him most attractive to the Law and Economics movement: it implies that human action can be coordinated without the use of a plan regulated by the state. However, the second half of his observation assumes that the structure of the system will actively discipline subjects in a certain way: "to make the individuals do the desirable things without anyone having to tell them what to do" (Hayek 1945, p. 527). This, in a nutshell, is Sunstein's desire in promoting "libertarian paternalism." Left undiscussed is what "right action" or "desirable things" are. It is simply assumed that implementing a system based on prices alone—that is, the market system with clear private property rights and protections disembedded from any other cultural norms—will ultimately create what Pierre Bourdieu calls "the enforced conversions" to the market modality (2005, p. 6). Yet the libertarian virtue depends on overlooking this process, seeing, instead, the "extended moral order" to be at once completely natural and the pinnacle of civilization. From this, Hayek concludes that we are communicating not only across space but also across time; his Whiggish history ends with a utopia where Jonathan Swift's "Modest Proposal" would be an entrepreneurial business plan.

For the market to be effective as an information, communication, and disciplinary mechanism, every possible object of value must be subjected to its valuation: every resource must be a commodity, and every object must be the alienable property of some individual who is able to calculate its value relative to all other values. Moreover, every individual must be forced to submit to this system in his or her every activity to properly calculate the value of his or her properties and communicate that valuation to other members of the market community. How much is your sleep worth? Your child's health? Your marriage? Your foot? These are no longer hypothetical questions. Insurance actuaries make calculations like these all the time, and it is increasingly possible to buy derivatives for anything imaginable. This system is clearly not the *way* those things are valued, but Hayek imagines that it should be.

Adam Smith's rendering of the market's disciplinary utility explores its grim implications. Writing in the absence of the welfare state that Austrian-inspired economists so deeply despise, Smith discusses the fairly direct way by which the demand for labor could create market equilibrium with its supply:

> Every species of animals naturally multiplies in proportion to the means of their subsistence, and no species can ever multiply beyond it. But in civilized society it is only among the inferior ranks of people that the scantiness of subsistence can set limits to the further multiplication of the human species; and it can do so in no other way than by destroying a great part of the children which their fruitful marriages produce. The liberal reward of labour, by enabling them to provide for their children, and consequently to bring up a greater number, naturally tends to widen those limits. It deserves to be remarked too, that it necessarily does this as nearly as possible in the proportion which the demand for labour requires. [. . .] It is in this manner that the demand for men, like that for any other commodity, necessarily regulates the production of men: quickens it when it goes too slowly, and stops it when it advances too fast. (2007 p. 52)

In other words, what Smith calls effectual demand works for every side of the equation: effectual demand by workers—that is, their ability to purchase goods on the market—is the inverse of the effectual demand for workers by capital. In managing this system of discipline, the state must therefore make every object of potential value a private, alienable property and make the rights in those properties clear and free of regulation. And it most certainly should not artificially prop up the labor market by preventing the deaths of poor children: this consideration creates inefficiency.

With Hayek, we have effectively jettisoned the notion that his liberal utopia is completely natural. The elegance of his understanding belies the coercive force of the market and the role of the state in managing the "enforced conversion" of any unruly citizens. The primitive accumulation—the "fire and blood" in Marx's terms—necessary to interpellate workers, raw materials, and the world at large into this exclusive modality is necessarily the result of a tremendous amount of state action and design. Hayek's price system requires a formal, juridical system that, as Wood says, makes the economic determine all social and cultural practices. The state is used to give all functional power to the force of the market, which then channels all the dynamic processes of culture into the single index of commodity price. And if *this* modality is seen, as in Hayek, as being beyond human design, then we cannot argue with the discipline that it enforces; it is more like a force of nature.

Aside from whether the market should or even can sort social values or arrange human interactions, neoliberal adherents cagily assume that it does. Smith, who was writing in the waning days of mercantilist absolutism, holds the market out as a unique area of society, an ideal space of freedom and resistance against absolutism. Mises, on the other hand, writing at the apex of robber-baron monopolies and state-led industrialization, looks at the market, ensconced in these social and political economic relations, and claims that it functions like the ideal of Smith's lore. The word "corporation" appears only four times in Mises's four-hundred-page text *Theory and History: An Interpretation of Social and Economic Evolution* (2001)—all in the same paragraph, refuting Marx's argument that monopoly would be the end result of this process.

Insofar as he is writing about industrial titans, Mises assumes they *must* have earned their place in the pantheon of capitalism by their superior insight and hunger for risk and reward. There are no accidents: each capitalist's success is the product of his or her superior engagement with the market. Thus, to quote from his manifesto *Liberalism*:

> In the capitalist system, the calculation of profitability constitutes a guide that indicates to the individual whether the enterprise he is operating ought, under the given circumstances, to be in operation at all and whether it is being run in the most efficient possible way, i.e., at the least cost in factors of production. If an undertaking proves unprofitable, this means that the raw materials, half-finished goods, and labor that are needed in it are employed by other enterprises for an end that, from the standpoint of the consumers, is more urgent and more important, or for the same end, but in a more economical manner (i.e., with a smaller expenditure of capital and labor). (1985, p. 71)

These idealistic descriptions are fanciful and abstract, taking into account very little in the way of the changes that were occurring in the organization of early-twentieth-century business enterprises.

Ironically, the example he gives—railroads—is the primary inspiration for what Michael Perelman calls "railroad economics," wherein the capitalists themselves realized that there could be no investment in such risky endeavors without some state guarantee of success. They did not conclude with Mises's imaginary calculation—"if the projected railroad promises no profit, this is tantamount to saying, that there is other, more urgent employment for the capital and the labor that the construction of the railroad would require; the world is not yet rich enough to be able to afford such an expenditure" (1985, p. 71). Instead, they colluded with one another and with politicians, helping engineer government bailouts of railroad speculators and guarantees of state protections and subsidies that helped them secure monopoly rights on certain train routes. In the process, a new cluster of "corporatist" economic theorists emerged who

> realized that the price system would be especially destructive in industries where firms have large fixed costs relative to the price of their product. Under such conditions [such as those prevailing in the, at that point, essential transportation industry of the railroad] competition will drive prices down below the level at which businesses can earn a profit, threatening widespread bankruptcy and economic chaos. [. . .] Because these nineteenth century economists recognized this defect in the market economy, they consistently promoted policy recommendations that violated the central tenets of ["pure capitalism"]. (Perelman 2006, p. 19)

If this theory had remained marginal, it might be a mere aberration in the "marginal revolution." But it became quite common in theory and in practice, having supporters in business, government, and the economic mainstream. Perelman even quotes John Bates Clark for his "rejection of laissez faire" (2006, p. 95), which was inspired by his observations on railroad. Clark was one of the most prominent U.S. economists of the nineteenth century. He was a founder and the referent of the highest honor awarded by the present-day American Economic Association. Perelman says, "Clark realized that much of modern industry was becoming more and more like the railroads. In Clark's words, 'competition of the individualistic type is rapidly passing out of existence' and giving way to consolidation and monopoly" (ibid.). As this outlook was adopted by corporate firms—along with corporate welfare schemes predating the government's sanctioning of collective bargaining—regulation by the price mechanism was replaced with a form of planning, a concern that animates Coase's early work, discussed later.

Mises seems blissfully unaware (or conveniently ignorant) of this history, assuming instead that railroads are solely the product of omniscient industrialists who clearly predicted the profitability of a projected railway line. The point here is less to question whether the price mechanism could or could not work: it is to point out that, contrary to Mises's example, it simply did not. And in the case of these communications technologies, it was better in the end that it did not. The national scope of the capital investment needed for railroads and telegraphs, as Dwayne Winseck and Robert Pike (2007) chronicle, necessitated state involvement. And, on the other hand, the market and nonmarket affordances provided by this infrastructure transformed the world on a scale that price simply cannot capture, a reality that we have seen echoes of in the fallout from the dot-com bust.

Instead of attending to these actual historical circumstances, Mises asserts the hypothetical logic of his theory. He points to this dramatic new technology, which completely transformed late-nineteenth-century life, claiming that omniscient industrialists and the price system actually brought it about rather than government subsidies, corporate consolidation, and the economic and political power of oligopolies. It is a classic libertarian defense: take something that people generally seem to like, ignore how it actually came about, and claim that it is the product of the imaginary system that you claim must now be perfected.

Bourdieu calls this neoliberal idealism an "amnesia of genesis" (2005, p. 5). It allows Mises to project abstractions of how social transformations actually occurred and for Hayek to project far into the past what he claims to be the pinnacle achievement of our contemporary culture: "We have developed these practices and institutions by building on habits and institutions which have proved successful in their own sphere and which have in turn become the foundation of the civilization we have built up" (1945, p. 528). As with Herbert Spencer and others who adopt organic metaphors for culture, there is no attempt to actually understand its history or account for the ways in which power—state or otherwise—has determined this system.

This amnesia of genesis creates a folly in the economic theory, illustrated by Hayek and Mises, who attempt to base their argument on an inherent human essence (proposition 1) that is the product of the system to which they hope to subject humans (propositions 4, 3, 2). But this contradiction is compounded when this faulty economic theory is then introduced into a philosophy of law. To reiterate, the goal of the Law and Economics movement is to show that liberalism in law (the purely economic state) is more efficient and that efficiency is the natural product of free, self-interested human economic interaction, absent the state. Therefore, this contradictory set of conclusions is produced:

5. All things being equal, the legal interference with private preferences will have no effect on the distribution of resources, which will tend, no matter what, toward efficiency
   5a. If a distribution of resources occurred, despite legal action, it was efficient.
6. The law should not try to dictate distributions or uses of property, since doing so will have an adverse effect on efficiency.

If conclusion 5 makes the state irrelevant to property distribution, conclusion 6 makes it all powerful. Sunstein (1986) describes these conclusions in terms of different objections to the "legal interference with private preferences," or the attempt to use statutes of the law to shape preferences rather than, as the liberal ideal would have it, to have the law reflect those preferences through its reliance on the private market. Sunstein categorizes these as objections from *futility* in the case of conclusion 5 and *liberty* in the case of conclusion 6, but in each case, the economic argument above is the fundamental assumption on which each objection relies:

> The objection from liberty has it that the government ought not, at least as a general rule, to be in the business of evaluating whether a person's choice will serve his or her interests, or even whether the choice is objectionable, except when the choice causes harm to others. The objection from futility emphasizes that in general, interferences with private preferences will be ineffectual, for those preferences will manifest themselves in responses to regulation that will counteract its intended effects. (Ibid., pp. 1129–1130)

It is important to keep in mind that, as it does for Hayek, the term "preferences" here refers to the self-seeking preferences of economic actors in terms of how they interact with private property in a market. In the liberal ideal, these are the only valid preferences, and the behavioral economics that Sunstein recommends are oriented to making more of our preferences conform to and explicable by this logic.

Liberal theorists simply assume that this world exists. The objection from liberty, following Hayek, Mises, Robert Nozick, and Epstein, among others, is that the government simply should not interfere with the "preferences" of economic actors. From this perspective, the state is an all-powerful entity that has the apparatus to coerce actors into changing these preferences or to otherwise restrict them from satiating these preferences. The state's omnipotence, therefore, is something to be feared, and citizens of the liberal polity should be leery of allowing the state to take any more power than is necessary. Liberty is precious and can easily be undermined.

From the perspective of futility, however, the state is starkly different. From this perspective, the private preferences of economic actors are so fundamental, so basic, so sovereign and natural, that even the full force of the state's omnipotent regulatory power can do nothing to alter them. On this count, the all-powerful state apparatus can successfully protect only one thing: the legal rules of property and contract. It is surprisingly successful in this task, which is a good thing, since protecting property is the natural, immutable foundation of the liberal state.

Within the Law and Economics tradition, both of these conclusions are often discussed in terms of the law's effect on economic efficiency. As Harold Demsetz puts it, "The output mix that results when the exchange of property rights is allowed is efficient and the mix is independent of who is assigned ownership" (1967, p. 349). In other words, so long as the state and the law provide a clear signal of who owns what property, the long-run effects of the distribution will be the same. Social costs—such as environmental degradation—will eventually be absorbed by one or another side of the transaction. Either a factory will continue to pollute, or the community that wants it to stop will pay it to stop polluting. Anytime the state gets involved in telling people what they can *do* with their property, it produces inefficiencies. The only thing the state, and the law, can do, therefore, is to enforce contracts and protect property rights as they have been allocated.

Again, this ideology must forget the history that created the present distribution. As Amadae says of Buchanan, the status quo is presumed to be just and efficient despite previous state interventions (i.e., primitive accumulation), and this presumed efficiency suggests that making further interventions would be ineffective. Paradoxically, if further interventions in the distribution or regulation of property seem imminent, the argument shifts to saying that the ineffective state is actually all powerful and that its interventions will result in the inefficient allocation of resources. The only way these positions are coherent is from the liberal perspective, which says that the state and the law should be used to protect only current distributions of resources. Following the dominant ideology of "improvement," the caveat is that if a better allocation would be more efficient, then the resources would naturally be shifted.

Liberty, in this regard, is equal to efficiency, and the efficiency of the liberal market economy makes any alternative legal intervention futile. Property will eventually find a way, as it should.

Property and the Social Cost of Neoliberal Efficiency

Coase (1988), writing at roughly the same time as Hayek, takes some of these liberal utopian economic ideologies and tries to square them with the actual practices of corporate capitalism by spending several months traveling around the United States to better understand the new economic organizations of U.S. businesses. He begins from the assumption of the efficiency of the market in liberal economics but finds that it does not explain the emergent structures of what Marxist economists Paul Baran and Paul Sweezy (1966) eventually termed "monopoly capitalism." Because of his travels, his conclusion is in stark contrast to those of Hayek and the price system, yet he finds a way to square the circle: citing an earlier article of Hayek's (1933), Coase says, "This theory assumes that the direction of resources is dependent directly on the price mechanism," but this gives "a very incomplete picture of our economic system. Within a firm, the description does not fit at all" (1988, p. 387). Within a vertically integrated firm, workers are regularly moved to different departments and factors of production are reorganized, based not on the external assessment of price but by the command of the management. Of this discovery, he says:

> Those who object to economic planning on the grounds that the problem is solved by price movements can be answered by pointing out that there is planning within our economic system which is quite different from the individual planning mentioned above and which is akin to what is normally called economic planning. (Ibid., pp. 387–388)

Planning done in the (monopoly) capitalist system is superior to socialist planning, because in the former it is done by "the entrepreneur," who is always a rational maximizer. Coase argues, "In a competitive system, there is an 'optimum' amount of planning" (1988, p. 389). His tautological reasoning is carried through to the theorem that results from his analysis. Corporate vertical integration, requiring the equivalent of command and control rather than organization using the price system, is used only to the extent that it is more efficient to do so in terms of the transaction cost of going outside the firm: therefore, if it is done, it must have been efficient. From within this tautology,

Coase sees no other possible reason for this arrangement: the market, which demands efficiency, would allow them to operate only on these terms.

In the article most closely associated with the Law and Economics movement, Coase (1960) approaches the problem of what he calls "social costs." Written while Coase was working with Buchanan at the University of Virginia, the product includes the intertwined ideology of both. If the purpose of "The Firm" is to write a caveat to premise 4—which says that, insofar as monopoly businesses forego the market, it is done because it is efficient—Coase's "social costs" article ultimately argues against regulation of any kind by introducing the idea of "joint costs," with all sorts of implications for the relationship between private property holders and the state.

Coase's argument is a version of what Sunstein calls the objection from futility: "Absent transaction costs in private bargaining, legal rules will have no effect on the ultimate allocation of resources" (Beecher-Monas 2002, p. 2n4)). To illustrate this argument, Coase produces a series of case studies. He begins with the case of a hypothetical farmer and a rancher. The farmer has crops on his property, which the rancher's cattle trample or otherwise destroy. Coase produces several separate scenarios: one in which a regulation mandates that the rancher fence his animals and two others in which the rancher and the farmer, absent any state regulation, simply contract with one another, agreeing to pay one another for the right to either continue ranching or to continue farming. The cost of this payoff—or the cost of fencing—is therefore included in the total accounting of each actor, making their respective decisions about whether they should continue their activities contingent on this calculation of overall economic efficiency. At the end of this thought experiment, Coase demonstrates mathematically that the effect is the same, meaning that the potential regulation of the hypothetical transaction makes no difference to the absolute efficiency of the situation: the most efficient outcome, as measured by the price system, is produced in either case. State regulation, in other words, is futile.

However, his unregulated outcome, like Mises's railroad example, does not take into account fixed or sunk costs yet to be amortized, the different skills that each player possesses, or these players' desires to maintain a certain way of life. In any case, the pure logic of the price system is not the only thing regulating these interactions. Absent some form of force, and even including it, a general understanding—the law of the prairie, perhaps—must lead them to come to some reciprocal agreement. This understanding is what Sunstein and Lessig mean when they call attention to the presence of social norms that might regulate in the absence of law—norms that, more than likely, "are part of a [legal] system that constitutes, and does not simply reflect, the social order" (Sunstein 1986, p. 1136).

If his first objective is to show that state regulation is futile, Coase's second objective is to argue for a theory of what critical legal scholar Duncan Kennedy (1998) calls "joint costs," a concept that effectively makes the state regulation of private property an economic transaction. Kennedy observes that Coase's innovation is not only to introduce the market mechanism in place of the legal mechanism but to point out that "if we are worried about how to allocate joint costs, with a view to efficiency, there is no reason to presume that the party we would intuitively identify as 'active' should have to pay, and that the intuitively 'passive' party should not" (ibid., p. 467). Or, as Coase says more succinctly, "in the case of the cattle and the crops, it is true that there would be no crop damage without the cattle. It is equally true that there would be no crop damage without the crops" (1960, p. 13). In other words, following somewhat from observations made by Hale, we cannot assume that the farmer is passive simply because he is there first and the rancher active because he appears on the scene later: both are actors engaging in economic activities.

In the theory of joint costs, every party to a transaction should be seen as bearing the costs of continuing his or her own activity. However, as with the price mechanism, or value in general, it is not for Coase to speculate about the mystical process whereby people will arrive at some agreement to pay for an infringement of what they previously regarded as a passive right. In other words, although the farmer is already involved in his industry, the fact that the costs he incurs suddenly increase (i.e., to pay off the rancher for not ruining his crops) should be seen not as a legal or even an ethical problem involving the abrogation of certain rights but as an economic one stemming from a change in the circumstances of his production. Or

> if we are to attain an optimum allocation of resources, it is therefore desirable that both parties should take the harmful effect (the nuisance) into account in deciding on their course of action. It is one of the beauties of a smoothly operating pricing system that, as has already been explained, the fall in the value of production due to the harmful effect would be a cost for both parties. (Coase 1960, p. 13)

A longer exposition of Coase's theory would more fully explore the implications of this second objective, which is ultimately essential to the shift in perspective he provides for the Law and Economics movement. Thinking about regulation in terms of joint costs is a wholly novel cultural assumption. It is above and beyond the economic presumptions that must be assumed to be active for his system to operate at efficiency, more akin to the system of voluntary payments for protection and presumed rights that operates behind the scenes in Nozick's *Anarchy, State, and Utopia* (1974). In the latter's ideal of state-free human action, he handily assumes that there is no question about what rights *are* and through what means they can be legitimately violated or enforced (ibid., ch. 4).

The notion of joint costs sets the ground for Epstein's argument in *Takings* (1985). His work is especially pertinent to the overall discussion of property rights in relation to economic value and the state. While it focuses on the policy of eminent domain, the upshot of Epstein's argument is that the government has no right to regulate even environmental standards unless it is prepared to pay businesses that *might* be hurt by those standards for all *potential* lost revenue. He therefore applies the Lockean argument about property in the extreme—that the owner has the natural right to the property and all potential value created from it—and applies it to conditions of eminent domain and, by extension, environmental regulation. And, as we will see, Epstein handily translates these arguments about private property in land to private property in "intangibles," aka IPR.

Coase does not go this far, but in presuming the hypothetical payment of these joint costs—or even their negotiation according to these terms—he is presuming an entirely novel cultural system where people will ignore even the existing arrangement in the interest of economic efficiency. Coase therefore presumes that this society, where the logic of market efficiency prevails and joint costs are understood by all parties, already exists. In these changed circumstances of market utopia, the government is given no credit for making the market function efficiently: as he puts it, "There is no reason to suppose that the restrictive and zoning regulations, made by a fallible administration subject to political pressures and operating without any competitive check, will necessarily always be those which increase the efficiency with which the economic system operates" (1960, p. 18). This observation is surely true, but there is also no reason to assume that economic efficiency is the only goal for the laws and regulations that societies choose to impose. More importantly, there is certainly no reason to imagine that the current distribution of property—what Marx calls "production-determining distribution"—is necessarily the result of decisions made with efficiency in mind. Nowhere is this more obvious than in the realm of IPR, particularly copyright, where we have seen several decades of so-called pirates finding more efficient ways to distribute culture than its ostensible owners.

If Coase were interested in looking at a *historical* rather than *logical* situation in which a conflict of interest existed between farmers and ranchers, he could have looked to Texas, where the enclosure of land with fences was one of the more arresting developments of the late nineteenth century. It involved just the kind of conflict between the older generation of cowboys and small agricultural holders, many of whom grazed their cattle on the "free grass," and a new class of large landholders, taking advantage of the new invention of barbed wire (patented in 1873) to consolidate and fence large holdings. After a series of violent confrontations—many of which were caused by the private security forces whom Nozick seems to find so endearing—the Texas state legislature voted in 1884 to make fence-cutting a felony; legend has it that it was illegal to even have wire cutters on your person in the state capital. As the *New York Times* noted at the time, this prohibition made one class of property owners "law-abiding citizens," while "those moved by a spirit of lawlessness and communism" would be turned over to the governor. As with the enclosures in England, ultimately the law and the state sorted the conflict between these cultures. One observer noted the way the legislature effectively mandated which culture would prevail:

> The fence-cutting which had caused so much trouble, he said, grew out of the conflict between the great interest of stock-raising and the lesser one of farming. The old civilization established the doctrine of free grass; the new asserts the rights of individual property. (*New York Times* 1884)

In other words, in practice, the problem of "social cost" is much more complicated than a simple, market-based transaction: when the basic agreement cannot be reached between the contracting parties; when one must admit that the culture does not function as automatically as a logic problem might indicate; when, to paraphrase Althusser, the ideological apparatus is insufficient, the repressive apparatus must be used in its place.

As this case illustrates, Coase is right to point out that the involvement of the law and the state often produces arbitrary judgments in favor of one set of rights over another. Yet even after that judgment is produced, as realists in the first Law and Economics movement argued, the efficacy of the law is shaky and arbitrary. People use loopholes, they pay off police, or they bribe their neighbors or intimidate them using their economic or political power to create advantages and "rearrange" rights—which, evidently, happened in Texas, where the "great interest of stock-raising" overruled the "civilization" of the "lesser interest" of farming. The court performs the role of sorting one claim against another; otherwise, as Marx puts it, "between equal rights, force decides" (1977, p. 344). The function of the law is an empirical question. In this sense, power can be used in a variety of ways by those who have it: the law is, in truth, only one such way. As a supposedly objective force, in its democratic ideal, the law is supposed to be used for securing rights; thus, it could be used by the less powerful party to secure some right in its interest. Indeed, the law must occasionally function that way if it is to remain legitimate. Horwitz (1977), paraphrasing Douglas Hay et al. (2011) and E. P. Thompson (1990), observes, "Use of legal ideology as a means of social control required that it be believed and acted upon by both higher and lower classes" (1977, p. 563). This observation means that the law must occasionally rule against property and efficiency if it is going to maintain legitimacy.

On the contrary, Coase says that we should not concern ourselves with this function of the law: it is usually ineffective anyway and, in the end, likely supports inefficient uses of materials. Thus, even if some apparent injustice might appear to be correctable by some reallocation of rights or resources, it should not be undertaken, because it might result in some unforeseen inefficiency. In the end, this narrow, economic concern is the only one anyone should worry about. Or, as Coase puts it:

> The economic problem in all cases of harmful effects is how to maximise the value of production. [. . .] The immediate question faced by the courts is *not* what shall be done by whom *but* who has the legal right to do what. It is always possible to modify by transactions on the market the initial legal delimitation of rights. And, of course, if such market transactions are costless, such a rearrangement of rights will always take place if it would lead to an increase in the value of production. (1960, p. 15; emphasis original)

For the Law and Economics movement, the ultimate point is that the law is, on the one hand, unjust when it intervenes in the economy and, on the other hand, ineffective because the market will always overrule it. This point highlights the specific articulation of the democratic paradox in the movement's framework. On the one hand, Law and Economics scholars want to present a deontological truth of liberty: the state should not intervene in "private contracts." This action, they say, is simply amoral. But since they also have to defend their creed to a wider audience, they appeal to this underlying utilitarianism: nonintervention produces efficiency and growth, and that's good for everyone!

But, to come full circle to the enclosures of the previous chapter and D. McCloskey's 1972 article, "The Enclosure of Open Fields: Preface to a Study of Its Impact on the Efficiency of English Agriculture in the Eighteenth Century," private property is not necessarily efficient in practice. McCloskey's presumption—traced here from Locke to Demsetz, Coase, Epstein, and the present Law and Economics movement—is that advancing and protecting the property rights of capitalist owners (who are, we are told, always improvers) necessarily results in an increase in the number of crops yielded. But this question, like the function of the law, is empirical. They assume their preferred articulation of liberty leads to actual utilitarian outcomes, which blinds the now hegemonic Law and Economics movement to the possibility that common pool resources can be maintained (as discussed in the work of Elinor Ostrom [2015]) and that private property may be less efficient (or at least less socially desirable) than other alternatives (as shown in the work of Carol Rose [1994] and Michael Heller [2006, 2008]). Epstein and others in the Law and Economics movement sometimes admit this possibility when pressed, but their reflex is to favor their capitalist inflection of liberty over political and economic democracy.

Indeed, McCloskey's primary hypothesis is that the enclosures did not happen earlier because the legal regime was not quite liberal enough: it was still too concerned with democracy and peasant rights in the common rather than the efficiency of enclosure. McCloskey's is an early variation of Hernando de Soto's (2000) argument, which asserts that the only variable holding back development in the early modern world—like de Soto says of the contemporary third world—is a lack of clear property rights. Likewise, McCloskey asserts that, before the mid-nineteenth-century Parliamentary enclosures, the legal regime created a cost that overrode possible efficiency gains. The need to unite the peasant population under common law prevented it from happening earlier. It is one of those unfortunate problems with democracy, as she points out early on:

> A conqueror can achieve by the threat of his sword and a stroke of his pen a result of eliminating inefficiencies of an earlier social arrangement on which a society of laws must spend many years and much expense. Legal constraints on enclosure preserved equity at the cost of making it more expensive than it need have been. (1972, p. 22)

Whatever the truth of this hypothesis about transaction costs and efficiency, it is wrong on the mutual exclusivity of conquering and the law. As Barrington Moore says, "Not all historically significant violence takes the form of revolution. A great deal may occur within the framework of legality that is well along the road to Western constitutional democracy. Such were the enclosures that followed the Civil War and continued through the early Victorian era" (1967, p. 20).

In any case, McCloskey's larger point—like de Soto's—is that the law was underdeveloped until it allowed for the efficient transfer of property as capital. The only disciplinary perspective capable of discerning this argument in full is some permutation of Law and Economics. Thus, McCloskey brushes aside claims of the venerated historians John and Barbara Hammonds most well known for their study of the broader social effects of the enclosures. McCloskey's myopic economic perspective suffices:

> Many students of the enclosure movement have emphasized not the size of the costs and benefits, but their distribution. A remark of E. P. Thompson could serve as a motto for the tradition of Marx and the Hammonds on this matter: "Enclosure (when all the sophistications are allowed for) was a plain enough case of class robbery." This judgment on the equity of enclosure would require no comment in an inquiry into its efficiency were it not that the incentive to enclose could have been affected, at least theoretically, by the distribution as well as the size of the costs and benefits. [. . .] As much as enclosure may have hurt the poor, however, it is doubtful that the hurt was large enough, relative to the net gain to be achieved by the larger owners of the land, that it influenced their decision to enclose. This is because the poor were very poor: the value of their land and other rights was small. In consequence, an equitable procedure, which compensated them fully for their ancient rights, would have changed the net benefits accruing to those who had the power to set an enclosure in motion very little. As a first approximation, then, the issue of equity may be set to one side. (1972, pp. 29–30)

In other words, it was not class robbery because the poor did not have much; thus, taking all their land would not have helped the enclosing landlords much. However, for the peasant, much more was at stake (as the previous chapter illustrates). As Moore puts it, "For the 'surplus' peasant it made little difference. [. . . H]e was caught in the end between alternatives that meant degradation and suffering, compared with the traditional life of the village community" (1967, p. 29).

Like Locke and the other followers of the Invisible College, McCloskey assumes that enclosure will be a more efficient economic model. And like the followers of the Law and Economic movement, McCloskey assumes that the real drag on efficiency was an excess of democracy—a problem solved by a change in Parliamentary procedures. Those changes effectively swept in McCloskey's preferred system of majority rule (as opposed to the unanimous system under common law). As always, the functional effects of formal law are often skewed by economic and social inequalities.

While McCloskey finds it a boon for efficiency that the rational calculators of the day finally remove the nuisance of the juridical transaction costs to enclosure, she fails to see that, as Moore contends,

> it was Parliament that ultimately controlled the process of enclosure. Formally the procedures by which a landlord put through an enclosure by act of Parliament were public and democratic. Actually the big property owners dominated the proceedings from start to finish. Thus the consent of "three-fourths to four-fifths" was required on the spot before Parliament would approve a proposal to enclose. But consent of what? The answer turns out to be property, not people. Suffrages were not counted but weighed. One large proprietor could swamp an entire community of smaller proprietors and cottagers. (1967, p. 42)

If McCloskey had actually read the Hammonds' work—which is where Moore gets this fact—instead of simply writing them off as irrelevant insofar as his discussion of efficiency is concerned, then perhaps the abstract calculation here would have had to deal with the messiness of historical facts. But, in the end, "the issue of equity may be set to one side" (McCloskey 1972, p. 30).

This is a clear example of where the argument for "liberty" seems suspiciously focused on a particular *kind* of liberty—one that Locke, as a large landowner, might have condoned. The shift in transaction costs (toward the liberty of property) was the result of the loss of political power by the peasants. In the end, it does not matter to McCloskey what that Parliamentary process looked like: the conclusion she proposes as a rational explanation for why this massive social undertaking occurred is an *ex post facto* justification for what even she seems to admit was a system that removed the democratic break on the wheels of capitalist development. In the end, the efficiency of enclosure is assumed: utility and the liberty of property are ultimately the same thing. In the market, after all, suffrage is weighed, not counted.

McCloskey does not attempt to prove this hypothesis empirically, but she is clear that it requires a narrowly defined metric utilized by a fellow economist. The Hammonds and E. P. Thompson will not do. She makes a suggestion for where one might look for proof of her assessments' accuracy:

> The increase in rent, then, is known in a general way, can often be known in detail for particular villages, and can be used as an estimate (although biased downwards by not including the value of the increased employment of the other, mobile factors of production) of the increase in the value of output resulting from enclosure. (1972, p. 33)

She then hypothesizes factors to be considered in using this index and sets up possible figures, ultimately saying—despite the fact that she has just asserted that efficiency was the motivating factor in the enclosures—that it would be difficult to determine just how efficient they were based on the fuzziness of the available data.

When Robert Allen, a fellow economist, takes McCloskey up on the challenge to look at the data, he actually finds not only that the enclosures were not necessarily more efficient than open fields but also that insofar as they created gains in rents, it was from the redistribution of income upward from the newly dispossessed peasants and cottagers to the landlords. He makes this discovery using the index that McCloskey recommends and data compiled by an advocate of enclosure during the period, a man named Arthur Young. Allen's conclusion (as an economist using the reductive, quantitative methods that McCloskey and Coase would insist on) is that the

> results would have surprised Young, who was an influential proponent of the view that enclosure increased efficiency, for they show that in the late eighteenth century, the enclosure of open field arable did not have that effect. Instead, enclosure caused a massive redistribution of income from farmers to landowners. (1982, p. 938)

In other words, that messy humanities scholarship that Thompson and others use produces accurate results, based, it is worth noting, on the views of people at the time. Enclosures were not a matter of efficiency or growth but a form of legalized class warfare that shifted resources from the poor to the rich.

Liberty is a concept that is already shot through with the contradictions of the contemporary status quo. It purports to be an absolute, universal value, the achievement of which all subjects should aspire to and demand. Yet when the lower classes, or women, or people of color see themselves as that subject of liberty, they are often faced with a political and socioeconomic status quo founded on their continued disenfranchisement, repression, and exploitation. The liberty of capitalist property—which has always been bolstered by the white-supremacist patriarchy—cannot be challenged without threatening the legitimacy of the state. The democratic paradox is fundamental to the capitalist order: the people can elect a government, but ultimately, property is king.

Lessig, Epstein, and the Law and Economics of Intellectual Property

These assumptions are not new. If we look back at what I call the "reified culture of property" in the previous chapters, it is no coincidence that it corresponds very closely to the assumptions Locke had to make to construct his liberal defense of the state. While Locke's philosophy might not have been injected directly into our current ideology of property, the Law and Economics movement attempted to complete the transfer of this reified culture of property from the seventeenth century to today. As one of the most successful academic endeavors of the late twentieth century, it has done a great deal to accomplish this transfer, and therefore discussing the reified culture of property today requires confronting this movement directly.

Within the United States, the allocation of IPR is understood as being a constitutional issue concerned with balancing the democratic values of freedom of speech and expression with, as stated in the Copyright Clause (Article I, Section 8, Clause 8), the need "to promote the progress of science and useful arts," a phrase that has an increasingly capitalist inflection in the twenty-first-century understanding of the global division of labor and power. As in every aspect of neoliberal governance, the connotation of economics dominates the conversation about this legal issue. The dominance of this language is especially evident in the international sphere, where absolute claims to ownership of IPR are more starkly defined, more often decried, and more strictly implemented. The maximalist position on IP is a direct descendent of the Law and Economics movement's position on the liberty and efficiency of property and the market. This relationship is made clearest later, in relation to the conservative views of the Progress and Freedom Foundation (PFF), for whom Epstein wrote briefly on IPR issues.

The Law and Economics movement has been one of the crucial intellectual and political influences on the debate over IPR. Its influence in the mainstream debate about IPR is indubitable. Mark Lemley argues that

> the rise of property rhetoric in intellectual property cases is closely identified not with common-law property rules in general, but with a particular economic view of property rights. This view, which emerges from the Chicago School Law-and-Economics movement, emphasizes

> the importance of private ownership as the solution to the economic problem known as the "tragedy of the commons." (1997, p. 37)

Lemley, like Lessig, objects to this "propertization," citing Carol Rose (1986) and noting that "it is not at all clear to me that commons are always a bad thing, even in real property law. I am further unconvinced that the Chicago approach to real property, even if valid in that context, maps well onto intellectual property" (1997, p. 45). Lessig generally agrees with the final clause of this sentence but usually refuses to broach the "even if" that Lemley mentions.

Before Lessig took up the cause of copyright, he was a tepid critic of the dominant Law and Economics movement. In fact, many of the observations he makes about the inadequacies of the property system in relation to copyright are borne from an earlier attempt to make the liberal and even libertarian premises of this movement more culturally effective. In the end, he bases his case for copyright reform on a fundamental agreement with Epstein and others on matters of property per se.

Thus, it should be no surprise to these scholars—and especially Lessig—that this perspective sees IP as equally absolute, advancing the arguments of liberty, efficiency, and the futility of altering the status quo in its defense. For example, when Law and Economics movement scholars William Landes and Richard Posner set out to investigate the copyright and trademark systems, they presume, from the outset, that these systems, as they have developed, are efficient—and that the question we should ask about copyright, for instance, is "to what extent copyright law can be explained as a means for promoting efficient allocation of resources" (Landes and Posner 1989, p. 325; see also 2004). In short, we know that property rights *must* be promoting the efficient allocation of resources—the question is how.

Elsewhere, when looking at the increased scope and scale of copyright and trademarks—since maximalist IPR is the status quo—Law and Economics movement advocates do not set out to investigate it according to the principles of freedom or democracy that balanced IPR critics like Lessig might; instead, they presume that the legal framework and the economic relations inherent in them are efficient. In response to Lessig—who argued the Supreme Court case (*Eldred v. Ashcroft*) against the constitutionality of the Copyright Term Extension Act (CTEA)—Landes and Posner use Lessig's data to argue not only that the additional twenty years granted through the CTEA were acceptable but also that "indefinitely renewable copyright" would be moral and efficient: if property, then right and efficient. As with the laws of property in general, shifting IPR law away from any relatively maximalist position could undermine what "improvement" has occurred: "We show that just as an absence of property rights in tangible property would lead to inefficiencies, so an absence of copyright protection for intangible works may lead to inefficiencies because of congestion externalities and because of impaired incentives to invest in maintaining and exploiting these works" (Landes and Posner 2003, pp. 474–475).

Landes and Posner are wrong on both counts. The congestion argument—that if Mickey Mouse were in the public domain, there would be so many Mickey Mouses that we would not know which one to pay attention to—is irrelevant when Disney itself sees to it that every possible space is saturated with its products. A few more could not possibly hurt. And as for the impaired incentives to invest, as Peter Menell (2007a) points out, there is no guarantee that the owner of a patent or copyright is necessarily the best positioned to exploit, maintain, or improve it. A case in point is the vast collection of orphan works—in film, books, and audio recordings—whose owners are not known but that could technically be under copyright. Here, property rights are arguably contributing to a less efficient market, with an almost completely impaired incentive to invest.

Patricia Aufderheide and Peter Jaszi (2011) highlight this serious issue in the copyright system, one that makes very limited—and legally risky—fair use the only possibility for potential reuse. Take for example the Google Books project (and eventually the lawsuit *Authors Guild v. Google*), for which the company scanned and digitized the contents of several major research libraries, initially estimating that it would make all twenty-four million books searchable online. Jonathan Band—a lawyer working with the Association of Research Libraries at the time—estimated that, although the cost of scanning and digitizing all the volumes could be in the area of $750 million, the potential liability (given a settlement of $150,000 for the infringement of each work) would be closer to $3.6 trillion. But the alternative of tracking down all the potential rights holders would still be enormous, with transaction costs closer to $24 billion (Band 2009, pp. 229–230).

Even this massive sum would not necessarily help the company locate the owners of orphan works. Band says the latter comprise between 1.5 and 6 million volumes, or between 6 percent and 24 percent of the total. But these numbers likely underestimate the problem. In 2011, John Wilkin, then the executive director of the HathiTrust—the nonprofit founded to collaborate with the Google Books project—examined its fraction of the Google Books corpus. Wilkin (2011) found that 35 percent of U.S. work after published 1923–1963 and 70 percent of work published outside the United States are orphan works. In short, IPR are far from the most efficient way to maintain our cultural commons. Yet according to the Law and Economics movement, the economic efficiency of the maximalist property regime is taken as a given—based largely on the assumptions of the reified culture of property.

The major deviation that Lessig makes from the Law and Economics tradition more generally is in making its reified culture explicit. He is best known for his discussions of copyright and the relationship of law to the Internet, but his first breakthrough book on this subject, *Code* (1999), was an expansion of the theory he worked out in an article on what he called "The New Chicago School" (1998). This work, in turn, built on a series of articles he penned in the 1990s critiquing the Law and Economics movement for overlooking social norms in simply asserting the "relatively autonomous and efficient regulations of a market relative to law" (Lessig 1995, 1996, 1998, p. 674). Far from replacing the economic assumptions discussed above or the general arguments of the Law and Economics movement, Lessig argues that more is needed to make this regulation happen: a variety of other modalities—what he calls norms, markets, architecture, and law—should be considered when writing regulations, using, of course, the same "rational choice perspective that would help understand these modalities alternative to law" (1998, p. 666):

> Law should understand, within these separate domains, its own insignificance and, the old school implies, should step out of the way. [. . .] But unlike the old school, the new school does not see these alternatives as displacing law. Rather, the new school views them as each *subject* to law—not perfectly, not completely, and not in any obvious way, but nonetheless each is itself an object of law's regulation. [. . . L]aw not only regulates behavior directly, but law also regulates behavior ***indirectly,*** by regulating these other modalities of regulation directly. (Ibid.; emphasis original)

Lessig is certainly correct that alternative regulators exist, as does a wider swath of social and cultural life than that captured by the impoverished, economizing lens of what he calls the "Old School." But in taking on most of the latter's goals and simply making the means by which they will be achieved more explicit, he breaks an unwritten rule.

Lessig begins by asserting that the Law and Economics tradition says that "forces outside law regulate, and regulate better than law," and thus "law should step aside" (1998, p. 661). On the contrary, the "Old Chicago School" holds the rule of law as paramount. The law exists for a very specific end: enforcing property rights, aka "natural rights." The adherents of the now hegemonic Old Chicago School say that enforcement is beyond questions of coercion or consent: the reified culture of property is right, and, due to what Wood (1981) calls the separation of the political from the economic, the ideal formal regulation of property merely amplifies the functional regulation of capital. As Hale points out in the first Law and Economics movement, this regulation means not just that "factors of production" will be employed most "efficiently" but that a variety of coercive mechanisms will compel those who do not have property to work for those who do. Hale says that while some people might be uncomfortable calling these mechanisms "coercive," "this can be explained, I think, by the fact that some of the grosser forms of private coercion are illegal, and the undoubtedly coercive character of the pressure exerted by the property-owner is disguised" (Hale 1923, p. 474).

In citing the lessons he has learned from the Chicago School, Lessig sings in a similar key to Sunstein in his article on "the paradoxes of the regulatory state." Sunstein begins from the Law and Economics conclusion that regulation is futile (an odd belief for a future regulatory czar!) Sunstein cites a handful of cases where regulation was effective and reached its goal, observing that "the view that regulation has generally proved unsuccessful is far too crude" (1990, p. 409); yet he ultimately focuses on the overarching assertion that a "large source of regulatory failure in the United States is the use of Soviet-style command and control regulation, which dictates, at the national level, technologies and control strategies for hundreds, thousands, or millions of companies and individuals in a nation that is exceptionally diverse in terms of geography, costs and benefits of regulatory controls, attitudes, and mores" (ibid., p. 412). Thus, despite Sunstein's critique of the neoliberal status quo in *The Partial Constitution* (1993), his commitment to forms of regulation that maintain libertarian values—what he calls "Libertarian Paternalism"—hampers any real chance at correcting many of the problems he claims to identify (Sunstein and Thaler 2003). With the scholarship of his coauthor Richard Thaler—a behavioral economist by training—Sunstein suggests that the margins of acceptable change are very narrow. To allude to the title of their recent popular tome, one cannot "nudge" one's way to social justice (Sunstein and Thaler 2008).

Lessig's and Sunstein's adherence to the libertarian underpinnings of the "Old Chicago School," on the other hand, wins them no friends among colleagues in that school. It is likely that part of Epstein's motivation to write *How Progressives Rewrote the Constitution* (2006a) was as a response to Sunstein's (2004) equivocal book on the New Deal. And it is especially the case in the area of the law that Lessig is now most known for: copyright. In both cases, Lessig and Sunstein renew something like the earlier progressive argument, which says that the regulatory arrangements we have today—about property, rights, contracts, and so on—are contingent and political: they are not natural and can be altered. Even though their stated goal is to make the liberal premises more culturally effective, the fact that they articulate this constructed nature at all suggests the return of the repressed of the democratic paradox, which Mouffe discusses in an earlier set of essays, *The Return of the Political* (2005). In short, in discussing the law in this way, Lessig and Sunstein challenge some of the fundamental assumptions of the Law and Economics movement. However, unlike the previous challengers to liberal understandings of the state—Hale and others at the turn of the century—they explicitly reject any sense that this "political" could challenge the reified culture of property. They attempt to move us in the direction of democracy and antagonism in the laws around IP but do so without lifting the liberal emergency brake. This limitation is especially the case in Lessig's arguments about IPR, in which property in general is sacrosanct. The political, in this sense, is returned to only the law and economics of copyright.

Closely hewing to the Old Chicago School property line, Lessig offers improvements to the contemporary copyright regime but still asserts that IPR should exist in some form—they should just be narrower and expire sooner. He justifies his heresy by insisting on that all-important distinction between real property and IP, as discussed in Chapter 1. He might veer slightly off the path of pure libertarian reason regarding copyright, but the change is warranted by the material under investigation: "In ordinary language, to call a copyright a 'property' right is a bit misleading, for the property of copyright is an odd kind of property. Indeed, the very idea of property in any idea or any expression is very odd" (Lessig 2004, p. 83). Like Peter Menell, Lessig sees the expansion of maximalist Law and Economics perspectives to IPR as a just bit too far. But this view means that he must regularly reaffirm his property rights bona fides: far from challenging the idea of property, Lessig explicitly affirms it. This stance is true even of the intangible products held under IPR. Thus, he says:

> But where the law does not give people the right to take content, it is wrong to take that content even if the wrong does no harm. If we have a property system, and that system is properly balanced to the technology of a time, then it is wrong to take property without the permission of a property owner. That is exactly what "property" means. (2004, p. 65)

In most of his books on copyright and IPR, Lessig (2001, 2004, 2006, 2008) suggests that this system is not balanced, especially given the technological changes that have ushered in a more participatory media system; but even in opening up these questions regarding IPR alone, Lessig takes his criticism a step too far for most in the Law and Economics movement.

Law and Economics stalwart Charles Fried, for instance, finds Lessig's work in the area of IPR interesting but says of *Code* (1999), "I quarrel with Lessig's barely explicit but detectable bias toward public decisionmaking—by which I mean political decisionmaking, as opposed to the disaggregated private decisionmaking of the market—about the design of code for the Internet" (2000, p. 614). Note that Fried's preference would be to leave this regulation of IPR and the Internet up to the market of private preferences, which he claims is free from politics. Fried says that he does not read "Lessig as hostile to the party of liberty, [but] he regularly invokes the virtues of democratic (that is, political) control over human interaction" (ibid., p. 607). This invocation, Fried believes, is evidence of Lessig's unfortunate influence not only by "ambivalent moderates" like Sunstein

> but also by the Critical Legal Studies movement and before it by Legal Realists such as Robert Hale and Morris Cohen: [these scholars say] there is no such thing as natural liberty. All choices, including the choice that government not regulate, are political choices establishing different political regimes. Correspondingly, the distinction between the public and the private, on which liberal theory depends, is an illusion. (Ibid.)

Fried contests this logic and finds Lessig's unfortunate use of it sufficient to render much of his argument suspect. In place of this entire body of reasoning, he merely contends that

> granted, the rules of private law—contract, tort, and property—are themselves rules of law and therefore public rules, but they represent a relatively stable (or at least slow-moving), natural-seeming, and therefore intuitively graspable (at least in their broad outlines) foundation on which individuals may securely plan their economic and personal lives. (Ibid., p. 617)

For Fried, as for scholars of the Law and Economics movement at large, the culture of property precedes the political—even in relation to only IPR. Even Lessig's tentative questioning in relation to regulation of the Internet and IPR is too much for him to handle.

Instead of looking at the "copyfights" of the early twenty-first century and seeing a vibrant resurgence of culture at its best, Fried thinks that the basic problems that Lessig discusses in relation to IPR are really just questions about property. Lessig may want to distinguish these issues, but Fried counters, "I would peel the subject all the way back to reveal what it would look like under the baseline intuitive concepts of property and contract" (2000, p. 622). And in a postindustrial global economy, much of the distinction that Lessig tries to draw between these concepts fades away. Multinational corporate conglomerates, such as the Walt Disney Corporation, value their IP—their trademarks and copyright libraries—in the same measure as they value any real estate property they hold; they should no more be forced to give up their holdings of Mickey Mouse than they should be to allow squatters to take over Disneyland. Property is property, particularly productive commercial property. The question that matters to Fried is how these commercial properties relate to what I have called the reified culture of property, which is the "baseline" of property and contract in the liberal tradition. Since Lessig fails to provide a coherent challenge to the latter, Fried easily picks off his arguments.

In other words, the basic outlines of the Law and Economics tradition—to which Lessig provides a useful corrective, but not a fundamental challenge—find the protection of property and the freedom from government intervention to be natural rights. This view is especially evident in the criticism that Lessig receives from the most active members of the movement to bolster the maximalist position against that of balanced copyright. For example, take the PFF: Vincent Mosco describes the philosophical position of this organization as exemplifying "the myth of the end of politics" in the Internet age (2004, p. 107). Based loosely on the theories of Alvin Toffler, with connections to conservative icons Newt Gingrich and George Gilder, the PFF was cofounded by Professor Jeffrey Eisenach of GMU, "where he has taught a course on the law and economics of the digital revolution" (ibid.).

The PFF shared Lessig's enthusiasm for the Internet, seeing it as a frontier for the rules of the liberal vision of stateless society to finally be fulfilled. The "end of politics"—or, as I have been discussing, the disavowal of the political—is achieved through the complete replacement of "old ways of government" such that the very idea of the public is eliminated. In Mosco's description, the PFF's vision is an early version of the now popular techno-utopia, which libertarian-minded Silicon Valley executives, such as Peter Thiel, believe will be brought about through the "sublime marriage between information technology and capitalism" (2004, p. 112). Thus, the Internet, like Hayek's market of information,

> provides us with the very basis of politics. The public no longer exists as an entity inasmuch as it is a collection of discreet individuals who are serviced. Under the auspices of efficiency, individuals reign triumphant as a corporatist ethic provides a roadmap of social design. (Ibid.)

In contrast to Fried, who claims that the "party of liberty" will respect (indeed depend on) "the distinction between the public and the private" (2000, p. 607), Mosco argues that, in practice, such visions as those of the PFF rely on the "privatization of both public space and public interest," supporting the enclosure of the public domain and reacting viciously to any challenge to the sanctity of private property in information. Like the maximalist position on IPR generally, theirs is not simply an ideological framework: it is also the dominant understanding of how the culture industries should work in the new "information economy." Thus, as Mosco notes, "the PFF's 2003 list of financial supporters finds 33 of the 53 located squarely in the media and information technology industries" (2004, p. 108). After its dissolution, many of those backers turned their attention to other similar organizations, such as the Center for the Protection of Intellectual Property (CPIP) at GMU's Antonin Scalia Law School, which recently hosted an event funded by the Motion Picture Association of America (MPAA) that featured Epstein as a keynote speaker.

The combination of an ideological commitment to the reified culture of property, translated to the online economy and fueled by material support from the content industries, makes even Lessig's extremely balanced position on copyright untenable. Thomas Sydnor's review of Lessig's *Free Culture*, written for the PFF, illustrates the continuity between this organization's position and that of the Law and Economics tradition that Lessig, Sunstein, and the rest of us should be criticizing more fundamentally:

> I submit that FREE CULTURE is a work that should be rejected by libertarians, conservatives, liberals, or anyone else concerned about reconciling the proven generative power of copyrights and other property rights with the now-obvious generative potential of the Internet. The many challenges inherent in that task *are* real, and grappling with them, *fairly*, is a job too important to be further delayed by collectivist histrionics. FREE CULTURE should thus be consigned to Trotsky's "dustbin of history"—along with PROMISES TO KEEP, KGB-style government surveillance of ordinary citizens, and "bland" communists like Stalin and Krushshev [*sic*]. (2008, p. 17; emphasis original)

Lessig, it seems, too openly "demonizes" property owners, and he advocates using the Internet to manage and distribute a government fund based on the popularity of free music rather than the proper digital rights management (DRM) proposals that private industry proscribes. The PFF and its corporate backers see no difference between these kinds of property; Lessig's interest in crafting a more balanced regulation as opposed to continuing to pretend that regulation does not exist is unacceptable.

Likewise, in one of Epstein's most-often-cited contributions to the PFF—a revised version of a piece written for the National Association of Manufacturers, which has long shared his ire at the earlier violation of its market sovereignty—he maintains "the structural unity of real and intellectual property" (Epstein 2006b). For Epstein, the question is the degree to which maximalist protection should exist for IP as opposed to real property: as with real property, his preference is to give the presumed owners complete control. This argument sits well with the PFF, whose reports have also been collected and shared by the Copyright Alliance, a public relations arm of the MPAA and the Recording Industry Association of America (RIAA) advocating for more stringent—absolutist—protections of copyright.

The next chapter considers the distinction between real property and IP as it currently exists in the rhetoric of the "balanced copyright" movement, particularly along the dimension of value—how it is produced and expropriated—and how the property system works alongside the social division of labor to maintain the incumbent hierarchy of mental and manual labor. In a liberal, digital, postindustrial, global capitalist democracy, it is difficult to sustain the distinction between real property and IP; the very notion of property and liberty assumes a certain division of labor guaranteed with laws that privilege owners of capital. Liberal democracy believes in this balance and will not discuss it, whether the topic is tangible or intangible property. This observation is made rather succinctly by Barbara Fried:

> "Liberty" and "property" were connected in narrow constitutional arguments through the doctrine of liberty of contract. As the dominant form of property rights shifted from possession and use to possession and exchange, an owner's right to contract for the use or exchange value of her property was acknowledged to be an important part of the total economic value of that property. At the same time, as the courts broke free of their historical conception of property as a tangible thing, they began to view the resulting contract itself as a form of intangible property presumptively entitled to the full-blown protections accorded other forms of property. (1998, p. 17)

Perhaps trying to preserve his libertarian credentials, Lessig (2015) has moved away from issues around copyright to look at an issue close to the heart of Coase, Epstein, and other scholars of the Law and Economics tradition: corruption in government.

The contemporary Law and Economics movement is a reaction against the appearance of an active U.S. welfare state and a radical set of legal ideas, both of which seemed to be kowtowing to militant pressure from below. The goal of this movement, like Locke's at the end of the English Civil War, is to reinstate the liberal understanding of the state. In Locke's time, the choice was to use the religious ideology ascendant in his culture; in the second half of the twentieth century, activist scholars in the Law and Economics movement have used what they argue is a scientific understanding of human behavior known as "economics." In both cases, these reactionary doctrines are largely successful because they help uphold—or, in the case of the Law and Economics movement, reinstantiate—the functional power of property owners. In short, both movements attempt to impose (or reimpose) a liberal doctrine of natural law that matches the dictates of what I have called "the reified culture of property."

We must not shrink from critiquing the more fundamental, neoliberal, Law and Economics ideology of property and its nearly authoritarian resistance to the democratic reorganization of society: they begin by defending class property but must end by bolstering the patriarchy, neocolonialism, and white supremacy that have helped bring current distribution of all property into existence. The power of property is not a neutral question of liberty, particularly when the effective liberty of the majority relies on stifling that power, ideally through the expropriation and redistribution of that property. This position is certainly political: it is supported by Piketty and other economists studying the toxic—and growing—social effects of inequality. Pretending that the defense of property rights—or IPR—is somehow innocent of politics overlooks the *longue durée* of the coercive, state-led imposition of capitalist social relations. The advent of participatory digital media—and the emergence of new forms of digital labor—should provide us an opportunity to look anew at the fundamental premises and faulty conclusions of the Law and Economics movement and to reconsider the role that the law and the state can play in helping secure a more just and humane society and culture, where the benefits of effective liberty are enjoyed by more than the top 1 percent of the population.

Lessig criticizes the Law and Economics tradition but remains steadfastly committed to the basic outlines of the reified culture of property that it promotes. However, in reintroducing politics to the law more generally, and in specifically questioning its relevance to IPR, he opens some conversation on the topic of property itself. While it is not enough to challenge this dominant logic, looking at his discussion about the law in relation to the movement most committed to property in general helps open the path for the next chapter. There, we consider the false distinction that he draws between IPR and property, but from another direction. The focus is on the aspect of IPR that Lessig has been quite vocal and eloquent in describing: its illumination of the extended process of social production.

4

Culture, Commodification, and the Social Production of Value

It has been a little more than a decade since *Time* magazine declared that its Person of the Year was "You," the connotation of which was illustrated by an image of a computer screen and an interface similar to that of YouTube, with reflective material in place of the screen: "For seizing the reins of the global media, for founding and framing the new digital democracy, for working for nothing and beating the pros at their own game, TIME's Person of the Year for 2006 is you" (Grossman 2006). This phrasing, this image, is a classic version of what Louis Althusser calls "interpellation," where an individual is hailed into a subject position. In Althusser's classic example, it is the policeman hailing us on the street, but the oracles of Web 2.0—from Tim O'Reilly, who popularized (if not coined) the term, to *Time* magazine and beyond—hail us as a convoluted challenge to conventional neoliberal subjectivity. Instead of working for money and profit, we work for clicks and likes. Early on, O'Reilly and others—including business gurus Don Tapscott and Anthony Williams (2010)—recognized that Web 2.0 subjectivity was not a challenge to the neoliberal order but a new way for businesses to capitalize on nominally free labor, with the latter noting that many companies and their leaders "have seized on collaboration and self-organization as powerful new levers to cut costs, innovate faster, cocreate with customers and partners and generally do whatever it takes to usher their organizations into the twenty-first-century business environment" (ibid., p. 2).

As José van Dijck (2013) observes in her book, the rhetoric of "connectedness," "interactivity," and "participatory media" contrasts contemporary social media platforms with what was possible in the previous era of media. I have discussed the potential of Web 2.0 in my previous work, noting it is less of a novel innovation than a return to how culture worked (at the C2 level) before the corporate hierarchy of mass media production and distribution made it impossible for the average user to produce media of the same temperature and bias as the dominant hegemonic media of the moment (Johnson Andrews 2016). We can see something similar to this situation in Chapter 2's discussion of the pirate publishers, who acted, in the words of Kathleen Kennedy, as "medieval hackers," articulating something like the ethos of contemporary hacker culture in response to Early Modern copyright and other "early attempts at information control" (2015, p. 4). The relatively rudimentary reproduction technologies of the time made piracy more of a threat to that control, even until the nineteenth century, when copyright in the United States offered little protection from unauthorized appropriations in print or the minstrel stage (Homestead 2010). In that sense, the true exception was in the antidemocratic, media oligopolies of the mid-twentieth-century culture industries.

Changes in media production and distribution technology and the emergent cultural practices around that technology have made visible the extended process of social valorization through which the properties in question have attained their valuable cultural efficacy. The process of globalization—the extended spatial organization of production that mirrors the distributed production of digital networks—exposes this further. Practitioners of the culturalist paradigm of cultural studies—including such scholars as Henry Jenkins—have long provided a rich description of these processes of cultural appropriation among audiences of mass cultural products and subcultural communities. While these processes of cultural appropriation have existed beneath the surface for some time, their visibility is highlighted by the widely discussed transformation of the relationship between consumers and producers—such that consumers are now producers, or "prosumers"—and the popular promotion of such ideas as Web 2.0 and distributed, nonhierarchical relationships among global producers in the "flat world," projecting them as an alternative interpretation of reality (within certain limits, that is).

Here, the "You" interpellated by *Time* magazine and others was quickly hemmed in by the already-existing culture of property and commodification. In a sense, this YouTube "You" was itself a form of what James Martel calls the "misinterpellated subject," a "subversive subject" that "responds to perceived calls" that are not meant for it (2017, loc. 143). Martel provides numerous examples from throughout history and literature: for instance, the Haitian Revolution's response to the call of the French Declaration of the Rights of Man and Citizen. In responding to this call for equal rights and freedoms, they took seriously the claims of liberalism, but in a way that was never intended and had worldwide revolutionary results. As Martel puts it:

> Liberalism occasionally enables an already-existent alternative, one that is not itself part and parcel of liberal subjectivity and authority, to be noticed, to emerge into visibility through liberalism's own internal breakdowns. [. . .] These subjects do not generally initially come with the intention to subvert and revolt; their radical response is the result of an increasingly legible mismatch between what they believe (what they think they have been called to do) and what those in power believe (who they have actually intended to call and why they have done so). (2017, loc. 167)

In accepting the call of the YouTube "You," users continue to produce content—meaning, power, and ultimately value for its parent corporation, Alphabet, the owner of Google and YouTube, which regularly derives upward of 98 percent of its revenue from search-related advertisements, including those prominently displayed on and around YouTube videos. But ten years after that call, despite implementing algorithmic filtering and copyright detection software on the platform and working with Universal Music Group (UMG) and other recording companies to launch the Vevo-branded subsite for official videos, "the RIAA [Recording Industry Association of America] says YouTube is operating a DMCA [Digital Millennium Copyright Act, aka copyright infringement] protection racket" (Andy 2016). These groups point to the ability of users to upload whole albums to the service and the growing practice (by other users) of "stream ripping" these albums and songs, downloading them as MP3s as efficiently as Napster used to allow (Sanchez 2017).

But as with Napster, because this piracy is so seamlessly integrated into the everyday practices of the average user, we do not see it as intentionally subversive, even if that is ultimately what it is. The phrase "no copyright intended" or "no copyright infringement intended" often appears in the description of illicit YouTube uploads, as if this declaration absolves the uploader of any wrongdoing, often with the confession, "I do not own the music." This misinterpellation is not just a misunderstanding of the law: in this performative "disowning" of some component of the culture they are sharing, they are also prefiguring what James Boyle (2003) and others might call "the opposite of property."

Two can play at this game. Corporate conglomerates and their subsidiaries, such as Warner Music Group (a subsidiary of Time Warner, the publisher of *Time* magazine and party to an attempted merger with the phone company AT&T that would have made it easier to monitor and monetize the mobile streaming that is now one of the main vectors of music consumption), hold copyrights to massive back catalogs of songs they had no role in producing. But this lack of creative involvement does not stop them from claiming the property rights over materials they do not actually own. The most famous recent decision—in *Good Morning To You Productions Corp. v. Warner/Chappell Music, Inc., et al.*—debunked Warner Music's long-held claim to own the rights to the song "Happy Birthday," with the company ordered to pay back $14 million in illegitimately collected royalties (Mullin 2016). In 2017, Warner made headlines for demanding that YouTube take down a video that was explicitly billed as having no music in it: the last few minutes of *Star Wars* "minus" the John Williams score that Warner/Chappel owns, but with the addition of the random sounds of an excruciatingly silent awards ceremony where Luke Skywalker and Han Solo receive medals from the rebellion. As *Wired* reports, "The copyright holder was claiming ownership of something that wasn't there. Under the claim, Warner would receive any future ad revenue the video earns, which has been viewed more than 4 million times" (Hsu 2017).

This algorithmically assisted corporate enclosure is increasingly common. After a supposedly offending video is discovered through YouTube's automated Content ID system, it is forwarded to the presumed copyright holder, usually resulting in the claimant's monetizing the video rather than taking it down. Hsu reports that more than 99 percent of these claims go uncontested. But even if they are contested—for instance, on fair-use or public-domain grounds (i.e., the opposite of property)—there is no consequence for Warner or its corporate conglomerate analogues. This corporate-friendly policy—by which owners get all the rights but none of the responsibilities—is e enshrined in (case) law, due to the conclusion of the case against one of most famous misinterpellated YouTube subjects: Stephanie Lenz, the mother who uploaded a video of her baby son dancing to the Prince song "Let's Go Crazy" (in February 2007—just a few months after *Time* celebrated her ilk for "seizing the reins of the global media"). With the help of the Electronic Frontier Foundation, Lenz sued Universal Music for its DMCA takedown of her video, a suit that has worked its way through the court system for the decade since. Lenz appealed to the Supreme Court to review a Ninth Circuit Court of Appeals ruling in *Lenz v. Universal Music Corp.* that says the "copyright owner [Universal] cannot be liable simply because an unknowing mistake is made, even if the copyright owner acted unreasonably in making the mistake" (Morran 2017). In June 2017, the Supreme Court declined her appeal, leaving this precedent in place.

This ruling is in stark contrast to the provisions of the DMCA that target consumers who may unknowingly redistribute content with altered digital rights protections: "People are liable for breaking this law even if they only had 'reasonable grounds to know' what they were doing. This sort of language is absent from the specific provision which holds copyright owners liable for frivolous DMCA claims" (Morran 2017). It may not be enough for a YouTube user to claim "no copyright infringement intended," but the property owner is free to claim "no fair use infringement intended."

The "You" interpellated through social media is subject to the demands of these platforms. As Robert Gehl (2013) highlights, the demand to share and feel through Facebook, Twitter, Google, and elsewhere is shaped by protocols set up by the Interactive Advertising Bureau, "a trade group that in the mid-1990s brought together content producers (such as Turner Interactive and Time, Inc.) and networks (such as Microsoft and Prodigy) to standardize the shape of the Web." But this subject is also supposed to respect the property rights of the corporate owners of the materials that "You" use. To ensure that the latter restrictions are observed, Facebook acquired Source3, a company with similar algorithmic rights management capabilities that was the brainchild of the same programmers who built (and sold) Google Content ID for YouTube (Freier 2017). This expansion of its algorithmic monitoring capabilities is in the service of the newly commoditized sociality (Huws 2014) that it peddles, which has supplanted the "You" of 2006 even as it subjects more and more people to its global reach. In the words of van Dijck:

> Commoditizing relationships—turning connectedness into connectivity by means of coding technologies—is exactly what corporate platforms, particularly Google and Facebook, discovered as the golden egg their geese produced. Besides generating content, peer production yields a valuable by-product that users often do not intentionally deliver: behavioral and profiling data. Under the guise of connectedness they produce a precious resource: connectivity. (2013, loc. 358)

User data and metadata have become the latest state-sanctioned form of intellectual property (IP), owned by some of the largest corporations in human history under the aegis of end-user agreements that only a handful of lawyers can parse.

Lawrence Lessig and other balanced intellectual property rights (IPR) scholars see the injustice of the appropriation of cultural property because they understand the broader process of production through which that property is valorized. As this book argues, this conflict, while ostensibly over IPR, is really over the culture of property more generally. Thus, the issue that these critics discover is really that they find the state to be protecting a group of monopoly rentiers. However, instead of seeing the increasing protection of all forms of property, as part of a general trend toward the neoliberal renovation of the state, they single out IP, claiming that it is so distinct that it must be cared for delicately.

This view takes us back to the previous chapter on the Law and Economics movement and Robert Hale's critique of private property at the turn of the twentieth century. In effect, Hale and Lessig are pointing to the same kind of problem, yet Hale sees the production of all kinds of value as having the same quality that balanced IPR critics do regarding their chosen cultural laborers. Both critique the power and unjustified appropriation of value by the juridical owner of the property. As we establish in Chapter 2, our conception of property is and was based on a Lockean notion of natural rights. Hale and other critics at the turn of the twentieth century reappropriated this argument based on what Barbara Fried calls "rent theory Lockeanism." Like those of Lessig and critics of balanced IPR, this theory "insists on a more exacting separation of the individual and social components in the creation of wealth" (B. Fried 1998, p. 75).

This theory basically says that John Locke's theory of property rights is meant only to reimburse owners/workers for their sacrifice—to help them recoup their costs in effort or capital; any more than this reimbursement, and the owner/workers are simply making money off certain circumstances: namely, the circumstances in which they own the productive property in question and are therefore able to exact a higher proportion of its rewards from the people who work for them or buy from them. This moral should be valid whether the workers are far-flung agricultural innovators, trade-polished workers on the shop floor, or creative prosumers activating the potential of Web 2.0. Therefore, rent theory Lockeanism claims that

> individuals have a moral right only to that portion of income that compensated them for costs of production: any unearned surplus above that amount was the moral property of the community, which it could appropriate and redistribute as it chose. [. . .] Surplus value was the fortuitous result of the market, in which demand exceeded available supply at constant costs. As a result, surplus value represented (as Henry George said of land rents) "a value created by the whole

> community." If anyone had a right to surplus value, the progressives argued, it was not any particular factor [i.e., not owners or workers in particular], but rather society at large, to do with as it saw fit to further the common good. (B. Fried 1998, pp. 74–75, 27)

Aside from the obvious difficulty of defining the "value created by the whole community," this theory helps tackle the thorny utilitarian issue of incentives, which always lay in the background of liberal arguments about property in general and IPR in particular. Namely, owners and innovators can be rewarded for their work (as an incentive for them to produce more), but after that point, the surplus should be redistributed—or, in the case of IPR, the work should enter the public domain. In short, there is an economic utility in social or common property and in private property. This approach is not all that different than Lessig's proposals in *Free Culture* (2004), except it applies to all productive property.

It is imperative that we see the contemporary dilemma of IP in this light. Seeing the issue of IPR as one of commodification and the culture of property in general helps illuminate the continuum on which these sit. As this chapter argues, making a distinction between the appropriation of property created by mental versus manual labor is arbitrary: in the end, mental labor needs physical resources to function, and manual labor always begins with a mental conception. The division between them that balanced IPR proponents support is not just between kinds of workers but between society at large and a rentier class that has appropriated the collective resources and energies of society to profit from them.

The absolutist position explored in the previous chapter—and reflected in trade policies and economic treaties at the national and international levels—defends a relationship of productive property to capital, labor, and the state that is essential to this reified culture of property. The point is not whether a property is tangible or intangible: these empirical qualities are just streaks on the materialist agar. The point is that the liberal state is dedicated to protecting the value of productive property in the interests of its owners. Our changed circumstances make the extended process of valorization visible again in relation to IPR and provide the justification for increased protection. To support—and incentivize—that economy, absolute property rights are absolutely necessary.

The balanced position of Lessig and others highlights the increased visibility of the social processes of valorization, which contradict that Lockean understanding and lend credence to some form of rent theory Lockeanism. But a sharp distinction between the expanded process of valorization in IP and that of "real" property rests on the spurious notion that these new discoveries about value and the process of valorization apply to only a particular set of cultural forms in a certain conjuncture. Because Lessig, Yochai Benkler, and their fellow critics do not challenge this more fundamental commitment to private property, the most that this alternative interpretation of reality—and of property—can promise is to carve out some limited space where different rules apply. This goal requires the conceptualization of an entirely separate realm where their arguments are valid. In Lessig's book *Remix*, he declares that "the market is an extraordinary technology for producing and spreading wealth" and recommends an interaction between this "sharing economy" and the "commercial economy," calling for a "hybrid economy" (2008, p. 121). Adam Arvidsson's (2006, 2008) notion of peer-to-peer (p2p) sharing and collaboration as an "ethical economy" builds off his earlier understanding of the consumer coproduction of brand values. Even Benkler (2002, 2003, 2007), whose elegant investigations of the widespread "nonproprietary production in information" illustrate a culture of "nonproprietary motivations, social relations, and organizational forms" on- and offline, explicitly rests his claims on their sharp distinction from "property in wristwatches and automobiles," thus affirming a continued commitment to the reified culture of property (2007, p. 461). Very few critics, including Michel Bauwens (2009), challenge the dominant neoliberal rhetoric infused in the descriptions of these processes. Bauwens speculates that p2p technology and the practices around it have created a crisis in the current elaboration of material and immaterial property. This position is closest to mine in this book, although, as this chapter contends, the technological transformation is only one catalyst for a more fundamental challenge to this neoliberal culture of property.

The neoliberal ideology of property in general provides crucial support for absolutist IPR. The continued expansion of IPR in this direction is nearly certain if there is not a more fundamental challenge to this reified culture of property. On one level, this challenge is posed by the bad or misinterpellated subjects of the contemporary global economy: the pirates and counterfeiters around the world who refuse to submit to this law. However, this challenge is mounted as a complete refusal of any law and thus without any specific target in the larger structure of cultural efficacy. It presents an energy that can certainly be harnessed for the rearticulation of the dominant paradigm of property; however, it can also be harnessed—as it has been already—by the maximalist position, whose main proponents (such as the late Jack Valenti of the Motion Picture Association of America [MPAA]) are prone to draw direct connections between piracy and terrorism. This connection presents a rich area of exploration in the history of Western capitalism, one that Marcus

Rediker (2004) has tried to turn on its head by looking at the democratic visions and organizations of actual pirates versus the terror imposed by the legal apparatus of early transatlantic capitalism. I have explored this position in several articles, especially in relation to how the pirates challenge the dominant systems of sovereignty—and how they helped mutually constitute that sovereignty in the Early Modern era (Johnson Andrews 2014).

In this book, the position I take follows from my work in *Hegemony, Mass Media, and Cultural Studies* (2016), which asks for a renewed synthesis in cultural studies between the two paradigms of structuralism and culturalism. The latter has been the most active in recent years, so renewing a synthesis between the two requires more of an emphasis on the former. I try throughout this book to do this, particularly within my conceptualization of culture in relation to the law and the state. At the same time, the culturalist position is essential to understanding the real, embodied processes of cultural efficacy. These are especially important in the current chapter, as they are also the processes that are now understood as producing social meaning, political power, and economic value in, around, and through cultural commodities. But we should also be attentive to the structural determinations of capitalist social property relations that helped channel these processes onto cultural commodities. These dual processes are joined in the branded commodities that now circulate as the material underpinnings of IPR, but focusing, as Arvidsson (2006) does, on only the immaterial developments misses the analogies that can be drawn to social production in general.

As this chapter demonstrates, several key concepts of Marxist political economy (and Marxian political economy of communication) are affirmed by those who resist the further commodification of culture through IPR. Attempts by balanced IPR critics to draw a sharp distinction between "real" and "intellectual" property are sustained by an understanding of the social division of labor, which largely ignores labor as such, and the global context of production and consumption these arguments rely on. Yet there is an enlightened kernel in their descriptions of the coproduction of meaning and value in the cultural realm (narrowly defined), similar to the early, path-breaking work in cultural studies on audiences and subcultures. These descriptions provide a useful entry point for discussions of value in general.

The next section outlines the theoretical framework of the chapter, focusing on three related processes: primitive accumulation, commodification, and the social division of labor. These Marxian concepts are useful for describing the historical development of the commodified culture of the United States from whence IPR springs—and its relation to earlier moments when capitalism engaged in these processes. The final section then demonstrates what understanding these fundamental processes of capitalism does for understanding the materialist situation of IPR in the current conjuncture.

Against contemporary critiques of IP, this chapter argues that the distinction between real property and IP cannot be maintained according to the proposed criteria. The descriptions these critiques offer of the total social production of meaning and cultural value map cohesively onto the Marxian analysis of production in general. The semiotic democracy that Lessig proposes could easily be expanded to include arguments about the total system of capitalist production; the legitimate observations that he and Benkler (2002) make about how meaning and value are collaboratively and collectively produced should make the concept of a socialist democracy a less radical proposition. Domestically and internationally, the U.S. state apparatus imposes a model of (intellectual) property and culture that protects incumbents and the value of their capital. This process is not an aberration of capitalist development but how large-scale capitalism functions and how its promoters intend for it to continue to develop. The next and final chapter looks at this system on a global scale, in relation to the concept of cultural imperialism.

Marx, Cultural Studies, and the Primitive Accumulation of Our Intellectual Properties

In *Remix* (2008), what Lessig bills as his final book on the topic of IPR, discussion centers around the distinction between Read/Only (RO) and Read/Write (RW) culture, a familiar designation for increasingly ancient storage media, such as CDs, that indicates whether the user is allowed to revise the inscribed data. Borrowing heavily from such cultural studies scholars as Jenkins, Lessig draws on the latter's understanding of the emergent "participatory culture" through which technology allows people to more easily interact with the media culture around them. Although Lessig sees technology as central to this distinction, for Jenkins and others, it is a distinction between how people approach culture and therefore is a subjective orientation in relation to culture. Jenkins (2006) insists that the "participatory culture" that he contrasts with older notions of "passive media spectatorship" is not a product of the "convergence" of media technology itself but a way of processing media that becomes increasingly necessary with the growing number of distribution and production platforms in what this study would understand as the mediated C2. Jenkins says:

> Convergence occurs within the brains of the individual consumers and through their social interactions with others. Each of us con-

> structs our own personal mythology from the bits and fragments of information extracted from the media flow and transformed into resources through which we make sense of our everyday lives. Because there is more information on any given topic than anyone can store in their head, there is an added incentive for us to talk among ourselves about the media we consume. This conversation creates buzz that is increasingly valued by the media industry. Consumption has become a collective process. (2006, p. 3)

Jenkins's concept of convergence—like Lessig's RO/RW—is constituted through an uneasy tension. "Convergence" sometimes refers to distinctions between subjective orientations to culture at any level, and at other times it results from different institutional arrangements of what Jenkins calls "delivery technologies." Elsewhere, in explaining the role that media plays in our lives, he describes television as "fodder for so-called water cooler conversations," while noting that "for a growing number of people, the water cooler has gone digital" through participation in online forums (2006, p. 26). Jenkins says that, for most people, viewing these media is a communal process where we discuss what we see with "friends, family members, and workmates," but now online forums provide new forms of social interaction. In other words, the orientation of "convergence" or "participatory culture" is less in the practices themselves than in their increased visibility through the networks of media convergence.

In this sense, the technological link is only marginally significant in terms of the practices in question. These practices are already ingrained in our everyday lives in concrete ways. The dominant culture of commodified media was already the stuff through which we related to others. One could even question whether we speak about TV around the water cooler because it is what we like to watch or whether we like to watch—feel compelled to watch, even—because that is what we talk about around the water cooler. It is hard to see this culture as RO until we look at what a RW culture would look like. Lessig posits that RO is related to only the kind of culture that circulates as a commodity—enabled by the "birth of technology to capture and spread tokens of culture"—and that RW is a more fundamental kind of creativity that has existed since "the dawn of human culture" (2008, p. 116). The latter is where the culture in circulation is actively appropriated, where prosumers "add to the culture they read by creating and re-creating the culture around them" (ibid., p. 28).

In making this distinction, Lessig draws on the early-twentieth-century composer John Philip Sousa, who testified before Congress in 1906 to ask for stricter copyright protections against makers of phonograph records who were unjustly appropriating the works of composers. While Sousa is an unlikely hero for a book questioning the merits of stronger copyright protection, Lessig finds in his example a ready distinction between these two approaches to culture. Sousa protested the use of phonographs because he saw the mass production of "tokens of RO culture" as being detrimental to the practice of culture production at the local level. Lessig accedes that Sousa's fear was well placed, claiming that "the twentieth century was the first time in the history of human culture when popular culture had become professionalized, and when the people were taught to defer to the professional" (2008, p. 29). On the other hand, as in Walter Benjamin's (2008) celebration of the democratization of culture brought by technological reproducibility, Lessig notes that this mass production "produced extraordinary access to a wide range of culture. Never before had so much been available to so many." (2008, pp. 29, 30).

If we project these positions onto the conceptualization of culture discussed in Chapter 1, RO sits rather well at the C2 level. RW is the culture of the culturalist vein of cultural studies. It is most at home in the C1 realm, but the ideal of culture to which Lessig aspires would make the C2 level readable and writeable. This process of interacting with culture, he claims, following Sousa, was common to "all of humanity from the beginning of human civilization" (2008, p. 28). If this process were so fundamental, what changed? Why were these tokens of culture, exchanged between and among communities, no longer readable and writeable?

The change, according Lessig, was primarily one of technology. The tokens of the culture industry (e.g., vinyl records, films, radio, TV) were created through expensive, centralized production and distribution systems, which were the "natural" limitations of analog technology. The law supported this natural technological limitation with copyright, but "it was the nature of the LP that really limited the consumer's ability to be anything other than 'a consumer'" (Lessig 2008, p. 38). Digital technology has remade nature: "What was before both impossible and illegal is now just illegal" (ibid.). Lessig's goal in the book is to help rewrite "the culture which regulates culture"—that is, copyright law as well as our "norms and expectations around the control of culture" (ibid., p. 275). This rewriting of the formal policy, he says, will allow the functional development of the hybrid economies that he sees as so promising.

For the purposes of this chapter, four factors stand out: (1) the continuity of the processes of RW culture; (2) the dominant RO culture that has existed in the United States for the past seventy-five years; (3) the culture's complete imposition as ultimately guided by some political, economic, and legal culture imposed from the top down; and (4) Lessig's and Jenkins's separation of culture and politics from each other. The processes that Lessig speaks about in relation to RW culture in the digital age are very similar to the creative process of appropriation through which communities of audience members have negotiated meanings since they were forced into the "consumer" relationship with RO tokens. Jenkins speaks about these practices in *Convergence Culture* (2006)—for instance, online fans who develop communities around discussing, reworking, and sometimes intervening in the production of network and cable TV shows. But he developed the idea of "participatory culture" more than two decades earlier in his book *Textual Poachers* (1992), alongside a host of other work in the culturalist paradigm of cultural studies. In his scholarship, Jenkins highlights the ways in which everyday users appropriate and incorporate the materials of the mass media in their lives, often in ways that challenge the original meanings and intents of their authors. This is the C1-level embedding that has long been essential to the efficacy of any cultural mediation. The difference now is that the efficacy is bilateral: consumers are more able to participate at the C2 level—and their participation in the process of embedding is more visible. Arvidsson (2006) provides more recent empirical evidence of this communal process in developing and activating culture around brands, but the process of creative reappropriation has been known by cultural studies scholars for some time. The difference today is in the scale of distribution and in the ability of more users to cheaply and easily produce media of roughly the same quality as the major media, sometimes at roughly the same scale as the major media.

This brings us to a second point: the dominant RO culture that has existed in the United States for the past seventy-five years was incomplete in that it allowed for only a one-way relationship with the content. As Lessig points out and as I argue elsewhere (Johnson Andrews 2016), this relationship is a break from the ways in which U.S. media culture worked in the past, when what we might call the master media (print) was, for better or worse, more malleable for the average user. Theodor Adorno and Max Horkheimer's (2007) critique of the culture industry is, in part, just this—that it encouraged people to merely consume culture. It was not just that the RO tokens were of crass, commercial quality; they removed the sense of agency and possibility in the RW mode of culture. Lessig's invocation of the yeoman sensibility inadvertently affirms this critique. The cultural yeomen, the makers who have the instruments and ability to craft a piece of culture—a song, a book, a pamphlet, a play—understand the malleability of culture and their potential agency in reappropriating the aspects of culture they want to alter. Lessig's point of reference is the yeoman self- sufficiency prized by Thomas Jefferson when he imagined the ideal citizen sprouting from the Virginia wilderness:

> Yeoman self-sufficiency was a virtue because of what it did to the self. [. . .] Just as Jefferson romanticized the yeoman farmer working a small plot of land in an economy disciplined by hard work and careful planning, just as Sousa romanticized the amateur musician, I mean to romanticize the yeoman creator. In each case, the skeptic could argue that the product is better produced elsewhere—that large farms are more efficient, or that filters on publishing mean published works are better. But in each case, the skeptic misses something critically important: how the discipline of the yeoman changes him or her as a citizen. [. . .] Speaking [through the RW mode of culture] teaches the speaker even if it just makes noise. (2008, pp. 27, 132)

While it is probably true that this version of the cultural process is more demotic than what Adorno would have embraced completely, it shares his emphasis on the transformative, malleable nature of culture and the individual subject. The point is that, before the culture industries effectively made culture at the C2 level an RO culture, people as well as culture could be changed—and both could be active subjects in that change.

Lessig acknowledges the importance of this shift but does not recognize the historical, political economic implications. If the nature of these RO tokens has been remade, and this new version allows for new, active consumers, the implication is that the mediated culture of the U.S. polity of the preceding era was effectively what Adorno calls "administered" culture. Even if we allow for the possibility—for the necessity, even—that there was a RW process of *embedding* the RO tokens, a process of making C2 effective at the C1 level at water coolers, knitting circles, and other face-to-face interactions, the fact is that the structure itself allowed only for a unilateral efficacy on a regular basis. In the U.S. context, this structure was itself the product of an explicit bargain between the U.S. state and the nascent culture industries that were licensed, promoted, and utilized by that same state.

As political economy of communication scholars have long argued, the dominance of RO media/C2 culture resulted from political, legal, and economic decisions—not the "nature" of the chosen technology. Robert McChesney (1993, 1999), for instance, argues that the early years of radio were far more RW than is usually acknowledged; amateur radio operators broadcast on the same airwaves as nascent national networks, the latter mostly sponsored by radio manufacturers like RCA and Westinghouse, the better to sell radio sets (see also Barnouw 1990). It was only due to the concerted efforts of those manufacturers, along with the demands of copyright holders (like Columbia Records) for protection from pirate broadcasts of their recordings, that Congress chose large, commercial networks of RO media for the national model of radio—a model that was then adopted for television as well.

Acknowledging this reality brings us to the third point we can tease out of Lessig's description. The state was as essential to the creation of the RO culture of the last half of the twentieth century as it has been to the development of the Internet, mobile phone technology, and the rest of the appurtenances of the RW culture of today. The components of C2—which were previously RO—are also now predominantly the wholly owned properties of a handful of major media conglomerates. Lessig's only explanation for this circumstance is that the technology of distribution—which he insists was very competitive—prevented any other relationship.

Several Marxian categories that are useful to understanding the culture he is describing are primitive accumulation, commodification, and the social division of labor. Each of these looks at the process of creating private property rights from a different dimension. Primitive accumulation is the process of dispossessing those who used a resource, usually in common. On the dispossessor's side of this relationship, this process means simply accumulating the property, often justified using the rhetoric of "improvement" and "efficiency." On the other side, however, it means transforming an essential resource into a property and a commodity, making it necessary for those who used that resource in common to approach it only as consumers, who must purchase it with money, most likely derived from selling their labor.

Karl Marx focuses on the commodity as the result of the production process, but this is only because commodification is a fundamental component of capitalist economic development. In the neoliberal "Washington Consensus" of economic development, this is described as "privatization," "capitalization," and even "financialization"; it means increasing the presence (and power) of private industry, subjecting more components of people's everyday existence to the objective valuation processes of the market, and, according to the theory, increasing the efficiency by which they are produced, exchanged, and distributed. In practice, commodification means subjecting more of people's means of existence to the rules of the cash economy, thereby decreasing their ability for self-provision outside the labor market and, in the end, increasing their dependence on credit, debt, and, in turn, capital. Primitive accumulation is the process of applying private property rights seen from the perspective of the dispossessor and the dispossessed; commodification is the same process seen from the perspective of the commodity itself.

If these two concepts represent different dimensions of the same process, the social division of labor is the relationship between social actors relative to the appropriated property after the fact. In its simplest formulation, primitive accumulation and commodification create a relationship where those who have legal ownership of property (or effective control, or both) make it necessary for nonowners to pay for the use of that property or, as Dallas Smythe discusses, otherwise work for the property owner to gain access. In other words, the extension of the social division of labor is implied in the process of the privatization of property. As Marx and Friedrich Engels say of their relationship:

> Division of labour and private property are, moreover, identical expressions: in one the same thing is affirmed with reference to activity as is affirmed in the other with reference to the product of the activity. Further, the division of labour implies the contradiction between the interest of the separate individual or the individual family and the communal interest of all individuals who have intercourse with one another. And *indeed* this communal interest does not exist merely in the imagination, as the "general interest," but first of all in reality, as the mutual interdependence of the individuals among whom the labour is divided. (2011, p. 52; emphasis original)

These three theoretical concepts—primitive accumulation, commodification, and the division of labor—are important to understanding the process of cultural enclosure that has occurred in the twentieth century. Thinking of these immaterial enclosures in relation to the actual "material interdependence of the individuals among whom the labor is divided" suggests that the cultural processes that Jenkins and Lessig highlight have long existed within the structure of this capitalist order. They consider this interdependence only in the properties of mental—not manual—labor but overlook the separation between mental and manual labor, seeing it as a product of our wider political economy and revealing the intensification of commodification in general. In other words, the increased visibility in one kind of property, and the moral indignation of its enclosure, should help us see the problem more generally.

This brings me to the final point: like scholars of the Law and Economics movement and neoliberal ideology more generally, Lessig and Jenkins effectively separate culture and politics. Although Lessig and other critics of IPR are ultimately targeting what he calls the "legal culture," he aims to change only the code of "the culture regulating culture," by which he means only the law that regulates media production and distribution. There is no sense that either the law from the top—or the cultural process from below—could effect any fundamental change to the neoliberal legal framework that increasingly determines the larger culture. As shown in the previous chapter, Lessig's critique of his Law and Economics colleagues demonstrates that he can imagine a way to use the law—along with our norms, expectations, and technological affordances—to change that culture: it is just that he does not believe a fundamental alteration in property or distribution structures is possible.

In this view, his appeal to the vitality and subjectivity of the individual yeomanry of RW culture appears to be an empty paean to democratic ideals. If the most fundamental questions shaping all of our lives have already been decided, it hardly matters that we can speak freely—particularly if the only goal of that speech is to create value in the sharing economy for the benefit of the commercial economy. Effectively, Lessig is asking for the intensification of the division of labor without formal private property—the prehistory of digital primitive accumulation. The RW culture, in other words, does not extend to rewriting the overall rules of the culture, particularly those of private property and free enterprise. These rules are the immutable constants in this endlessly shifting culture.

Jenkins is more upfront with how he sees this "participatory culture" relating to politics. Ideally, the cultural innovators that he champions are learning skills that they could apply to political activism. But I would argue, along with Bauwens, that these skills also teach them to think and act in this expanded process of social valorization central to Jenkins work, prefiguring a different version of themselves within that process. Their agency in that specifically cultural process (largely at the C1 and C2 levels) demonstrates the lacunae of the commodified system and their potential agency in transforming the social property relations (i.e., at the C3 level) that they are forced, formally and functionally, to inhabit.

When we shear away the façade of the social division of labor, we are better able to see what Marx calls "the mutual interdependence of the individuals among whom the labour is divided" (Marx and Engels 2011, p. 52). The process of commodification that is central to this chapter is directly related to the primitive accumulation associated with reinforcing the social division of labor, often by removing IP—ideas—from the direct producers of real property.

Innovation, Production, and Capitalist Property Relations: Social Division of Labor versus Extended Process of Valorization

Thus we return to one of the frequent characters in our story of reified culture of property: John Locke. Among other things, the idea of improvement is central to his doctrine of the liberal state. Prioritizing improvement implies that the yeoman farmer might need to be dispossessed to make way for a more efficient, productive, profitable farm. As Marx points out, proponents see enclosure and improvement as economically necessary: the direct producer must be dispossessed to allow for larger, more efficient farms. These larger farms might require employing more laborers, who then become parties to the creation of that increased product, but this scenario does not imply that those workers should then receive their share of the product. Instead, ideologically, the Lockean defense of private property says that the increased yield is solely owed to the owner: the division of labor between the owner of the property and the worker who creates value by denying the "mutual interdependence of the individuals among whom the labour is divided" (Marx and Engels 2011, p. 52). This relationship is as true of real productive property as it is of IP.

In *Capital,* volume 1 (1977), Marx provides detailed evidence that the benefits of modernity continue to flow mainly in one direction. This observation is proffered not only in the interest of promoting equality or engaging in class warfare; the observation takes seriously some of the key insights of what makes capitalist production valuable. In short, Marx took the liberal economists at their word, drawing out the implications of the reified culture of property in the long term. As Marx sees it, the key innovation of the capitalist system was that it brought together previously disparate laborers into a process through which they could collectively produce more—in factories and the fields. Although he criticizes the exploitative relations, he imagined the same processes of valorization—the same ability of collaborative, collective labor to produce more than its value—could be utilized for the benefit of all who helped produce that value. Like Benkler (2002), Marx and his co-author Engels see this value as produced in a social process:

> The production of life, both of one's own labour and of fresh life in procreation, now appears as a twofold relationship: on the one hand as a natural and on the other as a social relationship—social in the sense that it denotes the co-operation of several individuals, no matter under what conditions, in what manner and to what end. It follows from this that a certain mode of production, or industrial stage, is always

combined with a certain mode of co-operation, or social stage, and this mode of co-operation is itself a "productive force." (2011, pp. 48–49)

The social process of valorization, in this regard, is not just an economic issue. In one sense, the social production of value develops despite property relations rather than because of them. The surplus produced from this improved process of social production could be distributed in a variety of ways. Marx was not alone in this observation; even John Stuart Mill, a late-nineteenth-century liberal, says that once the surplus is produced, "mankind, individually or collectively, can do with [it] as they like" (2004, p. 210). Fried says that Mill understood that property and law determined distribution and thus "that the laws governing distribution were distinct from those governing production, and—unlike the latter—were mutable" (1998, p. 77). The division of labor under capitalism helped improve the productivity of the average worker, reduce the amount of work necessary to complete certain tasks, and hence create, in cooperation with others, more products with less effort.

But in reifying the notion that some forms of labor are less valuable, that they produce less value within this extended order, the underside of this particular arrangement has been that the majority of people employed have experienced little net change in their economic circumstances. Instead of working endlessly for a feudal overseer and paying their dues in kind, they have been coerced economically, by the dictates of the market, to sell their labor at a bargain to the people who happen to control the means of production. The injustice of this deal has been particularly evident for people who have been able to live outside this system, but who, as Chapter 2 catalogues, have been forced by the state to abandon their means of self-provision. Justifying this arrangement, therefore, has become an important political and cultural task, one that, in its practice, only further exacerbates the social division in question through the separation of mental and manual labor. The ideology of meritocracy asserts that the owners of these new means of production find themselves in their lucky position because they have had the imagination, courage, and mental capacity to forge innovative new production methods—and the capital with which to put them into effect. By risking their capital for the potential improvements of production, they are justified in receiving a vastly disproportionate share of the productivity gains.

Innovations in production—the knowledge necessary to produce—have therefore been assumed to be the product of an innovative class of engineers. While this is fundamental to the culture of capitalism, David Noble (1979) argues it has become more pronounced in recent years, exacerbating the social division of labor. In many cases, it may be correct that some tasks require especially skilled workers. But it does not necessarily follow from this presumption that the current social division of labor is the valid result of a meritocratic system that simply rewards innovations and innovators based on the amount of "value-added" labor they contribute.

Returning to Locke—one of the primary sources of this ideology—provides some insight into the roots of the current belief that a division exists between mental and manual labor and between real property and IP. As it turns out, the actual practice of agricultural improvement was based on the enclosure of not only the physical commons but the mental commons as well. While the actual enclosure might have yielded middling results in terms of agricultural productivity (see my discussion of McCloskey in the previous chapter), the agricultural practices used in that process were often derived from farmers and peasants, appropriated by Locke and others observing, querying, and collecting notes on their cultivation techniques. According to Neal Wood, Robert Boyle, one of Locke's associates, drafted what was "perhaps the first example of a systematic questionnaire for eliciting data of a technical nature" to be sent "to experienced farmers throughout England, Scotland, and Ireland" (1984, p. 26). Boyle encouraged his colleagues to "take pains to inquire a little more thoroughly into the ways of husbandry" (ibid.) by speaking to the laborers in their parts of the country. Boyle, Locke, and the other members of "the utopian and utilitarian group the 'Invisible College'" (ibid., p. 25) simultaneously advocated for enclosure of the land that those workers tended, ensuring that they would be working on enclosed land with techniques possibly dispossessed from them.

The process of enclosure explicitly relies on a social process of valorization: its benefits are contingent on workers' collectively laboring on a single crop, in a larger tract of land, even if the value produced goes back to the owner who hires that labor as a factor of production. Its increased efficiency depends explicitly on a multitude of others, compelled to labor by a commodity economy and an ever-more-totalizing state. Sir Francis Bacon and others saw enclosure and improvement as "a means of increasing the food supply and solving the unemployment problem" (N. Wood 1984, p. 24).

This recalls the full meaning of "primitive accumulation," which is never just that land or productive knowledge was concentrated into a few hands; it means the separation of workers from their means of production. As Michael Perelman (2000) points out, Adam Smith's understanding of how this meaning came about follows elegantly from Locke's labor theory of property. As observers from Marx to Karl Polanyi to Perelman have illustrated, this process was not natural. The "habituation of the laborer" to these new conditions was an imperative that only the guarantees of private property in the means of production could instill.

Likewise, the origins of Fordist production show a similar pattern of material dispossession and the primitive accumulation of knowledge. Harry Braverman's *Labor and Monopoly Capital* (1974) illustrates this point extensively. Here, Locke and the Baconian improvers are replaced by Frederick Winslow Taylor and the scientific management movement. In U.S. lore, Taylor is credited with single-handedly developing a more productive factory system. Supposedly expanding on Smith's pin-factory allegory, Taylor was able to subdivide the labor process so that it occurred faster and more efficiently. Hagiographies of the saving grace of "Taylorism" often present him as the source of essential innovations in the industrial labor process and give him credit for the increased productivity of modern industry.

Whatever the effects of his efforts on the improved output of the factory system, Braverman makes it clear that these efforts were not due to scientific or technological prowess on his part. More importantly, his primary goal was always political rather than economic—to increase management's control over labor. This change was possible only by wresting control of the labor process from the workers: "Workers who are controlled only by general orders and discipline are not adequately controlled, because they retain their grip on the actual processes of labor" (Braverman 1974, p. 100). Through the process of primitive accumulation, workers could be made to labor in the factory for the owners of the means of production, but Taylor realized that those workers still had an advantage over the owner because their specialized knowledge meant that only they understood how to complete these complex tasks. In an era of wildcat strikes, work stoppages, and militant labor solidarity, especially skilled workers were a dangerous factor of production. It was inarguable that the worker was a source of value, but that value gave them, collectively, a political force as well (in line with the autonomist Marxist understanding of Michael Hardt and Antonio Negri presented in *Labor of Dionysus* [1994] and elsewhere). The difficulty of training workers, of getting them to the point where they could be productively employed, militated against their easy replacement in the production line in the case of a strike. Thus, the science of management was invented to increase the division of labor incrementally until the power of management—in the form of knowledge over the labor process—became complete.

Again, the social process of valorization is incontrovertible: the mental and manual capacities of the workers are necessary for production to occur. They are, as in the capitalist agricultural improvement, the essential force of the more productive production process. Likewise, when Braverman quotes from

Taylor's own memoirs, it is clear that he realized that the workers possessed the essential knowledge that made even the machine industry function properly. As Taylor, in his proselytizing of scientific management, describes it:

> In the best of the ordinary types of management, the managers recognize frankly that the . . . workmen, included in the twenty or thirty trades, who are under them, possess the mass of traditional knowledge, a large part of which is not in the possession of management. The management, of course, includes foremen and superintendents, who themselves have been first-class workers at their trades. And yet these foremen and superintendents know, better than anyone else, that their own knowledge and personal skill falls far short of the combined knowledge and dexterity of all the workmen under them. The most experienced managers frankly place before their workmen the problem of doing the work in the best and most economical way. They recognize the task before them as that of inducing each workman to use his best endeavors, his hardest work, all his traditional knowledge, his skill, his ingenuity, and his good-will—in a word, his "initiative," so as to yield the largest possible return to his employer. (Braverman 1974, p. 101)

Taylor overcame this problem by closely studying the techniques that each of these workers used to efficiently and effectively complete their jobs. His study was focused on further separating the conception of the work from its execution—the division of mental from manual labor—thereby giving management more power over workers.

Even Taylor understood this process to be removing the traditional knowledge of the craft workers from their control and placing it solely in the hands of the management. Again, in Taylor's own words: "The managers assume . . . the burden of gathering together all of the traditional knowledge which in the past had been possessed by the workmen and then classifying, tabulating, and reducing this knowledge to rules laws and formulae" (Braverman 1974, p. 113). Work would be subdivided into minute tasks that would prevent workers from asserting their power over the production process through a walkout, strike, or other strategy. Using piece rates and wage fluctuations as a tool to motivate the workers to accept this condition of work, Taylor gave management increasing control over the work process. As Braverman points out, this shift allowed the purchaser of labor to "divorce conception from execution": "This dehumanization of the labor process, in which workers are reduced almost to the level of labor in its animal form, while purposeless and unthinkable in the case of the self-organized and self-motivated social labor of a community of producers, becomes crucial for the management of purchased labor" (ibid., p. 78).

As with the accumulation of agricultural data in the era of Locke, "systemization often means, at least at the outset, the gathering of knowledge which *workers already possess*" (Braverman 1974, p. 15; emphasis original). The division between mental and manual labor is artificial, maintained only after the traditional knowledge has been extracted from the dispossessed worker. And, as in the era of Locke, this new, common pool of technical, traditional knowledge is expropriated from the materially dispossessed workers. However, this extraction is no longer because laborers are assumed to be ignorant or debased, as they were in the late feudal studies of the natural scientists; this view would, after all, undermine the idea that scientific management needed to study laborers to control them. Still, the Lockean understanding of the labor theory of property is maintained. Braverman quotes Taylor, speaking to a U.S. House of Representatives Committee, as saying that although the workman has the knowledge, he cannot afford *not* to work long enough to develop a science of management. Consequently, those who *can* afford to do this become the rightful owners of the knowledge they are able to gather. The implications are clear to Braverman, and they bear directly on the previous argument about primitive accumulation:

> The possessors of labor time cannot afford to do anything but sell it for their means of subsistence. It is true that this is the rule of capitalist relations of production, and Taylor's use of the argument in this case shows with great clarity where the sway of capital leads: Not only is capital the property of the capital, but *labor itself becomes part of capital*. Not only do workers lose control over their instruments of production, but they must now lose control over their labor and the manner of its performance. This control now falls to those who can "afford" to study it in order to know it better than the workers themselves know their own life activity. (1974, p. 116; emphasis original)

Thus, alongside the more complete socialization of the creation of value, the separation of mental from manual labor—the origin of the assumption of division of labor that is fundamental to most IP scholars—lays the groundwork for the very forms of control that they rail against. Braverman points out that this separation is effectively the dispossession of trade secrets and, in an era before the widespread use of patents, a progenitor of the practices that Lessig observes in *Free Culture* (2004): the current holders of copyright properties often build their products on the cultural commons that they later try to lock down through maximalist rights.

In this vein, one of Lessig's favorite anecdotes from *Free Culture* involves Walt Disney's original "invention" of Mickey Mouse as well as most of Disney's early movie-length cartoons. All of these cartoons were based, in one way or another, on folk music, communal fairy tales, and early animated characters, such as Steamboat Willie. Lessig (2002) argues that this example illustrates that "creativity and innovation always builds on the past." Yet once Disney appropriated that culture under a particular set of social property relations, once it had been turned into a commodity under capitalist production relations, this earlier process of social valorization—and any process afterward—was effectively negated. Future appropriations like Disney's, from either the common culture that existed before he commodified it or the cultural commons that he helped produce through his appropriation, were closed off to future creators. As with the enclosure of land and the separation in the factory, these relations became reified and bound by law.

In the cultural sphere, the difference is that we currently lack the controls to solidify these relations completely: the initial distribution can be undermined by new production and new distribution techniques outside the supposedly legal frameworks of value. But in this regard, the distinction between real property and IP is more historical and cultural than ontological. Yes, the current technology prevents the complete locking down of nominally immaterial culture, but likewise, until the invention of barbed wire, it was difficult to fence in the prairie in Texas. After the patent for barbed wire was issued in 1874, its widespread use was greatly responsible for the "transformation of the cattle kingdom from a free range to one of enclosed pastures" (Hayter 1963, p. 20). The subsequent legalization of the practice of fencing—and the criminalization of fence-cutting—is not all that different than the DMCA restrictions on the distribution of the method for cracking DVD encoding: the mere possession of wire cutters was, for a time, enough to charge the holder with intent to rustle the contents of the enclosed area; likewise, under the DMCA, the possession of the illegal code to crack DVDs is interpreted as evidence of intent to pirate. That the legal control of the material distribution of property is currently hampered by the lack of adequate enforcement techniques should not give us the illusion that it represents a serious ontological difference. It is true that the contents of the DVD and the enclosed prairie are quite different in terms of the joint consumption properties of nonrivalrous goods. As critics of IPR as far back as Jefferson have pointed out, the distribution or derivative production of an intangible product leaves the original intact. But this interpretation misunderstands what is actually being bought and sold in the culture industry.

Commodification and the Cultural Production of Intellectual Property

As a way of connecting this discussion of commodification and the division of labor with the observations of the balanced IPR critics in relation to the social process of production, I find Dallas Smythe's (1977) concept of the "audience commodity" useful, even if it is inadequate. He elaborates on what he calls the "blindspot" of media studies to expose important facets of the emergent culture of the social order of postwar capitalism. By attempting to discuss the broader labor process of production for the value of cultural goods, he illuminates—in some cases unintentionally—the link between this extended process of cultural production and the social processes that helped create economic value and cultural efficacy.

His incomplete conceptualization points to the ways in which a strictly empirical distinction between real property and IP overlooks their material similarity. However, to see the relevance of his points, it is important to read Smythe in the context in which he was writing: he was a Marxist critic of communications networks under monopoly capitalism. Most cultural studies critics of this system had focused on the products distributed through these communications networks in a narrow structuralist or culturalist fashion. In effect, Smythe argues that both approaches were true. This perspective is best summed up by Eileen Meehan, who uses Smythe to talk about the value produced by fans of popular cultural products: "Our enculturation [. . .] generates direct and indirect revenues for media corporations" (2000, p. 79).

The social production of meaning is important—as in Jessica Litman's (2007) concept of "creative reading"—but Smythe articulates this social production from within a Marxist problematic, retaining the importance of the social division of labor within this production process. Because he cannot see the ways in which the value created in this process will be appropriated through the expansion in scope and scale of IP, he cannot fully conceive of the property relations that anchor it except in terms of the system of monopoly capital that he sees around him. In retrospect, we can see the system in its totality and engage more fully with these various iterations of Marxist understandings of cultural production. Entertainment, news of the world, community interaction, the material of water cooler conversations—the raw matter from which these are produced slowly have become the properties of large corporations, the source of our common national culture, for which we must pay, through money or audience "labor," for access. These tensions run through the critical cultural approach to communication, and they map the basic tensions of cultural studies' two paradigms of culturalism and structuralism (Hall 1980a).

Smythe is not engaged directly in these theoretical debates, but he nevertheless touches on both. From the culturalist side, in his longer explanation of what he means by the work of the audience, he considers the work that consumers do from childhood—learning how to buy commodities to satisfy their needs—which allows the smooth functioning of advertising as demand management (Smythe 1981). However, as an economist (akin to the structuralist paradigm), he is far more interested in the economic consequences of this transition, objectively and for Marxist theory. In Smythe's assessment, the theoretical difficulty is that

> in "their" time which is sold to advertisers workers (a) perform essential marketing functions for the producers of consumers' goods, and (b) work at the production and reproduction of labour power. This joint process, as shall be noted, embodies a principal contradiction. If this analytical sketch is valid, serious problems for Marxist theory emerge. Among them is the apparent fact that while the superstructure is not ordinarily thought of as being itself engaged in infrastructural productive activity, the mass media of communications are simultaneously in the superstructure and engaged indispensably in the last stage of infrastructural production where demand is produced and satisfied by purchases of consumer goods. (1977, p. 3)

The idea that the superstructure could be productive in the same way as the infrastructure defies easy explanation in orthodox Marxist terms. Although he is not entirely clear on how he would rewrite this model, Smythe sees something very different in the social formation as it existed at the time he was writing. The use of commodities to satisfy needs, the political effects of the psychology promoted through advertising, the regular cultural processes into which this new system was being injected—all of these pointed to something more intensive occurring. The infrastructure was interpenetrating the superstructure, and vice versa.

Smythe thus conceptualizes the economic effects of the power of media in culture in the same ways in which Jürgen Habermas sees the political effects of commodified culture. In *The Structural Transformation of the Public*

Sphere, Habermas concludes that the major change is the transformation "from a culture-debating to a culture-consuming public":

> So-called leisure behavior, once it had become part of the cycle of production and consumption, was already apolitical, if for no other reason than its incapacity to constitute a world emancipated from the immediate constraints of survival needs. When leisure was nothing but a complement to time spent on the job, it could be no more than a different arena for the pursuit of private business affairs that were not transformed into public communication between private people. To be sure, the individuated satisfaction of needs might be achieved in a public fashion, namely, in the company of many others; but a public sphere itself did not emerge from such a situation. When the laws of the market governing the sphere of commodity exchange and of social labor also pervaded the sphere reserved for private people as a public, rational-critical debate had a tendency to be replaced by consumption, and the web of public communication unraveled into acts of individuated reception, however uniform in mode. (1989, pp. 160–161)

The mistake that Smythe makes is to assume that the consumption of branded commodities is the unique transformation of this moment—that the issue of leisure time spent learning about branded commodities is separate from the "free lunch" portion of consuming media. From a long, historical view, we can now see the significance of both sides. Not only were the needs being met by commodities, and not only was demand management creating new needs and attaching new desires to the commodities that could fill them; a whole new set of social processes above and below, also attached to the cultural efficacy of demand management, was being commodified.

These were, in part, reactions to the double movement that emerged in response to the Great Depression and World War II. These changes did not dissolve the market mechanism or the reified culture of property. In fact, they attempted to render moot the most problematic attributes of capitalism to salvage it as a sustainable model—attempting to solve such problems as credit liquidity, frictional unemployment, labor/capital conflicts, imbalances in income, erratic elastic consumption patterns, and the periodic devalorization of fixed capital. These attempts, however, required a return to the political. Again, a full accounting of this scenario is beyond the scope of this book. For now, I mention only the role that the state played in helping encourage commodity consumption.

In this case, what we find is not just a superstructural aspect to the reproduction of the infrastructure but the use of the economy itself in an ideological way. The political force of this ideological use of the economy was what Antonio Gramsci (1972) describes as the genius of "American Fordism." Michel Aglietta, a French regulationist economist, observes that there was certainly an increase in what Georg Lukács would have called reification in that "the time devoted to consumption witnessed an increasing density in individual uses of commodities and a notable impoverishment of non-commodity interpersonal relations" (2015, p. 159). However, despite the truth of many of the theories of the increased role of advertising in consumption—he looks expressly to Jean Baudrillard (2006) as an important progenitor of these observations—Aglietta cautions that "it cannot be stressed too greatly that the role of the image in consumption, which many sociologists have made into a fundamental explanatory principle of capitalist development, is strictly subordinate to the material and social conditions we have discussed" (2015, p. 161). Many of the material and social conditions wrapped up in the change in the working conditions and consumption patterns of the wage-earning classes are identified by critics of monopoly capitalism at the time, but the mechanisms of efficacy are largely assumed to be narrowly concerned with the "spectacular" aspects of the changes.

In effect, the postwar state did what the earlier liberal state could not. Just as the Tudor and Stuart regimes helped, in the words of Barrington Moore, slow the pace of the enclosures, postwar Fordism helped ease more and more citizens into commodity consumption. By guaranteeing wage security through collective bargaining, unemployment insurance, and Social Security and by encouraging home ownership and the purchase of large appliances by providing cheap, federally subsidized or sponsored loans, the U.S. government helped create an ambient cultural sphere in which all the production and consumption that Smythe discusses took place. This situation led to what Aglietta calls "*the predominantly intensive regime of accumulation*," which "create[d] a new mode of life for the [predominantly white] wage-earning class by establishing a logic that operate[d] in the totality of time and space occupied or traversed by its individuals in daily life. A social consumption norm [wa]s formed which no longer depends in any way on communal life, but entirely on an abstract code of utilitarianism" (2015, pp. 71–72; emphasis original). In short, while these were economic transformations, they had a cultural component: they made it possible for the average citizen to believe in the justness of the system and to feel safe in their increasing reliance on commodities. This form of primitive accumulation was softer but had many of the same effects: these policies continued to support the capitalist process of accumulation (although under altered, monopoly conditions), but they also helped remove other options for satisfying needs outside the market/property nexus. This time, however, it was not necessarily compelled by the market. Instead, it necessitated the process of establishing cultural efficacy in all its complexity.

The habitus necessitated by this new regime of accumulation had to be supported by definite social and cultural norms that were reestablished alongside or on top of existing ones. Using the Bourdieuian term "habitus" here is apt. Alain Lipietz, another regulationist economist, describes the "mode of regulation" that a "regime of accumulation" requires using just this term, elaborating it as "norms, habits, laws, and regulating networks which ensure the unity of processes and which guarantee that its agents conform more or less to the schema of reproduction in their day-to-day behaviour and struggles" (1987, p. 14). The "mode of regulation" is, therefore, "the set of internalized rules and social procedures which incorporate social elements into individual behaviour" (ibid., p. 15). This socialization process cannot occur from the top-down alone and must be integrated into the microlevel C1 interactions of individuals within the social formation. Scholars in the discipline of administrative communication studies (e.g., Katz and Lazarsfeld 1955) well understood the need to have local cultural valorization of these new rules—including the new rules about which aspects of life and labor should be commodified and/or incorporated into the process of commodification by necessitating commodified inputs, including, and especially, women's housework.

Within these changed circumstances, brought about through the state/corporate implantation of a model of culture, Smythe and others observe that previous forms of leisure entertainment were being overtaken by mass forms of communication. On a practical level, this technology was injected into the already vibrant local forms of communication and cultural association, embedded in a community, a network of interaction with those nearby and, in the case of the national media, with an "imagined community" that now demanded interaction, even if only superficially, through the mediums of commercial broadcasting (B. Anderson 2006; Morley 1992; Morley and Brundson 1999). This sociological process of individuated, interpersonal interaction with mass-produced cultural products certainly had its ideological and political dimensions, but Smythe loses the focus on these in trying to isolate its economic dimension.

While the metaphor of the audience commodity is insufficient in itself, Smythe's focus on labor in general provides a welcome contrast to what he calls "idealist" notions of how ideological apparatuses work. As an economist, he sees something different occurring in the process of valorization: he cannot quite put his finger on it, but he knows it is there. But if we look at this process as the habituation of workers to an increasing social-consumption norm, we can see the general economic environment he was considering. What Smythe detects was the parallel processes of cultural validation/valorization that were necessary for this new system to function and take hold. In other words, for the system that was imposed from the C3 level to have cultural efficacy, it required labor and efforts—the labors of appropriation—throughout the cultural hierarchy to instantiate it into everyday life. What Smythe—and the combined paradigms of the culturalist and structuralist cultural studies—recognizes and tries to articulate is the complex process whereby the capitalist mode of production, altered in its purity, is politically installed in the social formation, yet the only way it is effective is if it engages the participation and captures the energy of the collective cultural and communal process of meaning making.

At the time Smythe was writing, this understanding was simply a matter of noting that, along with the variety of negotiated meanings produced throughout the cultural circuit, along with the ideological role these intended meanings played in their support of the revised capitalist order—along with these, to paraphrase Meehan, our enculturation produced value. Now, with the increasing importance of IPR, it is evident what this primitive accumulation has done. As I elaborate further elsewhere (Johnson Andrews 2016), the control of this common culture is in the hands of a few media corporations. But before it drifted into their possession, before we "worked" as audience members on its materials, we ceased to participate in our own cultural rituals at the local level. As Lessig laments, we became a nation of consumers. This recognition returns us to the discussion at the beginning of this section about what IP owners actually claim to be their property.

The fact that the term "intellectual property" covers the copyrighted materials of commercial television *and* the trademarked products of their advertisers could alert us to homologous processes: a similar course of cultural valorization was necessary *even as both sets of producers were apparently given complete control over the material means of production*. In both cases, what eventually occurred was the complete commodification of not only consumption in terms of use values necessary for life but also the process of cultural meaning making. From the producer side, this shift meant that the average citizen would increasingly meet these needs for community and communication through the purchase of one of their commodities. But for this purchase to happen, there needed to be a general social and cultural appropriation of these as the objects of what Lessig would call RO culture. The latter was essential for the integration of branded commodities into everyday life; as mass-mediated products—throughout the flow of commercial media—became cultural commonplaces in themselves, social and political forces transformed them into instruments of meaning themselves, thus valuable as social and cultural signifiers far beyond the contributions of their owners.

From a certain empirical perspective, there is something distinctive about the products protected by what we call IP. Patents, copyrights, and trademarks all have what is referred to as a nonrivalrous quality. In the words of Lessig, discussing the difference between music piracy and shoplifting, "When you take a book from Barnes & Noble, it has one less book to sell. By contrast, when you take an MP3 from a computer network, there is not one less CD that can be sold. The physics of piracy of the intangible are different from the physics of piracy of the tangible" (2004, p. 64).

However, this example focuses too closely on the empirical qualities of the object rather than the materialist understanding of it as property. What is owned is not a particular object—obviously, the intangible, nonrivalrous good can be reworked, redistributed, remixed, and so forth without harming the original. Derivative uses may theoretically do nothing to destroy the nonrivalrous quality of the cultural token—more copies could still be made—but it might destroy the affective capital that has become attached to it or prematurely harvest it, destroying the "cool" it might have before its owner can profitably parlay it. Derivative uses can either degrade the cultural value—capitalized in the form of the perceived value of a corporate stock of copyrighted libraries—or it can pilfer the profits perceived to be owned solely by the title holder.

Thus, what is owned is the semiotic connection between the sign of the property (its signifier) and the mental image created in the minds of the viewers (its signified). In short, the claim is not on the empirical property itself but on the section of our collective consciousness devoted to that trademark, copyright, or patented idea—and its possible material revenues. This claim is explicit in trademark law, where owners must prove that this association is active—that the mark has what I have called "cultural efficacy." By this term, I refer to a given range of references and meanings that inspire memories, emotions, and personal and interpersonal identification within a certain cultural inside. Until now, we have mostly focused on the dimensions of meaning and power related to these objects of the C2 level. But Smythe and others help us see the ways in which these articulations and appropriations also have—and collectively produce—value. And because they have value, the liberal orthodoxy proclaims that they should be property and that they should be owned by those with the means to "improve" on them.

The property of IP is semiotic. It is a claim to ownership not just of the signifier but of the complete process of signification that results in the sign. As V. N. Vološinov points out, "Signs can arise only on *interindividual territory*" (1973, p. 12; emphasis original). Only in the social process of communication can the signifier of the branded, copyrighted work or even patented product acquire its full valorization as a commodity. To put it another way, we all engage in anthropologically given human processes (cf. Jhally 1990, ch. 1). The move to more intensively commodify the basic processes—from life necessities to forms of entertainment and art—is unique in human history and has long been one of the preoccupations of cultural studies. Scholars have focused on the more superficial changes, reading the more fundamental economic processes as contextual background. Graham Murdock and Peter Golding criticize Western Marxists—all the way back to Adorno—for this approach, saying, "Instead of starting from a concrete analysis of economic relations and the ways in which they structure both the processes and results of cultural production, they start by analysing the form and content of cultural artifacts and then working backwards to describe their economic base" (1977, p. 17). Although this method might have been inadequate from an economic perspective, it made a great deal of sense culturally—quite a bit when one factors in the ways in which the results of these cultural processes are now claimed as economic capital. The meaning of language and social practices not only directs our activities; it affects our understanding of the world. As Vološinov argues, "The individual consciousness is a social-ideological fact" (1973, p. 12). By this statement, he means that all our inner speech, all our personal reflections, will be refracted through the social language of signs we share with others:

> Consciousness takes shape and being in the material signs created by an organized group in the process of its social intercourse. The individual consciousness is nurtured on signs; it derives its growth from them; it reflects their logic and laws. The logic of consciousness is the logic of ideological communication of the semiotic interaction of a social group. (Ibid., p. 13)

In other words, insofar as the value of IP is based mostly in its meaning, in its semiotic attachments, it is—and can only be—valorized in a social process. Not only is the social value that IP accretes due to countless people's picking up that meaning and using it; when one looks closely at the cultural products that have the most staying power—those that, as marketer Alex Wipperfürth says, "stick"—they most often must use the cultural materials already available. Their cultural efficacy relies on the repertoire of previously created meanings and references.

This is as true of the brands Wipperfürth discusses, such as Hush Puppies and Pabst Blue Ribbon, as it is of blockbuster motion pictures. In their study of why U.S. movies and television shows are dominant globally, Colin Hoskins, Stuart McFadgen, and Adam Finn (1997) point out that it is often possible to recoup most production costs within the domestic market because it is so enormous; exports, therefore, can be priced lower (almost to the point of "dumping"). But they rationalize the latter—particularly in non-Anglophone, non-Western/Northern countries—because the language and references do not have as much purchase with those audiences. They term this difference in value the "Cultural Discount," arguing that the full value can be recouped only in environments where these cultural references dominate the national consciousness. As Vološinov puts it, "No cultural sign, once taken in and given meaning, remains in isolation: it becomes part of the *unity of the verbally constituted consciousness*" (1973, p. 15; emphasis original).

When IP owners claim title to the sign value that they are given legal rights over, they are not claiming ownership of the material in question: it could obviously be reused, remixed, and so on, nearly infinitely, without technically degrading the original material. Instead, they are claiming ownership of the little section of the individual and collective consciousness that contains those references to their property, that shared cluster of memories and memes that has cemented the relationship between their signifier and all the positive, emotionally charged, signifieds attached to it. This piece inevitably includes a wide variety of things the producers never intended, but the force of nostalgia works in their favor: childhood memories of movies watched at sleepovers; water cooler conversations about prime-time TV programs; social interactions that happened to the soundtrack of recorded music. These cognitive connections, populated by the properties in question, are ultimately owned by the same clique of corporate individuals who were given control over the technology that made the national community possible in real time.

This is not to say that the original authors had no agency, but that these properties would never have acquired their associated values were it not for the social valorization in question. If anything, as Clay Shirky suggests in his book *Cognitive Surplus* (2010), an entire generation (two or even three now) had the bulk of its collective creative energy channeled into these endeavors. Enormous intellectual effort was committed to reinforcing and controlling these associations—in some cases through propaganda alone, but often using the law itself. As critics of the use of IPR to stifle free speech point out (although not in these terms), the ownership is over the specific signification as the owners have articulated it and/or as it benefits them. It becomes less important whether, for instance, people have a different interpretation of a film or whether they have a certain opinion about Colgate toothpaste; in either case, the goal is for people to pay for them both, as many times as possible. The DMCA was passed with the explicit goal of allowing copyright owners to exploit the multitude of new formats, even as digital encoding and global distribution would make the control even harder to enforce.

IPR ownership therefore exists on a continuum between the ethereal semiotic qualities orbiting this section of the consciousness and its instantiation in an actual medium. For analytical purposes, taking the three major forms of IP, this continuum runs from trademarks to copyrights to patents. Trademarks, even in the legal definition, deal mostly with the cultural associations of their products. Even here, the particular articulations and enunciations are important—for instance, the trademark owners must prove that their registered marks and phrases are understood by consumers as referring to their specific products but are not so closely associated with the general commodities in question that the marks become synonymous with the products (e.g., "Xerox," "Kleenex," or, more recently, "Google"). They must ensure, in Roland Barthes's (1972) terms, that the marks remain connotative rather than denotative. Patents obviously have the most material basis, but, as the preceding sections on agriculture and industrial labor illustrate, they are no less a part of the social process of valorization.

Copyrights, however, are given the most long-lasting protection. Trademarks can be registered for only ten years at a time and are renewable only if the marks are still used in commerce and actively recognized; patents can last up to twenty years. But copyrights last for the full life of their authors *plus* 70 years, or up to 120 years from the time of creation for corporate works for hire. The longevity of their protection as property makes them a valuable form of commodified culture, which synergistic telecommunications corporations are discovering new ways to turn into streams of revenue.

The process of extending copyright terms is an attempt to apply the rules of the welfare state—where the state helped the corporation prevent the devalorization of its fixed capital investment—to the *ex post facto* capitalization of corporate libraries of copyrighted works. As Mark Lemley (2004) contends, this process has little to do with inspiring what the relevant article of the U.S. Constitution describes as "the creative arts and sciences" and more to do with securing the continued global monopoly of media industries. In this case, their previous monopoly was often effective only in that it was prohibitively expensive to create distribution networks of the scale necessary to broadcast TV/radio programs and to replicate films for theaters; at times, this effective monopoly was assisted by state licenses or challenged by antitrust legislation or lawsuits. But the changing means of distribution—meant originally to help preserve their bottom line by making distribution cheaper—has undermined their effective monopoly altogether, making the state-supported monopoly of IPR the primary means of securing their profitability. Smythe was interested in looking at the ways in which the media industry functioned as an industry: what did it sell? In effect, it sold the audience attention that it was able to garner from its "free lunch" of TV shows, movies, and so on. The contradiction is that these cultural products simultaneously undermined and relied on previous systems of meaning and processes of valuation—a process I have elaborated on elsewhere as the "valorizing of hegemony" (Johnson Andrews 2016).

IPR used to be a bulwark against tangible competition—whether in the copyrights of LPs that Lessig mentions or the webs of patents securing the monopoly control of an industry that Noble discusses at length; now it is the material basis of intangible capitalism. While I would argue that we have every reason to regard the idea of a "weightless economy" with extreme skepticism—as Doug Henwood (2003), Christopher May (2002), and James Boyle (1996) all do in some respect—the fact is that this is the dominant model of capitalist accumulation and regulation. Pushing back against this model means resisting not only the imposition of the narrow problem of IPR but also the social division of labor and the reified culture of property that this latest push for maximalist property hopes to recreate in the global, digital era.

The difference on an international scale is that the reification of commodification is incomplete in many nation-states; therefore, international policy has to work to push not only the increased commodification of IPR on other cultures but also the intensification of commodification in general. If the former push has created anxieties for domestic critics of IPR in the United States, it should come as no surprise that the latter has created a reaction of much more monumental proportions on a world scale. Just as the study of our own cultural history teaches us much about our cultural present, the study of present alternatives gives us some notion of the alternatives for considering our cultural future. The latter is the subject of the final chapter.

5

Culture, Property, and the Ends of Progressive Neoliberalism

In the spring of 2007, the Ecuadorian Institute of Intellectual Property (Instituto Ecuatoriano de la Propiedad Intelectual [IEPI]), set up to enforce new World Intellectual Property Organization (WIPO) and Trade-Related Aspects of Intellectual Property Rights (TRIPS) riders to the World Trade Organization (WTO) rules, made a very public threat to the media retailers operating in the southern port city of Guayaquil: start selling legally imported merchandise or be shut down. In their threat, the IEPI targeted fifteen merchants operating near the Malecón 2000, a tourist-oriented commercial center built through public/private partnerships on the banks of the Guayas River in an effort to increase the profile of the city. In the coverage of the threatened crackdown, IEPI officials said they had found forty-two such merchants in the Malecón and nearby Bahia shopping centers: they did not explain why less than half were being asked to change their wares. The merchants themselves denounced the policy, declaring their "right to work" and insinuating that, far from being an attempt to bring Ecuador's antipiracy efforts on par with those of their neighbors in Colombia and Brazil, this demand was really just a power grab by the single, unnamed importer with the authority to supply them with legal CDs and DVDs (*El Universo* 2007).

By 2010, the IEPI began periodic raids of the so-called illegal media merchants—"so-called" because, although many of them sold goods that global corporations would call pirated or counterfeit, the merchants were technically legal at the municipal level, permitted by and paying taxes to the city of Guayaquil. In response, the vendors and the merchants organized themselves into a collective—La Asociación Ecuatoriana de Comerciantes y Distribuidores de Productos Audiovisuales y Conexos (ASECOPAC)—led by Omaira Moscoso. Moscoso, a former filmmaker, ran a shop in Guayaquil called El Coleccionista (The Collector) and claimed her shop was addressing a significant market failure: there was "no place in town where you could find good movies, the movies that don't come from Hollywood":

> Soon, El Coleccionista became a place where intellectuals from Guayaquil sought films by Godard, Bresson, Jodorowski, and the like, which Moscoso copied from her personal collection. "El Coleccionista made me realize that, as a state, we were really doing things the wrong way because we were denying people access to culture," she said. (Heidel, Acuña, and Karaganis 2014)

But, as one of the estimated sixty thousand storefronts in Ecuador selling copied movies, El Coleccionista faced a common problem: these shops, hawking mostly pirated copies, were the only places those media products could be bought. These informal distributors, although not licensed by the studios in question, were doing the work of spreading Anglo-American media culture as efficiently as the U.S. pirate TV broadcasters in the 1960s whom Herbert Schiller (1992) denounces as tools of the American Empire.

Moscoso said that she and her colleagues eventually asked the question that the Motion Picture Association of America (MPAA) and the Recording Industry Association of America (RIAA) do not usually have to answer: "How do we pay? Where do we have to go to pay?" It is a good question, for despite the shearing of the material and immaterial qualities of the products sold by the content industries, if one wants to sell a physical copy, it is still supposed to be an artifact that the industries produced—or at least directly licensed. Could these "pirate" merchants be licensed by the global corporations threatening to shut them down in the same way they were licensed by the city? Moscoso took her case—along with that of three thousand other merchants—to Quito, where she met with Rafael Correa, then the president of Ecuador. He agreed to launch an initiative, but it has been difficult to get off the ground. According to the head of the IEPI, while the initiative has successfully channeled all the domestic cinema products into the licensing scheme, "it has been very difficult to get international rights holders to authorize licenses" (Heidel, Acuña, and Karaganis 2014). In part, this delay is because the vendors would sell their wares at a significant discount. As Evelin Heidel, Ezequiel Acuña, and Joe Karaganis (2014) put it, "Hollywood studios may not like the old status quo of token enforcement and high piracy, but a successful challenge to their global pricing power could be much costlier."

A few hundred miles to the southeast, Bolivian apparel workers are also engaged in labor, primarily in "unregistered, small, family-owned shops" established in private homes, independently and part of loose networks; at the same time that the Bolivian Chamber of Commerce reported 235 legally registered textile companies, estimates put the number of unregistered apparel factories at 10,000 or more. "Some may perform contract work for larger, legitimate firms," but "some of the workshops produce counterfeit apparel products, which are sold in the local market shops or transported to Bolivian towns near the Argentinean and Brazilian borders" (Frazier, Bruss, and Johnson 2004, pp. 439–440). Although all of these workshops operate outside state regulation, the same TRIPS rules that Ecuador is trying to enforce would apply to these distributed workshops of clothing manufacturers: trademarks are part of the same international bargains as copyrights. Ecuador has its share of trademark counterfeiters as well: the town of Pelileo is legendary for its counterfeit denim products. As noted in a World Bank report:

> In Pelileo there are around 400 enterprises engaged in the tailoring of jeans. This activity started in the early 1970s when an entrepreneur started sub-contracting out to households. Rapid expansion of tailoring activities took place during the 1980s. While Pelileo has specialized in jeans tailoring, other communities in [the region] have focused on shoe-making, knit-wear and shirt-making. In total some 3,000 people are employed in one capacity or another by the jeans economy. A few firms are large (about 15 out of the 400 in Pelileo, employing around 70 people each), but most are household based, with an average of no more than 5 members. Most of the household-based enterprises operate in a subcontracting relationship with larger firms. (Lanjouw 1996, p. 157)

Notable in each case is the fact that the local laborers claim ownership—or a right of some kind—to the work that they do. This claim is explicitly in response to efforts to curb these practices because they do not conform to the particular articulation of property rights in the Lockean vein. As I have mentioned, although the latter is supposedly based on the labor of the direct producer, it is actually a defense of the capitalist expropriation of the direct producer. In any case, the labor of the actual producer is ignored by the ideological and juridical defense of private property. The expanded production of trademarked garments in the global commodity chain blurs the line between tangible and intangible property. It also raises the question of whose labor produces more value in the final product—and thus whose property rights in either tangible or intangible commodities should be defended by international law.

A 2004 report on Bolivia, from scholars writing for the *Journal of Fashion Marketing and Management*, touches on the dimension of labor that would likely apply equally to the formal and informal producers in Ecuador and throughout the developing world. Barbara J. Frazier, Mozhdeh Bruss, and Lynn Johnson, in attempting to portray the skills of this labor pool that would make them "attractive to foreign apparel firms because they would need to invest less in training," relay the following assessment, based on observations and interviews with the producers themselves:

> The president of an apparel manufacturer association explained with considerable pride that Bolivian apparel workers are masters at duplicating brand-name products. He explained that many apparel manufacturers in his trade association are able to disassemble a pair of famous brand jeans, make a pattern from its pieces, and then duplicate the item flawlessly—right down to the trademark label. There were many examples of this skill in the local markets, where vendors offered counterfeit clothing with popular trademark labels for $6–$10. Although trademark owners would probably not be impressed by this practice, the comment illustrates the skill that apparel workers have, and the pride that they take in their craft. Bolivians also take pride in the quality of their alpaca and llama wools. There is a rich culture of artisan handwork using these fibers to produce hand-knitted garments that have found their way to upscale markets in the US and Europe. (2004, p. 441)

The singular difference between licit and illicit producers is in the consecration given by a license from the trademark owner to some other producer up the supply chain. The careful reverse engineering mentioned above is not necessary in the case of, for instance, counterfeit Oscar de la Renta jackets sold in the square in La Paz: the same producer made them on a subcontract from the official company. Once the contract ran out, the small manufacturer simply purchased some fake labels from a Chinese supplier, and the otherwise identical jackets were sent to the local square rather than to the contractor, the company, and the North American retailer who would otherwise have sold the jackets.

In cases like these, the purpose of trademark—to ensure that you are getting the authorized *quality* of product—is still being fulfilled to some extent; it just is not authorized by the branded marketer that is the legal owner of the "mark." Jane Collins coins the term "branded marketer" in distinction from the earlier model of "branded manufacturers": the latter actually owns some aspect of the production process, while the former concentrates on "high-value-added" labor, such as "research, design, sales, marketing, and financial services [. . .] while farming out riskier and lower-return tasks such as manufacturing itself" (2003, p. 44).

The quality of the labor involved in these products is not lost on the consumers—nor is its local origin. Nina Laurie contends that to call them merely replicas or counterfeit does not capture either the value that is created through the labor or the exchange value as perceived by consumers. Also speaking about Bolivian counterfeiters, she says:

> In fact, they are not replicas at all but originals designed for the local market but with a designer label included because otherwise they would not sell. [. . .] "The quality of the fakes has improved so much that they are proud of their products as being better than the originals." [. . .] An example is Tunari/Wrangler jeans, made in Bolivia. They are made by a Bolivian cooperative in the shadow of the Tunari Mountain so people know they are getting local quality, not badly produced fakes. (Brown 2003)

A similar dynamic is found in China, where Fan Yang reports that bandit "Shanzhaiji" cell phones—along with many other counterfeit and pirated commodities—are produced and sold not only because they are cheaper but also because they have features (longer battery life and enhanced signal strength) that are especially attractive to Chinese working-class consumers "because they allow continuous use in factories and rural areas where signals are weak and battery charging difficult" (2015, pp. 71–72).

On the other hand, the costs and features of these locally produced Shanzhaiji products are sometimes secondary to a "law defiant ethos," collectively produced through Chinese social-media representations, which positions Shanzhaiji as "cutting into the profits sought by global brands, which depend on the IPR regime to lay claim to their intangible values" (Yang 2015, p. 70) Within the developing world, Chinese bandit phones are widely popular, "from Southeast Asia and India to the Middle East, Russia, and Africa. In Dubai, an entire street is reportedly set up as part of the Shanzhaiji sales network" (ibid., p. 72). As Yang puts it, "The embrace of Shanzhaiji by the transnational 'information have-less' points to a sort of 'globalization from below,' a 'dark flow' that 'appropriates globalization, repetitively reduplicating and deconstructing it'" (ibid.).

It does not hurt, on the other hand, that the counterfeit products sell for a fraction of the cost of an authentic brand original. Trademark, in this case, serves as an ambivalent signifier of some cultural value: part created by the local producers, part created by the designers of the branded manufacturer, part created in the larger social context where the brand circulates to indicate both. It is attached, however, to a product that can be used: whatever the value of the trademark, its being attached to a shoddy piece of clothing would make a mere kitsch object, particularly in societies where consumption proceeds first of all from need. In other words, the labor of these producers is creating most of the value of the product, particularly for the customers and in the markets where they are sold; its relation to the brand is ambivalent, even if international law claims it is not. This distinction is lost on the International Criminal Police Organization (INTERPOL), which launched Operation Jupiter III from October 1 to December 31, 2007, to crack down on pirates of all kinds, arresting and deporting Bolivian workers (among others) who had moved to Argentina to work in larger counterfeiting operations (INTERPOL 2008). Although this operation did not target Ecuador, more than 50 percent of the goods it confiscated were CDs, DVD, or other media products.

These short anecdotes highlight several of the key themes and questions that fill this book. The central topic of the anecdotes and this larger project is the reason *qua* culture determining the process through which Anglo-American, capitalist-oriented understandings of IPR are being imposed on other countries. Here, I mean "reason" in two ways. On the one side, there is the cultural production of the idea of IPR, which, as I discuss in the early chapters of the book, is the product of a certain rationality developed through the history of Western/Northern political and economic cultures. On the other hand is the more conjunctural reason for the rearticulation and promotion of this rationality of property rights, discussed below.

For instance, INTERPOL reported that its action was praised by David Hirschmann, the president and CEO of the U.S. Chamber of Commerce's Global Intellectual Property Center, who said, "By working together, the business community and INTERPOL are striking severe blows against criminal counterfeiters and pirates, while protecting the innovators, workers and consumers who rely on legitimate and safe products and technologies" (INTERPOL 2008). If we read this statement as an inflection of the Northern/Western culture of property I have discussed throughout this book, it is easy to assume that what he calls the "business community" is not a network of households in Bolivia; the "innovators" are not the apparel workers in these networks; the "workers" are not the media merchants in Guayaquil; and the "consumers" are not the shoppers who prefer the local, cheap, well-made fakes to the overpriced products consecrated by the corporate owner. Thus, the entire culture at the sites of these interactions is discounted from the cost-benefit analysis of using an international police force to shut them down. Bolivia, Ecuador, Shanghai—the very basis of their means of subsisting at the bottom rungs of the global capitalist economy is undermined by the enforcement of IPR. The everyday life of the culture is a synthesis between their own local cultures and what development economist Richard E. Peet calls "sub-hegemonic" iterations of neoliberalism. As he puts it, "Hegemony conceived in the centre has to be creatively 'translated' to fit many local contexts. The term 'sub-hegemony' refers to the semi-autonomous strata and locations that translate broad hegemonic ideals into particular ideologies suited to more discrete audiences" (2007, p. 13). Without the material promises of Fordism, this sub-hegemonic embedding is left with only the apparatuses of ideology and repression. If we were truly interested in fostering local cultures—in valuing the creative potential of individuals and communities—then we would surely think twice about destroying what appear to be the most loyal partners in the instantiation of Northern capitalism as a global mode of production.

If you are a Western media company, do not shut down the only distribution network that exists in a country you have little interest in formally serving: co-opt the Ecuadorian pirate co-op; turn "the collectors" into your codistributors. Use the "rent theory Lockeanism" discussed in the previous chapter and give them what they demand: a financial share for their labor in producing that value. And, likewise, have them help foster the local movie industry, which could then provide new content—new IP. The institutional features already exist for great partnerships, even in the business-oriented meaning of partnerships. Instead, these forces are seen as a threat, made an example of, and prevented from any form of self-sustaining livelihood in the interstices of the global, capitalist market society. And here we see how simultaneously central and peripheral the IP is per se. It is ultimately about enforcing a political economic regime that quarters no threats to the legitimacy of property rights, up to and including IPR. The only "workers" are the "innovators" in the "business community" who figure out how to maintain and expand the realm of commodification in what one would hope to the last version of the late capitalism era.

Hirschmann's definitions hinge on the distinction he assumes between "criminal" and "legitimate." This perspective ultimately comes back to a

Lockean understanding of value, private property, and the state. This understanding necessitates a powerful state with complete, unrivaled sovereignty over its territory and the capability to functionally execute law on a national basis. This structure of law is then given specific content through a class-oriented definition of property. This capital-friendly definition of property justifies ownership over formerly common resources based on a reified cultural understanding of how value is produced and distributed. The presumed agreement on these points is the result of hundreds of years of struggle over law, theories of law, and their relation to local cultural practices. Henri Bergson once said, "It takes centuries of culture to produce a utilitarian such as John Stuart Mill" (1977, p. 122); in like fashion, it takes centuries of culture to produce a statement like Hirschmann's. The production of this fundamental culture is the first type of reason behind this imposition.

The second reason is more conjunctural, but it is related to the reification of the former reason. The reasoning above creates a view of the world, an international division of labor, in which the United States and the West are at the pinnacle of a contemporary hierarchy of producers that corresponds to their being the pinnacle of development. The "creative industry" work done in these countries is presumed to have a higher ratio of "value-added" labor. Therefore the (primarily) first-world workers engaged in this labor—and the companies who employ them—should receive a greater proportion of the profits. There is not necessarily anyone making these calculations in quite this way, although reading between the lines of business journal articles would probably reveal that many are coming close to such an argument. From the perspective that sees this Lockean reasoning as natural and reasonable, increasing the scope and scale of IPR domestically and globally is doubly reasonable. By this explanation, I mean "reason" more directly: why is this being done? As A. Samuel Oddi (1996) points out, until the TRIPS regime, the rule of IP was basically that "foreigners be treated like nationals," with each state free to establish its own rules. With TRIPS at the international level, this flexibility is no longer the case. The Digital Millennium Copyright Act (DMCA) points to the domestic version of this treatment within the United States.

These policy instruments are necessary because the current conjuncture has unsettled what were assumed to be natural laws. So-called globalization and the widespread availability of digital technology, networked and produced on a global scale, have undermined the functional monopoly of capital owners in postindustrial economies. Here, I focus on IPR, but the full extent of the legitimation crisis is much worse: it is a crisis in the fundamental rationality of the Northern/Western culture of property and the international division of labor and power that it helps maintain.

It is problematic to uncritically celebrate the actors of informal spaces, such as the pirate media merchants in Ecuador or the producers of counterfeit clothing in Bolivia. In all cases, it is likely that they remain enmeshed in systems of unequal power and wealth. As Yang says of Shanzhaiji production in general, "Its real working conditions are often no better than those facilities subcontracted by global brands" (2015, p. 70), making Shanzhaiji production just as enmeshed in the system of what Jack Qiu (2016) calls "iSlavery." The expansion of IPR is best understood as an attempt to suture a juridical patch over the more fundamental rupture in property rights and the international division of labor that they presume to reinforce. In previous chapters, I outline what I see as the fundamental reason of this imposition—the rationality of what I have called the "culture of property" as it operates within the dominant, hegemonic ideology of Western and especially Anglo-American culture. Charting a path through the development and instantiation of this culture, I have attempted to show how it is able to have what I call cultural efficacy within U.S. society, despite the apparently dynamic changes that have occurred in that country and its relationship with the world over the past half century. I have argued that most critics of IPR fail to see this reification as the underlying context of their objections. Instead "balanced copyright" critics presume neoliberal capitalism to be a natural state of affairs.

The reification of this culture of property, in other words, often prevents critics from seeing this more fundamental reason for the imposition of IPR. Perhaps even more problematically, they pose their criticism of IPR by perceiving the reified culture of property to be beyond question. The problem as they see it is not with the fundamental cultural assumptions—stretched throughout the levels of culture at the top (C3) and bottom (C1); their issues are with the unique characteristics of the material to which property rights are being applied—the materials that would normally be a part of the "free flow" of cultural mediation and dialogue at C2. This criticism sidesteps the process discussed in Chapter 4 whereby these materials, along with all other materials satiating needs at the level of C1, became commodified. Distributed by monopoly corporations, alongside soap and soda, these materials of the ambient culture have been the property of someone for the better part of the past two centuries. Valorized through a collaborative, interactive process of social interaction—similar to that of the symbolic interactionism of the early Chicago School—they became valuable in just the same way that fixed capital or machine equipment would have been in an earlier age, listed as assets on the company balance sheet.

In these terms, it is a distraction to focus too much on the distinctive qualities of IP as opposed to other forms of industrial or otherwise socially produced and productive property. In the dominant liberal economics and political theory, real property and IP share the two most important qualities. First, the value in the property is produced socially—either directly, through the employment of multiple persons in the actual production process, or indirectly, through the social division of labor or the emergent system of distributed, social production—but the surplus must always flow back to the owner. In the liberal paradigm, the very fact of this valorization justifies individual ownership: if the value is "improved," it must be due to the owner's "labors of appropriation." Paradoxically, the *ex post facto* ownership supposedly creates the incentive for this valorization: regardless of how many other laborers have now been robbed of the value they created, the system is valid so long as the owner is getting paid. Second, this form of property justifies the state, which exists solely to protect this understanding of property rights and their relationship to the production of value. While globalization can be said to mean many things, it is most effectively viewed—at least in its neoliberal guise—as an attempt to universalize this understanding of property, value, and the state throughout the world. As such critics as David Harvey (2005), looking at neoliberalism more generally, have observed, this is what "leaving development up to the market" means in its deep logic: submitting more aspects of natural, social, and cultural life to the dictates of commodification, privatization, and market exchange.

"Globalization," in this sense, primarily refers to the globalization of private property. Apologists for this imposition argue that the legal structure of the nation-state, the reified content of the culture of property, and the capitalist understanding of value are essential to development, modernity, progress and a variety of other oblivious Western myths. From this perspective, IPR are simply another channel through which these processes of social valorization can be captured by private individuals—and through which this process of accumulation can be protected by the disciplinary functions of the state. As Richard Epstein puts it, "Whatever the difference between tangible and intangible property, none of them matter for the urgent problem of devising effective countermeasures to piracy and counterfeiting" (2006b, p. 58).

But the Ecuadorian pirates and the Bolivian counterfeiters see a different kind of urgency: they are less concerned with paying exorbitant fees to northern rentiers than with improving the property available to them, riffing off the designer clothes they have produced for multinational corporations, and distributing the "long tail" of culture industry products in markets that copyright lobbyists would prefer to treat as criminals rather than partners. Peter Menell (2007a, 2007b), a legal scholar at the University of California, Berkeley, criticizes how what he calls the "Property Rights Movement" (which

I have mostly referred to as the "Law and Economics movement") embodied by Epstein has embraced IPR, recommending the kinds of absolute protection they believe that real property should enjoy. Taking Epstein's comments on the Supreme Court's opinion on *eBay Inc. v. MercExchange, L.L.C.*, Menell outlines this intellectual imperialism perfectly:

> Professor Epstein's expansion of his property rights advocacy into the intellectual property domain over the past several years coincides with the growing importance of intangible assets in the modern economy. The digital revolution has displaced General Motors and other manufacturing enterprises from the top of the economic food chain. Knowledge-based companies such as Google, Microsoft, and Apple reflect the new economic order. (2007a, pp. 36–37)

But unlike Lawrence Lessig or other advocates of the balanced copyright movement, Menell goes beyond highlighting the differences between these kinds of property to also note that, even with so-called real property, absolute ownership comes with a variety of caveats.

Writing in the *Ecology Law Quarterly*, Menell notes the emergence of the collaborative creation (discussed in the previous chapter) that illustrates the "increasingly interdependent nature of information ecosystems," which "points away from the PRM's [Property Rights Movement's] conception of property" (2007b, p. 753). But not only is it a bad fit; because we are now able to see the ways in which communities on social media, in open access publishing, and in the free software movement (Benkler 2002, 2007) are able to create, produce, distribute, and maintain culture without the dogmatic insistence on private property rights,

> [by] expanding the property tent to encompass intellectual property, property rights enthusiasts run the risk of diluting the distinctive attributes of real property that brought it special attention at the founding of the nation. Such a conception has been on the decline and the growing importance of intellectual property seems likely to hasten that trend. As Justice Benjamin Cardozo remarked in describing the development of water rights in the American West, "[h]ere we have the conscious departure from a known rule, and the deliberate adoption of a new one, in obedience to the promptings of a social need so obvious and so insistent as to overrun the ancient channel and cut a new one for itself." The rise of intellectual property, like water resources, highlights both the complexity and interdependence of resources in mod-

> ern societies. Efforts to shoehorn legal protection for such resources into the real property mold will undoubtedly fail and may well hasten the demise of the rigid conception of private property rights. (Menell 2007b, p. 753)

I imagine that it will take a bit more to encourage a broad movement to turn against the neoliberal vision of property per se, but as I contend in the Introduction, it is certainly the case that we are seeing the pushback against neoliberal globalization as a whole. The question on the table appears to be whether this emergent "double movement" for social protection—seen in the Donald Trump administration's claims to economic nationalism—will be able to preserve the progressive gains of the "triple movements" of the liberation movements of the 1960s. In short, will we be able to have a progressive form of social protection—a New Deal that would work for everyone—or will reactionary protectionism preserve privilege and property?

One Statue, "Both Sides," and the Next Triple Movement

Here, I must pause and assume that, if you have reached this point in the book, you are at least mildly sympathetic to a socialist perspective, or at least you see the value in fostering what Stuart Hall calls a more humane, democratic society. We see some potential for a hegemonic crisis in this culture of property and the possibility that any resistance to it will be implicated in the dramatic rise of fascism that appears to be marching forward with great speed. This development means reviving the call for the abolition of slavery—as Qiu so helpfully outlines in his book *Goodbye iSlave* (2016)—and restoring the commons to ensure that the formal abolition is functional. Yet for this shift to be successful in a global space shot through with racial and regional divisions, this call must also appeal to those who falsely believe that the current mode of production has something to offer them due to the privileges and prejudices generated by the ideological apparatuses to legitimate the culture of property almost from its beginning. To return to the framework set up in the Introduction, following Nancy Fraser, we must articulate a politics and culture that can restore the double movement of social protection and the triple movement of emancipation without succumbing to the reaction against either. IPR are only one of the institutions that will need to be seriously revised, but clearly the global elite understand IPR to be central to the continuation of this mode of production.

As an illustration of these strategic limits, the conundrum we face, and the ways in which both are intercalated with the issues of property, culture, and power discussed in this book, take the protests (and counter-protests) that took place in Charlottesville, Virginia, on August 12, 2017, over the removal of a statue of Robert E. Lee. There are many dimensions to explore, some of which I have clearly neglected throughout this book. Most obviously, I have not focused nearly enough on the ways in which real property and IP are interpenetrated with issues of race, gender, and sexuality. I have traced some of these traits in my previous book (Johnson Andrews 2016) and could have written a much longer book here to evaluate the issues of property and class in a more intersectional way.

For instance, there is a direct connection to the racist forms of segregation that this statue is meant to celebrate, which, as Richard Rothstein (2017) has chronicled, is clearly evident in the ways in which real property—that is, real estate—was restricted along color lines. The process he examines—which involves laws and policy decisions passed by local, state, and federal governments—began in the 1920s, around which time the number of statues like this one rose precipitously, according to the Southern Poverty Law Center (Parks 2017). This *de jure* segregation was legal, as was the effective disenfranchisement of African Americans for more than one hundred years after their supposed emancipation. Statues like this one were meant not as a celebration of "tradition" or, as Trump declared, "culture" but as a warning, one perhaps best summarized by the now-infamous chant of the white supremacists who gathered, nearly a century after its erection, to protest the removal of the Lee statue: you will not replace us.

Charlottesville provides another connection along these lines: James Buchanan and R. H. Coase worked here when the latter wrote his article on social cost. Buchanan was invited here, as Nancy MacLean documents, to help start what we can now call a Law and Economics program that would "'train a line of new thinkers' in how to argue against those seeking to impose an 'increasing role of government in economic and social life'" (2017, p. xvi). Chief among the government incursions that concerned Buchanan's patrons (if not Buchanan himself) was the then-recent ruling on school desegregation. The implications of the ruling—which effectively voided states' rights arguments along with the notion of "separate but equal"—were especially troubling:

> It was not difficult for either Darden or Buchanan to imagine how a court might now rule if presented with evidence of the state of Virginia's archaic labor relations, its measures to suppress voting, or its efforts to buttress the power of reactionary rural whites by underrepresenting the moderate voters of the cities and suburbs of Northern Virginia. (Ibid., p. 12)

Buchanan saw this threat less in terms of the government per se and more in the possibility that social movements—such as the "labor monopoly movement," aka unions—would demand that the government intervene on their behalf. He called this democratic dynamic (whereby citizens demand something of their elected officials) "government corruption." "The enemy," recounts MacLean, "became 'the collective order,' a code phrase for organized social and political groups that looked to the government" (2017, p. 23).

MacLean's description of Buchanan's perspective accords with my account of the Law and Economics movement's Lockean conception of liberty, which puts the breaks on democracy in the protection of property. But MacLean is helpful in highlighting the uniquely racist ways in which this ideology has been articulated in the American context: through John C. Calhoun. For not only did the U.S. law of the twentieth century make it harder for black people to own property; the same legal system made it possible for black people to be owned as property. Calhoun, a South Carolina senator after serving as vice president in the 1820s, aimed to preserve his defense of private property rights against the meddling abolitionist agitators: whipping his slaves or otherwise disciplining his labor force "fell under the heading of the property rights that Calhoun was trying to make absolute" (MacLean 2017, p. 45). She notes that two recent George Mason University professors allege that Calhoun, Buchanan, and by extension the Law and Economics movement that I critique in Chapter 3 were united in their concern with the "failure of democracy to preserve liberty" (ibid., p. 35).

MacLean's book became a lightning rod in the weeks after it was released—a few weeks before the Charlottesville protests—particularly for her suggestion that Buchanan's support of segregation was racially motivated. One critic is familiar from Chapter 3: David Bernstein. Bernstein claims that MacLean misrepresents his own fondness for the *Lochner*-era court, a claim explored (and basically refuted) in that chapter (Bernstein 2017). But more importantly, he does not seriously refute her overall claim, featured in the title of the book, that Buchanan and others wanted to put "democracy in chains." In fact, in trying to address Buchanan's motivation for helping craft an ideology that aided Virginia's struggle against desegregation, he characterizes *Brown* as an "anti-majoritarian, anti-democratic supreme court decision" (ibid.). In short, Buchanan was not simultaneously antidemocratic and anti-*Brown*: he was just the former.

This point is important for considering the dynamic on the ground in Charlottesville and the dynamic of progressive neoliberalism at large. Michael Munger, a colleague of MacLean's at Duke University and a scholar in

Buchanan's intellectual tradition, elaborates further on these dynamics in his response to the book, saying that MacLean herself is likely antidemocratic on this point as well:

> Jim Crow was a majority rule policy. The Constitution, or at least the Bill of Rights and Amendments 13–15, exist precisely to *suppress* the murderous and racist impulses of majorities. [. . .] Buchanan often rightly said, nobody believes in unlimited majority rule. Democracy is and must be a balancing of, on the one hand, the rights of minorities, and, on the other, the ability of the majority to have its way within the domain established as "political" by the constitution. (Munger 2017; emphasis original)

Munger's response is largely beside the point in relation to Buchanan and desegregation. He might well have supported the school choice movement and the voucher system in a "moral commitment to individual liberty" (MacLean 2017, p. 56), but, in the context of Virginia, which used this system to continue to educate white students in segregated schools nearly a decade after *Brown*, it is a thoroughly racist morality of individual liberty. It took two more Supreme Court rulings, the Civil Rights Act of 1964, and the Elementary and Secondary Education Act of 1965 to finally desegregate Virginia's schools and give black students any hope of receiving a quality education.

But it is also the case that Buchanan and the Law and Economics tradition more generally are not overtly concerned with race as a primary issue: they, like Ireton, have an eye to property. But, as George Lipsitz argues, "White supremacy is usually less a matter of direct, referential, and snarling contempt and more a system for protecting the privileges of whites by denying communities of color opportunities for asset accumulation and upward mobility. Whiteness is invested in, like property, but it is also a means of accumulating property and keeping it from others" (2006, p. viii). In this sense, the argument for "individual liberty" in a class-dominated, white-supremacist, patriarchal society effectively supports the status quo. As Robert Hale puts it in relation to class, "There is no a priori reason for regarding planned governmental intervention in the economic sphere as inimical to economic liberty, or even to that special form of it known as free enterprise" (B. Fried 1998, p. 36). The same could be said for policies of active desegregation, reparations, and affirmative action.

Here, one of the bright spots missed in the coverage of the events in Charlottesville is that, in the deliberations over whether the statue should be removed, the city council also approved a $4 million reparations package. Wes Bellamy, the African American vice mayor and youngest city council member ever elected in Charlottesville, spearheaded both efforts:

> All of this is about equity. We need equity, and not equality. Those are two different things. Equity is giving everyone what they need in order to have the same playing field. Equality is just giving everyone the same thing. I don't want equality. I want us to have equity. And we're going to push for equity in every space, whether that's public parks, whether that's in our city budget. (Charlottesville VA Backs "Reparations" 2017)

Bellamy is not alone in this revived push for equity and social justice. The tools of collaboration and social coproduction praised by Lessig and others in the previous chapter are now being used to critique the white-supremacist culture that is as deeply embedded—if not mutually constituted—with the culture of property in U.S. society. As Keeanga-Yamahtta Taylor captures in the title to her book *From #BlackLivesMatter to Black Liberation*, the Black Lives Matter movement has picked up the mantle of the "Triple Movements" of the 1960s. It is merging the nonviolent organizing techniques of the civil rights era with the multimedia, networked communications of today to great effect.

But, as Angela Nagle points out in her book, *Kill All Normies* (2017), this online culture has also spawned the violent subcultures of reactionary white males, many of whom identify with the alt-right. Most of the leaders of the "Unite the Right" march in Charlottesville were able to amplify their message through YouTube, social media, podcasts, and websites. Nagle traces some of this movement's members from Reddit, Anonymous, and 4chan, saying they "had little in the way of a coherent commitment to conservative thought or politics but shared an anti-PC impulse and a common aesthetic sensibility" (2017, p. 24). This nascent movement, in turn, was mobilized in the Gamergate saga, which highlighted the extremely vulgar gender politics of the moment:

> Gamergate brought gamers, rightist chan culture, anti-feminism and the online far right closer to mainstream discussion and it also politicized a broad group of young people, mostly boys, who organized tactics around the idea of fighting back against the culture war being waged by the cultural left. (Ibid., p. 30)

Keeanga-Yamahtta Taylor has been one of the most recent victims of their tactics, forcing her to cancel several speaking appearances due to threats of being shot or lynched. But in contradiction to the supposed hegemony of the "cultural left," as Sarah Taylor (2017) notes, her cancelations received far less attention than those of our dear friend Charles Murray (see Chapter 1), who merely faced picketing college students.

This cohort of what I call the "counter triple movement" does not appear to have any overt complaints about globalization or IP. In contrast, Arlie Russell Hochschild's *Strangers in Their Own Land* (2016) highlights the ways in which many on the right see the problems of economic degradation—supposedly caused by such treaties as the North American Free Trade Agreement (NAFTA) or the potential Trans-Pacific Partnership (TPP)—on a continuum with divisions of race and urban elites. According to Hochschild, these voters—many of whom might have voted for Barack Obama's vision of "Hope and Change"—are more concerned with being left behind economically. In this sense, they could be part of the double movement, but they have been led to believe what she calls a "deep story" that helps explain their experience as victims of the triple movement. As she puts it, "The deep story of the right, the feels-as-if story, corresponds to a real structural squeeze. People want to achieve the American Dream, but for a mixture of reasons feel they are being held back, and this leads people of the right to feel frustrated, angry, and betrayed by the government" (2016, loc. 2252). This feeling of betrayal comes from the deep story that says "Others"—blacks, women, immigrants, refugees—are getting preferential treatment, "cutting in line," and someone (liberals?) in the government is helping them. But, ironically, because its members are led to distrust the government, "the right sees the free market"—the very free market that has led to a stagnation of wages and increasing inequality over the past thirty years—"as its ally against the powerful alliance of the federal government and the takers" (ibid., loc. 2321).

These members of the right quite literally represent Steve Bannon's "forgotten man." The economic nationalist agenda he purports to believe is premised on helping these "working hobbits," and "deplorables" once again take their place at the front of the line: to have, in Buchanan's terms, their personal liberty (aka white male privilege) restored. This double movement is contingent on undermining the triple movements by repressing minorities and especially immigrants. But it appears to be a counter triple movement only insofar as the liberation of the "Other" is a threat to their own security.

While the Gamergate goons do not appear to have a great deal of concern over these bread-and-butter issues, they fit into the larger political—and cultural—strategy for Trump, and especially Bannon. The pivotal figure here is Milo Yiannopoulos, who used Gamergate "to shoot to mainstream celebrity status" (Nagle 2017, p. 30). Bannon, as *Breitbart*'s editor, hired him as a columnist

> to entice the online legions into the *Breitbart* fold. "I realized Milo could connect with these kids right away," [Bannon] said. "You can activate that army. They come in through Gamergate or whatever and then get turned onto politics and Trump." In this way, Breitbart became an incubator of alt-right political energy. (Green 2017, pp. 137–138)

This energy, in turn, could be harnessed to build online campaigns, like those Nagle charts in her book. Importantly, though, this movement was not, as Nagel assumes, another version of the "Leaderless Revolution": it was a well-organized operation, receiving hefty infusions of cash from the right-wing billionaire Robert Mercer, whose firm Cambridge Analytica also helped manage the microtargeted online campaigns for Trump and Brexit.

Few of these alt-right or 4chan denizens were present in Charlottesville. They might have helped fertilize seeds sown by the neo-Nazi and white-supremacist groups who showed up, but dedicated groups, including Vanguard America, actually have provided a more explicit linkage between the right-wing double movement and the counter triple movement. If that group sounds familiar, it is likely because it was aligned with the man who murdered Democratic Socialist activist Heather Heyer with his car. Vanguard America's manifesto reads as a twisted indictment of progressive neoliberalism, infused with juvenile rantings about racial supremacy and "Blood and Soil." I quote at length in the following paragraphs, as its website has been taken offline:

> A multicultural nation is no nation at all, but a collection of smaller ethnic nations ruled over by an overbearing tyrannical state. Our America is to be a nation exclusively for the White American peoples who out of the barren hills, empty plains, and vast mountains forged the most powerful nation to ever have existed. Vanguard America stands indomitably opposed to the tyranny of globalism and capitalism, a system under which nations are stripped of their heritage and their people are turned into nothing more than units of cheap, expendable labor. Vanguard America, and our nationalist allies across the Western world, see a world of nations ruled by their own people, for their own people. (Vanguard America n.d.)

On one level, the reaction to the liberation movements that Fraser discusses as "the Triple Movement" is front and center. Cultural Marxism and the Frankfurt School are also blamed for the degradation of the culture, the isolation and atomization of white men, and "[rendering] our women race mixers and promiscuous rags." (They offer no citation for this claim. I certainly have not read that essay by Theodor Adorno; perhaps it is Herbert Marcuse.) But their screeds are also interspersed with evidence of the double movement. The arguments here about "globalists" are not-so-thinly veiled rearticulations of Nazi-era anti-Semitic stereotypes. Further down, they spell out this connection more clearly, saying, "America should strive for a truly national economy. An economy that is self-contained, and free from the influence of international corporations, led by a rootless group of international Jews."

Although Vanguard America criticizes the left, it is telling that the ideological commonplaces that its followers rely on to critique contemporary corporate globalization are recycled from the 1930s. But in any case, this pattern fits into the frame of Karl Polanyi's understanding of the double movement, even if, like Bannon and Hochschild's informants, they have a romanticized view of the role of the free market. On this point, we return, circuitously, to the issue of IP and the global implementation of the culture of property. Here, we should look to Trump's response to an activist's death and to the actions and statements of his administration in the days following it.

Trump was rightly castigated for his statement on August 12, 2017, when he said that there was violence "on both sides" at the Charlottesville protest, especially after the broadcast of images of heavily armed militia in military hardware facing off against barely armed antifascist demonstrators. There are not many things most Americans will agree to, but denouncing Nazis is a pretty easy call. And, of course, the fact that an unhinged white supremacist committed the murder would seem to mitigate against much nuance, particularly for a speaker so prone to hyperbole.

Clearly, Trump was speaking to his base in that statement. The antiliberation, counter triple movement supporters have introduced laws in North Dakota, Texas, Florida, North Carolina, and Tennessee that would protect drivers who kill protesters, largely in response to the Black Lives Matter and Dakota Access Pipeline protests (Grabar 2017). But the rest of his statement was obviously mocked for being off topic: I would argue that it told the deep story that Hochschild recognized among her informants.

After gently condemning the protesters "on both sides," Trump pivoted to focus on the positive:

> Our country is doing very well in so many ways. We have record—just absolute record employment. We have unemployment, the lowest it's been in almost 17 years. We have companies pouring into our country. Foxconn and car companies, and so many others, they're coming back to our country. We're renegotiating trade deals to make them great for our country and great for the American worker. (Cillizza 2017)

In other words, for those not enticed by the overt appeal to reactionary white supremacy, perhaps an appeal to economic nationalism might just help "Unite the Right."

The latter became the theme for the rest of the week, save when Trump was forced to revisit (and then double down on) his "both sides" comment. On Monday, August 14, Kenneth C. Frazier, the African American chair and CEO of Merck, a pharmaceutical company, became the first executive from Trump's American Manufacturing Council to resign in protest over that statement. Trump's response was to tweet, "'Now that Ken Frazier of Merck Pharma has resigned from President's Manufacturing Council, he will have more time to LOWER RIPOFF DRUG PRICES!'" (Thrush 2017). On Tuesday, August 15, Secretary of Commerce Wilbur Ross published an op-ed in the *Financial Times* titled "American Genius Is under Attack from China." He asserts, "Intellectual property theft and expropriation costs US businesses up to $600bn a year," and says that the following day, Trump will direct the U.S. trade representative to begin an investigation of "Chinese policies, practices, or actions that may be harming US companies' intellectual property, innovation and technology by encouraging or requiring the transfer of technologies to China" (W. Ross 2017). And the following day, on August 16, 2017, Bannon participated in a recklessly on-the-record interview with Robert Kuttner, advocating a trade war on China, beginning with Section 301 complaints regarding IPR: "'To me,' Bannon said, 'the economic war with China is everything. And we have to be maniacally focused on that'" (Kuttner 2017).

Of the white supremacists and ethno-nationalists he has housed and fed for the past few years, so recently seen marching with torches, chanting racist slogans, and killing with cars, Bannon says, "'It's losers. It's a fringe element. [. . . W]e gotta help crush it.'" Bannon recites the catechism that any mainstream commentator would have believed a decade before, but he is not a true believer, supporting such policies as a reduction of legal immigration, the travel ban, the end of Deferred Action for Childhood Arrivals (DACA) and praising, as he (and Attorney General Jeff Sessions) did on his show, the ethnic quotas in the U.S. immigration policy of 1924, a policy that James Q.

Whitman (2017) says helped inspire the Nazi jurists' own anti-Semitic race laws. But as the political landscape above illustrates, like the supporters of the National Socialists of the 1930s, the resurgent right is only marginally concerned with race per se. It is a signifier of the failures of globalization from the perspective of the Middle American, straight, Christian, white man. But the more the organs of progressive neoliberalism kick back on race, even as they insist on the continuation of the status quo by any means necessary, the more they fuel the counter triple movement articulated to the emergent double movement. Or, as Bannon puts it, "'The Democrats' . . . 'the longer they talk about identity politics, I got 'em. I want them to talk about racism every day. If the left is focused on race and identity, and we go with economic nationalism, we can crush the Democrats'" (Kuttner 2017).

By the end of the week, on August 18, 2017, Bannon was no longer employed by the White House and was back at his job as the editor of *Breitbart*. His return coincided with the website's first reaction to the wave of corporate CEOs and nongovernmental organization (NGO) leaders exiting Trump's two business advisory panels, leading Trump to dissolve both. The *New York Times* contextualized the exodus alongside recent corporate threats—in Arizona, North Carolina, and Texas—to boycott states passing antigay or antitrans legislation, saying the business community is "testing its moral voice more forcefully than ever" (Gelles 2017). Cultural issues, it seems, are even more important than market imperatives—or, perhaps, they are increasingly the same thing.

It is a welcome development, to be sure, and one that indirectly affirms one of the more noxious libertarian canards of recent years, for which Rand Paul made headlines when he said he would not have supported the 1964 Civil Rights Act because it forced private businesses to serve those they did not want to. Instead, the government should have left it to the market and the conscious of the community: "In a free society we will tolerate boorish people who have abhorrent behavior, but if we're civilized people we publicly criticize that and don't belong to those groups or associate with those people" (Roth 2010b). This position is supported by Bernstein, who says, "The foundation of libertarian thinking is private property as a limit on state action. [. . .] So if a private business chooses to discriminate, a typical libertarian would say that's a business owner's right to do so" (Roth 2010a). The mainstream reaction was to find this position as illogical today as when Barry Goldwater first popularized it in 1964. But with the corporate support of progressive positions, the logic seems finally affirmed: the market has finally delivered on its liberal promises. Of course, this delivery has followed five decades of state support for the cultural position, but libertarians should take their little victories where they can.

Meanwhile, at *Breitbart*, John Carney's interpretation of these corporate CEOs' moral position went on to affirm the double movement in the counter triple movement—and Bannon's assertion that economic nationalism is the strategically superior position: "Corporate Antifa: CEOs Revolt Against American Democracy" (Carney 2017). Democracy here is represented by the figure of Trump, who is the elected leader of the country these CEOs agreed to serve. In our topsy-turvy political scene, Carney compares this corporate action to the era of "Robber Barons" when "Railroad mogul Cornelius Vanderbilt once bosted [*sic*], 'Law! What do I care about law? Haint I got the power?'" (ibid.). He continues:

> Vanderbilt's son William would go even further, announcing that his motto was "The People be Damned!" But the people wouldn't be damned. Within a generation, they were electing progressive politicians who broke up the 19th century equivalents of today's corporate giants. This is a clarifying moment in American politics. The confederacy of the media institutions, the American left, and Corporate America has aligned itself against the populist uprising that brought Trump to the White House. The battle lines are clear. (Ibid.)

It is absurd to imagine that Trump will end up as a trust-busting progressive, but his hawkish stance on trade appears to be cut from some derivative of its protectionist cloth. In any case, for our purposes, it is more important to see the ways in which these political positions are articulated against the backdrop of progressive neoliberalism.

The challenge, therefore, is to articulate a counterargument that manages to remain true—and continue to expand—the liberation movements for race, gender, sexuality, prison abolition, and indigenous rights that arose in the 1960s, but to do so from a refounded form of social protection that combats the unprecedented precarity and inequality of class that is toxic to our long-term survival and inimical to our ability to maintain solidarity on any of these fronts. In short, this challenge requires dismantling the reified culture of property that remains fundamentally unexamined in American society even as we confront the resurgent reaction of patriarchal, heteronormative, white supremacy.

Labor, Global Production, and Intellectual Property

But as fraught as our domestic politics are, the international scene compounds them. Here, the contradictions of the social division of labor that haunt the "democratic paradox" are global in scale, harder to square with a simple move to economic nationalism, and, as suggested at the start of the chapter, tenuously secured through IPR. To illustrate this difficulty, note Secretary of Commerce Ross's (2017) explanation of the problem the United States faces in its relationship with China on the topic of IPR: "Rather than building a globally competitive free market economy in order to compete, China has chosen instead to compel American companies that want to operate in China to turn over proprietary technology and intellectual property." As in the Vanguard America manifesto, Ross's understanding of the "free market" is decidedly limited, but it ironically echoes Hale's reappropriation of the term from the libertarians of his day.

The use of the word "compel" here is curious—after all, no company is forced to go to China. Until two decades ago, in fact, almost no American company did: only the very structured opening of the market internally in the 1980s and the acceptance of China into the WTO in the late 1990s made it possible. Offshoring production to China was a conscious strategy from which U.S. businesses disproportionately profited for the better part of the next decade (see Harvey 2005). Taking advantage of the cheap labor and lax enforcement of labor, health, and environmental standards was hailed as the next chapter in the ruthless genius of the neoliberal corporate playbook. It is counterintuitive to imagine that China now holds the upper hand, not because it has helped finance this expansion but simply because it has made certain demands for businesses that want to operate within its borders.

As Barry Lynn (2002) has noted, the spread of skills and knowledge was the advantage supposedly accruing to countries that accepted U.S. corporate investment as part of the bargain of globalization. But even more than a decade ago, Lynn identifies the potential geopolitical and political economic outcome of this arrangement:

> At the end of the day, who "owns" the actual semiconductor plant [or, we should now add, the patents for those semiconductors] matters far less than where the plant is located, because whoever physically controls the production of semiconductors can paralyze thousands of the world's assembly lines with the flick of a switch. Beijing need not even declare a blockade of Taiwan, backed by a threat to use its missiles, in order to cause economic havoc. If it succeeds in luring enough key manufacturing capacity, Beijing will need only to threaten a peaceful closure of its own border, a sit-down strike if you will, organized by the most powerful labor syndicate in the world. (Ibid., p. 40)

And, at the end of the day, this power is what Ross means by "compel." Despite the fact that Apple owns the patents to specific components of the iPhone or iPad, despite the fact that its trademarks and copyrights aid in an unprecedented tax-avoidance scheme that has accrued the company nearly $200 billion in offshore accounts, China houses the workers capable of producing its products. This labor, the supply chains in the country, the rare earth elements available in nearby mines, are all essential to Apple's timely production of the next utopian device. And, as with the Ecuadorian film distributors or the Bolivian textile manufacturers, the only means Apple has of maintaining its superiority is through the casually enforced laws of IPR.

But despite Ross's pleadings, even this leverage will not suffice for long. The Chinese company Huawei recently surpassed Apple as the second-largest cell phone manufacturer in the world, after Samsung. This title is really a misnomer, however, because unlike Huawei, Apple owns almost none of its manufacturing capacity. Like Huawei, the tacit knowledge for the assembly of its major products resides in the minds and hands of Chinese workers. As Frederick Winslow Turner recognized in the early twentieth century—and as Ross is wont to admit today—the power of this labor confronts the corporate owners. This power, in the end, is what increasingly compels Apple, Boeing, and other Fortune 500 companies to do business in China—and to provide those workers with the technical schematics and legal permissions to assemble their products.

American citizens should resist the temptation to fall for Ross's call to arms. For in the end, the advancement of Chinese corporations and workers was supposed to be the result of the globalization process. The fact that the "knowledge economy" here at home has failed to develop at anything like the necessary scale was all but predictable for anyone looking at the ways in which the social division of labor works in any factory or factory town. Just as we should resist the impulse to side with the reactionary counter triple movement, closing borders to immigrants or deporting those formerly covered by DACA, we should also resist the attempt to use IPR to enforce a paradoxically autarkic imperialism that attempts to maintain the U.S. position at the top of the international division of labor and power.

Instead, we should attempt to organize for a new, postcapitalist world, seeing the ways in which our collective labors are unjustly appropriated by corporate conglomerates across the borders between nations and the increasingly hazy division between mental and material labor, cyberspace and meatspace. As Ellen Meiksins Wood reminds us, the more cherished goal of enlightened modernity was supposed to be the improvement of humanity, not property (2002, p. 189). As we live in a world with fewer jobs available for

U.S. workers, we should not attempt to wrest them back from China; instead, we should reimagine our culture of property and reorganize the distribution of the resources such that fewer people here or there *need* to work. Or, in James Livingston's more succinct version: "Fuck work" (2016, loc. 44).

Although the calls for full automation and a universal basic income (UBI) (Srnicek and Williams 2016) may be premature—and problematic in the ways in which they subtly maintain the very social division of labor that is the root of the problems we face—the movement for something like these changes is clearly possible. But as with the imposition of capitalism in its early days, this call is far more of a political and cultural problem than an economic or technological one. As evidence, take the recent attempt by the rabidly antilabor Wisconsin governor Scott Walker to bring a Foxconn factory—the company that manufactures Apple's products—to his state. To facilitate the bargain, he offered the company $3 billion in tax incentives for the thirteen thousand jobs it would bring. As *Reason* points out, this sum is the equivalent to $231,000 per job (Britschgi 2017), or almost $20,000 per worker annually for each job paying $55,000 (Schwartz, Cohen, and Davis 2017).

If the state of Wisconsin—and especially Walker, one of the most public proponents of the Tea Party agenda—can be persuaded to fork over $20,000 to subsidize workers for a Chinese corporation, then it is not unreasonable to imagine that it could be persuaded to simply give that amount (which is in the ballpark of figures suggested for a UBI) to its citizens; it is simply a matter of organizing power in that direction. On the other hand, as Qiu has extensively documented, Foxconn's labor and human rights practices in China are some of the most reprehensible in the world: suppressing wages, threatening journalists, and doing nothing to improve "a merciless 'flexible' labor management regime, which [has] led to the suicide of several Foxconn workers since June 2007" (2012, p. 182). This regime of accumulation is secured by the repressive apparatus of the Chinese state and the legal suture of global IPR.

How will transplanting this model of labor management to the U.S. Midwest transform it? What will be the response of the everyday culture to the imposition of what will be only the latest regime of merciless labor management? Thanks in part to Foxconn and its Chinese workers, we have more tools available than ever for organizing that culture. Even in the supposedly controlled Chinese media environment, "the new wave of labor-capital clashes was triggered by the suicides—helpless individual acts in the beginning but with powerful butterfly effects within and beyond Foxconn—the tools of everyday connectivity were converted, almost instantly, into tools of labor solidarity," with cell phone cameras and text messaging helping workers organize strikes at a Chinese Honda factory; and concerts, folk theater performances, and "most importantly hundreds of poems expressing their emotions at the time [. . .] easily circulated through mobile phone (especially through SMS) and Internet among workers and concerned citizens" (Qiu 2012, p. 184). The key now is to penetrate that great Chinese firewall, to include those workers in our struggle and include ourselves in theirs. As Qiu reminds us:

> No matter how "immaterial" the iPhone culture seems to be, its material dimension is always indispensable, depending, first of all, on the physical labor of Foxconn workers. Labor is also integral to the research and development of the iPhone, the production, testing, and installation of its software, and even the consumption of the fingertip economy. Labor is not a thing. It is a perspective. Only by using this perspective can we start to treat the workers with dignity and extend this dignity though our activities online and offline. (Ibid., p. 186)

IP is one tool among many for dividing not only the fruits of our collective labors but also the laboring classes, undermining our potential solidarity and legitimate demands. But with these emergent tools and platforms, the workers of the world can unite as never before, and thanks to the increasingly punitive, unequal neoliberal state, we truly have little to lose but our chains.

References

Adorno, Theodor W. 2001. *The Culture Industry: Selected Essays on Mass Culture.* 2nd ed. London: Routledge.

Adorno, Theodor W., and Max Horkheimer. 2007. *Dialectic of Enlightenment.* Translated by Edmund Jephcott. Stanford: Stanford University Press.

AFI. 2005. "AFI's 100 Greatest Movie Quotes of All Time." *American Film Institute.* June 21. http://www.afi.com/100years/quotes.aspx.

Aglietta, Michel. 2015. *A Theory of Capitalist Regulation: The US Experience.* Repr. ed. London: Verso.

Aksikas, Jaafar, and Sean Johnson Andrews. 2014. "Neoliberalism, Law and Culture: A Cultural Studies Intervention after 'The Juridical Turn.'" *Cultural Studies* 28 (5–6): 742–780. doi:10.1080/09502386.2014.886479.

———, eds. 2016. *Cultural Studies and the "Juridical Turn": Culture, Law, and Legitimacy in the Era of Neoliberal Capitalism.* London: Routledge.

Allen, Robert C. 1982. "The Efficiency and Distributional Consequences of Eighteenth Century Enclosures." *Economic Journal* 92 (368): 937–953. doi:10.2307/2232676.

Althusser, Louis. 2001. *Lenin and Philosophy, and Other Essays.* Translated by Ben Brewster. New York: Monthly Review Press.

———. 2007. *Politics and History: Montesquieu, Rousseau, Marx.* Translated by Ben Brewster. London: Verso.

———. 2014. *On the Reproduction of Capitalism: Ideology and Ideological State Apparatuses.* Translated by G. M. Goshgarian. London: Verso.

Amadae, S. M. 2003. *Rationalizing Capitalist Democracy: The Cold War Origins of Rational Choice Liberalism.* Chicago: University of Chicago Press.

Anderson, Benedict. 2006. *Imagined Communities: Reflections on the Origin and Spread of Nationalism.* Rev. ed. London: Verso.

Anderson, Perry. 1964. "Origins of the Present Crisis." *New Left Review* 1 (23): 26–53.
———. 1976. "The Antinomies of Antonio Gramsci." *New Left Review* 1 (100): 5–78.
———. 1979. *Lineages of the Absolutist State.* London: Verso.
———. 1996. *Passages from Antiquity to Feudalism.* London: Verso.

Andy. 2016. "RIAA Says YouTube Is Running a DMCA Protection Racket." *TorrentFreak,* April 12. https://torrentfreak.com/riaa-says-youtube-is-running-a-dmca-protection-racket-160412/.

Arnold, Matthew. 2009. *Culture and Anarchy.* Edited by Jane Garnett. Reissue ed. Oxford: Oxford University Press.

Arvidsson, Adam. 2006. *Brands: Meaning and Value in Media Culture.* London: Routledge.
———. 2008. "The Ethical Economy of Customer Coproduction." *Journal of Macromarketing* 28 (4): 326–338. doi:10.1177/0276146708326077.

Aufderheide, Patricia, and Peter Jaszi. 2011. *Reclaiming Fair Use: How to Put Balance Back in Copyright.* Chicago: University of Chicago Press.

Baker, Philip. 2007. *The Levellers: The Putney Debates.* London: Verso.

Band, Jonathan. 2009. "The Long and Winding Road to the Google Books Settlement." *John Marshall Review of Intellectual Property* 9:227–329. http://bit.ly/q46VDf.

Barakat, Matthew. 2016. "George Mason University Becomes a Favorite of Charles Koch." *AP NEWS,* April 1. https://apnews.com/613470e79eb64a5f9a4880996e0fd7c5.

Baran, Paul, and Paul Sweezy. 1966. *Monopoly Capital: An Essay on the American Economic and Social Order.* New York: Monthly Review Press.

Barnouw, Erik. 1990. *Tube of Plenty: The Evolution of American Television.* 2nd ed. New York: Oxford University Press.

Barone, Michael. 2007. *Our First Revolution: The Remarkable British Uprising That Inspired America's Founding Fathers.* New York: Crown.

Barthes, Roland. 1972. *Mythologies.* Translated by Annette Lavers. New York: Farrar, Straus and Giroux.

Baudrillard, Jean. 2006. *The System of Objects.* Translated by James Benedict. 9th ed. London: Verso

Bauwens, Michel. 2009. "Class and Capital in Peer Production." *Capital and Class* 33 (1): 121–141. doi:10.1177/030981680909700107.

Becker, Howard S. 1997. *Outsiders: Studies in the Sociology of Deviance.* New York: Free Press.

Beecher-Monas, Erica. 2002. "Challenging Coase: Socioeconomic Explanations in the First Year Contracts Course." SSRN Scholarly Paper ID 306565. Rochester, NY: Social Science Research Network. https://papers.ssrn.com/abstract=306565.Beecher-Monas

Bell, Daniel. 1962. *The End of Ideology: On the Exhaustion of Political Ideas in the Fifties: With "The Resumption of History in the New Century."* Cambridge, MA: Harvard University Press.

Benjamin, Walter. 1969. *Illuminations: Essays and Reflections.* Edited by Hannah Arendt. Translated by Harry Zohn. New York: Schocken Books.
———. 2008. *The Work of Art in the Age of Its Technological Reproducibility, and Other Writings on Media.* Edited by Michael William Jennings, Brigid Doherty, and Thomas Y. Levin. Cambridge, MA: Harvard University Press.

Benkler, Yochai. 2002. "Coase's Penguin, or, Linux and The Nature of the Firm." *Yale Law Journal* 112 (3): 369–446.

———. 2003. "Freedom in the Commons: Towards a Political Economy of Information." *Duke Law Journal* 52 (6): 1245–1276.

———. 2007. *The Wealth of Networks: How Social Production Transforms Markets and Freedom.* New Haven, CT: Yale University Press.

Bergson, Henri. 1977. *The Two Sources of Morality and Religion.* Translated by R. Ashley Audra and Cloudesley Brereton. New ed. Notre Dame, IN: University of Notre Dame Press.

Berlin, Isaiah. 2002. *Liberty: Incorporating Four Essays on Liberty.* Edited by Henry Hardy. 2nd ed. Oxford: Oxford University Press.

Bernstein, David. 2006. "*Lochner v. New York*: A Centennial Retrospective." SSRN Scholarly Paper ID 918404. Rochester, NY: Social Science Research Network. https://papers.ssrn.com/abstract=918404.

———. 2017. "Yet More Dubious Claims in Nancy MacLean's 'Democracy in Chains.'" *Washington Post*, July 6. https://www.washingtonpost.com/news/volokh-conspiracy/wp/2017/07/06/yet-more-dubious-claims-in-nancy-macleans-democracy-in-chains/.

Blumenthal, Sidney. 1986. *The Rise of the Counter-Establishment.* New York: Crown.

Blyth, Mark. 2002. *Great Transformations: Economic Ideas and Institutional Change in the Twentieth Century.* Cambridge: Cambridge University Press.

Bourdieu, Pierre. 2005. *The Social Structures of the Economy.* Cambridge: Polity.

Boyle, James. 1996. *Shamans, Software, and Spleens: Law and the Construction of the Information Society.* Boston: Harvard University Press.

———. 2003. "The Second Enclosure Movement and the Construction of the Public Domain." *Law and Contemporary Problems* 66 (33): 33–75.

———. 2008. *The Public Domain: Enclosing the Commons of the Mind.* New Haven, CT: Yale University Press.

Braverman, Harry. 1974. *Labor and Monopoly Capital: The Degradation of Work in the Twentieth Century.* New York: Monthly Review Press.

Brennan, Jason. 2017. *Against Democracy.* Ed. with new preface. Princeton, NJ: Princeton University Press.

Brenner, Robert. 2006. *The Economics of Global Turbulence: The Advanced Capitalist Economies from Long Boom to Long Downturn, 1945–2005.* London: Verso.

Britschgi, Christian. 2017. "$3 Billion Foxconn Deal Is Biggest Corporate Subsidy in Wisconsin History—Hit and Run." *Reason.com*, August 1. http://reason.com/blog/2017/08/01/3-billion-foxconn-deals-is-biggest-corpo.

Brooks, David. 2001. *Bobos in Paradise: The New Upper Class and How They Got There.* 1st pbk. ed. New York: Simon and Schuster.

Brown, Paul. 2003. "World's Poor Prefer Fake Designer Gear." *The Guardian*, September 3. http://www.guardian.co.uk/uk/2003/sep/04/clothes.lifeandhealth.

Burgin, Angus. 2012. *The Great Persuasion: Reinventing Free Markets since the Depression.* Cambridge, MA: Harvard University Press

Caplan, Bryan. 2011. *The Myth of the Rational Voter: Why Democracies Choose Bad Policies.* New ed. with a new preface by the author. Princeton, NJ: Princeton University Press.

Carney, John. 2017. "Corporate Antifa: CEOs Revolt Against American Democracy." *Breitbart.com*, August 17. http://www.breitbart.com/big-government/2017/08/17/corporate-antifa-ceos-revolt-against-american-democracy/.

Certeau, Michel de, Luce Giard, and Pierre Mayol. 1998. *The Practice of Everyday Life.* Minneapolis: University of Minnesota Press.

"Charlottesville VA Backs 'Reparations' Fund for Black Residents and Votes to Sell Robert E. Lee Statue." 2017. *Democracy Now,* August 7. https://www.democracynow.org/2017/8/7/charlottesville_va_backs_reparations_fund_for.

Cillizza, Chris. 2017. "Donald Trump's Incredibly Unpresidential Statement on Charlottesville." *CNN Politics,* August 13. http://www.cnn.com/2017/08/12/politics/trump-charlottesville-statement/index.html.

Coase, R. H. 1937. "The Nature of the Firm." *Economica* (New Series) 4 (16): 386–405

———. 1960. "The Problem of Social Cost." *Journal of Law and Economics* 3:1–44.

———. 1988. "The Nature of the Firm: Origin." *Journal of Law, Economics, and Organization* 4 (1): 3–17.

Collins, Jane L. 2003. *Threads: Gender, Labor, and Power in the Global Apparel Industry.* Chicago: University of Chicago Press.

Coombe, Rosemary J. 1998. *The Cultural Life of Intellectual Properties: Authorship, Appropriation, and the Law.* Durham, NC: Duke University Press.

———. 1999. "Culture: Anthropology's Old Vice or International Law's New Virtue?" *Proceedings of the Annual Meeting (American Society of International Law)* 93:261–270. doi:10.2307/25659311.

Couldry, Nick. 2000. *Inside Culture: Re-imagining the Method of Cultural Studies.* Thousand Oaks, CA: Sage Publications.

Cowie, Jefferson. 2016. *The Great Exception: The New Deal and the Limits of American Politics.* Princeton, NJ: Princeton University Press. Kindle.

Davis, Julie Hirschfeld. 2017. "Obama, Out of Office 10 Days, Speaks Out against Immigration Ban." *New York Times,* January 30. https://www.nytimes.com/2017/01/30/us/politics/obama-trump-immigration-ban.html.

Davis, Mike. 1986. *Prisoners of the American Dream: Politics and Economy in the History of the US Working Class.* London: Verso.

Dean, Jodi. 2005. "Communicative Capitalism: Circulation and the Foreclosure of Politics." *Cultural Politics* 1 (1): 51–74. doi:10.2752/174321905778054845.

Debray, Régis. 2000. *Transmitting Culture.* New York: Columbia University Press.

Demsetz, Harold. 1967. "Toward a Theory of Property Rights." *American Economic Review* 57 (2): 347–359.

Denning, Michael. 2004. *Culture in the Age of Three Worlds.* New York: Verso.

de Soto, Hernando. 2000. *The Mystery of Capital: Why Capitalism Triumphs in the West and Fails Everywhere Else.* New York: Basic Books.

Dewey, Caitlin. 2016. "Facebook Fake-News Writer: 'I Think Donald Trump Is in the White House Because of Me.'" *Washington Post,* November 17. https://www.washingtonpost.com/news/the-intersect/wp/2016/11/17/facebook-fake-news-writer-i-think-donald-trump-is-in-the-white-house-because-of-me/.

"Donald Trump." 2016. *Last Week Tonight with John Oliver.* HBO.

Drahos, Peter, and John Braithwaite. 2003. *Information Feudalism: Who Owns the Knowledge Economy?* New York: New Press.

Dreyfuss, Rochelle Cooper. 1990. "Expressive Genericity: Trademarks as Language in the Pepsi Generation." *Notre Dame Law Review* 65:397–424.

Duménil, Gérard, and Dominique Lévy. 2004. *Capital Resurgent: Roots of the Neoliberal Revolution.* Cambridge, MA: Harvard University Press.

El Universo. 2007. "Un cerco para los CD piratas." April 17.

Epstein, Richard. 1985. *Takings: Private Property and the Power of Eminent Domain.* Rev. ed. Cambridge, MA: Harvard University Press.

———. 1997. "Law and Economics: Its Glorious Past and Cloudy Future." *University of Chicago Law Review* 64 (4): 1167–1174.

———. 2001. "Intellectual Property: Old Boundaries and New Frontiers." *Indiana Law Journal* 76 (4): 803–827. http://www.repository.law.indiana.edu/ilj/vol76/iss4/1.

———. 2006a. *How Progressives Rewrote the Constitution.* Washington, DC: Cato Institute.

———. 2006b. *The Structural Unity of Real and Intellectual Property.* Washington, DC: Progress and Freedom Foundation.

Foster, Hal. 1985. *Recodings: Art, Spectacle, Cultural Politics.* Port Townsend, WA: Bay Press.

Foucault, Michel. 1980. *The History of Sexuality.* Vol. 1. New York: Vintage Books.

Fraser, Nancy. 2013a. *Fortunes of Feminism: From State-Managed Capitalism to Neoliberal Crisis.* New York: Verso. Kindle.

———. 2013b. "A Triple Movement?" *New Left Review* 2 (81): 119–132.

Frazier, Barbara J, Mozhdeh Bruss, and Lynn Johnson. 2004. "Barriers to Bolivian Participation in the Global Apparel Industry." *Journal of Fashion Marketing and Management* 8 (4): 437–451.

Freier, Anne. 2017. "Facebook Has Acquired Copyright Protection Start-up Source3." *MobyAffiliates*, July 28. http://www.mobyaffiliates.com/blog/facebook-has-acquired-copyright-protection-start-up-source3/.

Fried, Barbara H. 1998. *The Progressive Assault on Laissez Faire: Robert Hale and the First Law and Economics Movement.* Cambridge, MA: Harvard University Press.

Fried, Charles. 2000. "Review: Perfect Freedom or Perfect Control?" *Harvard Law Review* 114 (2): 606–638.

Gehl, Robert William. 2013. "What's on Your Mind? Social Media Monopolies and Noopower." *First Monday* 18 (3). http://firstmonday.org/ojs/index.php/fm/article/view/4618.

Gelles, David. 2017. "The Moral Voice of Corporate America." *New York Times*, August 19. https://www.nytimes.com/2017/08/19/business/moral-voice-ceos.html.

Gibson, James. 2007. "Risk Aversion and Rights Accretion in Intellectual Property Law." *Yale Law Journal* 116 (5): 882–951.

Giles, Jeff. 2007. "Lionsgate Says: 'Nobody Puts Baby on a T-Shirt.'" *Rotten Tomatoes*, August 22. http://www.rottentomatoes.com/m/dirty_dancing/news/1664954/.

Goldstone, Jack A. 1983. "Capitalist Origins of the English Revolution: Chasing a Chimera." *Theory and Society* 12 (2): 143–180.

Grabar, Henry. 2017. "'Run Them Down.'" *Slate*, August 14. http://www.slate.com/articles/business/metropolis/2017/08/driving_into_crowds_of_protesters_was_a_right_wing_fantasy_long_before_charlottesville.html.

Gramsci, Antonio. 1972. *Selections from the Prison Notebooks of Antonio Gramsci.* Edited by Quintin Hoare. New York: International Publishers.

Grant, Melissa Gira. 2014. *Playing the Whore: The Work of Sex Work.* London: Verso.

Green, Joshua. 2017. *Devil's Bargain: Steve Bannon, Donald Trump, and the Storming of the Presidency.* New York: Penguin Press.

Grossman, Lev. 2006. "You—Yes, You—Are TIME's Person of the Year." *Time*, December 25. http://content.time.com/time/magazine/article/0,9171,1570810,00.html.

Guardian, The. 2007. "Lawsuit Launched over 'Stolen' Dirty Dancing Line." August 22. http://www.theguardian.com/film/2007/aug/22/1.

Habermas, Jürgen. 1989. *The Structural Transformation of the Public Sphere: An Inquiry into a Category of Bourgeois Society.* Cambridge: Massachusetts Institute of Technology Press.

———. 1998. *Between Facts and Norms: Contributions to a Discourse Theory of Law and Democracy.* Translated by William Rehg. Cambridge: Massachusetts Institute of Technology Press. Kindle.

Hale, Robert L. 1920. "Law Making by Unofficial Minorities." *Columbia Law Review* 20 (4): 451–456.

———. 1923. "Coercion and Distribution in a Supposedly Non-coercive State." *Political Science Quarterly* 38 (3): 470–493.

Hall, Stuart. 1980a. "Cultural Studies: Two Paradigms." *Media, Culture and Society* 2 (1): 57–72. doi:10.1177/016344378000200106.

———. 1980b. "Encoding/Decoding." In *Culture, Media, Language: Working Papers in Cultural Studies, 1972–1979*, edited by Stuart Hall, Dorothy Hobson, Andrew Lowe, Paul Willis, 128–139. London: Hutchinson.

———. 1982. "The Rediscovery of 'Ideology': Return of the Repressed in Media Studies." In *Culture, Society, and the Media*, edited by Tony Bennett, James Curran, Michael Gurevitch, and Janet Woollacott, 56–90. London: Methuen.

———. 1986. "The Problem of Ideology-Marxism without Guarantees." *Journal of Communication Inquiry* 10 (2): 28–44. doi:10.1177/019685998601000203.

Hannerz, Ulf. 1992. *Cultural Complexity: Studies in the Social Organization of Meaning.* New York: Columbia University Press.

Hardin, Garrett. 1968. "The Tragedy of the Commons." *Science* 162:1243–1248.

Hardt, Michael, and Antonio Negri. 1994. *Labor of Dionysus: A Critique of the State-Form.* Minneapolis: University of Minnesota Press.

Harsin, Jayson. 2010. "The Lost Histories of American Economic Rights." *Cultural Studies* 24 (3): 333–355. doi:10.1080/09502381003750294.

———. 2012. "Cultural Studies and/of Economic Rights: Neglect and Promise." *Communication and Critical/Cultural Studies* 9 (2): 115–145. doi:10.1080/14791420.2012.675077.

Harvey, David. 1990. *The Condition of Postmodernity: An Enquiry into the Origins of Cultural Change.* Oxford: Blackwell.

———. 2005. *A Brief History of Neoliberalism.* Oxford: Oxford University Press.

———. 2006. *Spaces of Global Capitalism: Towards a Theory of Uneven Geographical Development.* London: Verso.

Hay, Douglas, Peter Linebaugh, John G. Rule, E. P. Thompson, and Cal Winslow. 2011. *Albion's Fatal Tree: Crime and Society in Eighteenth-Century England.* 2nd ed. London: Verso.

Hayek, Friedrich A. von. 1933. "The Trend in Economic Thinking." *Economica*, no. 40 (May): 121–137.

———. 1945. "The Use of Knowledge in Society." *American Economic Review* 35 (4): 519–530.

———. 1989. *The Fatal Conceit: The Errors of Socialism.* Chicago: University of Chicago Press.

———. 1994. *The Road to Serfdom.* Chicago: University of Chicago Press.

Hayter, Earl W. 1963. "Livestock-Fencing Conflicts in Rural America." *Agricultural History* 37 (1): 10–20.

Heidel, Evelin, Ezequiel Martin Acuña, and Joe Karaganis. 2014. "Can Former 'Pirates' Fix a Broken Movie Market?" *Ars Technica*, January 21. https://arstechnica.com/information-technology/2014/01/where-movie-makers-and-former-pirates-are-starting-to-get-along/.

Heller, Michael. 2006. "The Rose Theorem." *Yale Journal of Law and Humanities* 18:29–48.

———. 2008. *The Gridlock Economy: How Too Much Ownership Wrecks Markets, Stops Innovation, and Costs Lives.* New York: Basic Books.

Henwood, Doug. 2003. *After the New Economy.* New York: New Press.

Hill, Christopher. 1972. *The World Turned Upside Down: Radical Ideas during the English Revolution.* New York: Penguin Press.

———. 1982. *The Century of Revolution, 1603–1714.* New York: Norton.

Hobbes, Thomas. 1968. *Leviathan.* Edited by C. B. MacPherson. London: Penguin Books.

Hochschild, Arlie Russell. 2016. *Strangers in Their Own Land: Anger and Mourning on the American Right.* New York: New Press. Kindle.

Homestead, Melissa J. 2010. *American Women Authors and Literary Property, 1822–1869.* Reprint, Cambridge: Cambridge University Press.

Hoppe, Hans-Hermann. 2001. *Democracy—The God That Failed: The Economics and Politics of Monarchy, Democracy and Natural Order.* New Brunswick, NJ: Routledge.

Horwitz, Morton J. 1977. "The Rule of Law: An Unqualified Human Good?" Edited by Douglas Hay, Peter Linebaugh, John G. Rule, E. P. Thompson, and Cal Winslow. *Yale Law Journal* 86 (3): 561–566. https://doi.org/10.2307/795801.

Hoskins, Colin, Stuart McFadgen, and Adam Finn. 1997. *Global Television and Film: An Introduction to the Economics of the Business.* Oxford: Clarendon Press.

Hsu, Jeremy. 2017. "The Star Wars Video That Baffled YouTube's Copyright Cops." *Wired*, August 2. https://www.wired.com/story/the-star-wars-video-that-baffled-youtubes-copyright-cops/.

Huws, Ursula. 2014. *Labor in the Global Digital Economy: The Cybertariat Comes of Age.* New York: Monthly Review Press.

Inayatullah, Naeem, and David L. Blaney. 2004. *International Relations and the Problem of Difference.* New York: Routledge.

INTERPOL, Intellectual Property Crimes Unit Sub-regional Bureau for South America. 2008. "Operation Jupiter III—South America." Lyon, France: INTERPOL. http://www.interpol.int/Public/ICPO/PressReleases/PR2008/PR200821.asp.

Jameson, Fredric. 1984. "Postmodernism, or the Cultural Logic of Late Capitalism." *New Left Review* 1 (146): 52–92.

Jenkins, Henry. 1992. *Textual Poachers: Television Fans and Participatory Culture.* New York: Routledge.

———. 2006. *Convergence Culture: Where Old and New Media Collide.* New York: New York University Press.

Jhally, Sut. 1990. *The Codes of Advertising: Fetishism and the Political Economy of Meaning in the Consumer Society.* Rev. ed. New York: Routledge.

Johnson Andrews, Sean. 2014. "Modernity, Law and the Violence of Piracy, Property and the State." In *Piracy: Leakages of Modernity,* edited by Martin Fredriksson and James Arvanitakis. http://litwinbooks.com/Piracy-Andrews.pdf.

———. 2016. *Hegemony, Mass Media and Cultural Studies: Properties of Meaning, Power, and Value in Cultural Production.* Lanham, MD: Rowman and Littlefield International.

———. 2018. "Property, Sovereignty, Piracy and the Commons: Early Modern Enclosure and the Foundation of the State." In *Property, Place, Piracy,* edited by Martin Fredriksson and James Arvanitakis, 36–49. London: Routledge.

Jones, Daniel Stedman. 2014. *Masters of the Universe: Hayek, Friedman, and the Birth of Neoliberal Politics.* Updated ed. Princeton, NJ: Princeton University Press.

Katz, Elihu, Paul Felix Lazarsfeld, and Columbia University Bureau of Applied Social Research. 1955. *Personal Influence: The Part Played by People in the Flow of Mass Communications.* Glencoe, IL: Free Press.

Katznelson, Ira. 2013. *Fear Itself: The New Deal and the Origins of Our Time.* New York: Liveright.

Kennedy, Duncan. 1998. "Law-and-Economics from the Perspective of Critical Legal Studies." In *The New Palgrave Dictionary of Economics and the Law* 2:465–474. London: Macmillan Reference.

Kennedy, Kathleen E. 2015. *Medieval Hackers.* New York: Punctum Books.

Klain, Ronald A. 2017. "The One Area Where Trump Has Been Wildly Successful." *Washington Post,* July 19. https://www.washingtonpost.com/opinions/the-one-area-where-trump-has-been-wildly-successful/2017/07/19/56c5c7ee-6be7-11e7-b9e2-2056e768a7e5_story.html.

Klein, Naomi. 2002. *No Space, No Choice, No Jobs, No Logo.* New York: Picador.

———. 2017. *No Is Not Enough: Resisting Trump's Shock Politics and Winning the World We Need.* Toronto: Knopf Canada. Kindle.

Kruse, Kevin. 2015. *One Nation under God: How Corporate America Invented Christian America.* New York: Basic Books.

Kuttner, Robert. 2017. "Steve Bannon, Unrepentant." *American Prospect,* August 16. http://prospect.org/article/steve-bannon-unrepentant.

Laclau, Ernesto, and Chantal Mouffe. 2001. *Hegemony and Socialist Strategy: Towards a Radical Democratic Politics.* London: Verso.

Lærke, Mogens, ed. 2009. *The Use of Censorship in the Enlightenment.* Leiden, Netherlands: Brill.

Landes, William M., and Richard A. Posner. 1989. "An Economic Analysis of Copyright Law." *Journal of Legal Studies* 18:325–364.

———. 2003. "Indefinitely Renewable Copyright." *University of Chicago Law Review* 70 (2): 471–518.

———. 2004. *The Political Economy of Intellectual Property Law.* Washington, DC: American Enterprise Institute Press.

Lanjouw, Peter. 1996. "Poverty in Rural Ecuador." In *Ecuador Poverty Report,* by World Bank, 141–182. A World Bank Country Study. Washington, DC: World Bank Publications.

Laslett, Peter, ed. 1988. "Introduction." In *Two Treatises of Government*, by John Locke, edited by Peter Laslett, 3–127. Cambridge: Cambridge University Press.

Lee, Dave. 2011. "You Have a Regional Dialect—Even on Twitter." *BBC News*, February 12. http://www.bbc.com/news/technology-12381912.

Lemley, Mark. 1997. "Romantic Authorship and the Rhetoric of Property." *Texas Law Review* 75:873.

———. 2004. "Ex Ante versus Ex Post Justifications for Intellectual Property." *University of Chicago Law Review* 71 (1): 129–149. doi:10.2307/1600514.

Lessig, Lawrence. 1995. "The Regulation of Social Meaning." *University of Chicago Law Review* 62 (3): 943–1045. doi:10.2307/1600054.

———. 1996. "Social Meaning and Social Norms." *University of Pennsylvania Law Review* 144 (5): 2181–2189.

———. 1998. "The New Chicago School." *Journal of Legal Studies* 27 (2): 661–691.

———. 1999. *Code: And Other Laws of Cyberspace.* New York: Basic Books.

———. 2001. *The Future of Ideas: The Fate of the Commons in a Connected World.* New York: Vintage.

———. 2002. "Keynote Address." Presented at the Open Source Convention, San Diego, CA, July 24.

———. 2004. *Free Culture: How Big Media Uses Technology and the Law to Lock Down Culture and Control Creativity.* New York: Penguin Press.

———. 2006. *Code: Version 2.0.* New York: Basic Books.

———. 2008. *Remix: Making Art and Commerce Thrive in the Hybrid Economy.* London: Bloomsbury Academic.

———. 2015. *Republic, Lost: Version 2.0.* Rev. ed. New York: Twelve.

Liebelson, Dana. 2015. "Leaked Email Reveals How Hollywood Opposed 'Fair Use' Protections in Secretive Trade Agreement." *Huffington Post*, April 17. http://www.huffingtonpost.com/2015/04/17/sony-emails-tpp_n_7088580.html.

Linebaugh, Peter, and Marcus Buford Rediker. 2000. *The Many-Headed Hydra: Sailors, Slaves, Commoners, and the Hidden History of the Revolutionary Atlantic.* Boston: Beacon Press.

Lionsgate Entertainment Inc. v. Carter's Inc. et al. 2007. California Central District Court.

Lipietz, Alain. 1987. *Mirages and Miracles: The Crises of Global Fordism.* Translated by David Macey. London: Verso.

Lipsitz, George. 2006. *The Possessive Investment in Whiteness: How White People Profit from Identity Politics.* Rev. and exp. ed. Philadelphia: Temple University Press.

Litman, Jessica. 1991. "Copyright as Myth." *University of Pittsburgh Law Review* 53:235–1061.

———. 2007. "Creative Reading." *Law and Contemporary Problems* 70:175–184.

Littler, Jo. 2017. *Against Meritocracy: Culture, Power and Myths of Mobility.* Abingdon, UK: Routledge

Livingston, James. 2016. *No More Work: Why Full Employment Is a Bad Idea.* Chapel Hill: University of North Carolina Press. Kindle.

Locke, John. 1988. *Second Treatise of Government.* In *Two Treatises of Government*, edited by Peter Laslett, 265–428. Cambridge: Cambridge University Press.

———. 1997. "Liberty of the Press (1694–5)." In *Locke: Political Essays*, edited by John Goldie, 329–339. Cambridge: Cambridge University Press.

Lukács, Georg. 1971. *History and Class Consciousness: Studies in Marxist Dialectics.* Cambridge: Massachusetts Institute of Technology Press.

Lury, Celia. 2004. *Brands: The Logos of the Global Economy.* London: Routledge.

Lynn, Barry. 2002. "Unmade in America." *Harper's Magazine* 304 (1825): 33.

MacLean, Nancy. 2017. *Democracy in Chains: The Deep History of the Radical Right's Stealth Plan for America.* New York: Viking.

Macpherson, C. B. 1962. *The Political Theory of Possessive Individualism: Hobbes to Locke.* Oxford: Clarendon Press.

———. 1977. *The Life and Times of Liberal Democracy.* Oxford: Oxford University Press.

Manjoo, Farhad. 2017. "I Ignored Trump News for a Week. Here's What I Learned." *New York Times,* February 22. https://www.nytimes.com/2017/02/22/technology/trump-news-media-ignore.html.

Martel, James R. 2017. *The Misinterpellated Subject.* Durham, NC: Duke University Press. Kindle.

Marx, Karl. 1972. "On the Jewish Question." In *The Marx-Engels Reader,* edited by Robert Tucker, 26–52. New York: Norton.

———. 1973. *Grundrisse: Foundations of the Critique of Political Economy (Rough Draft).* Translated by Martin Nicolaus. London: Penguin Books, in association with New Left Review.

———. 1977. *Capital: A Critique of Political Economy.* Vol. 1. New York: Vintage Books.

Marx, Karl, and Friedrich Engels. 2011. *The German Ideology, Including Theses on Feuerbach.* Amherst, NY: Prometheus Books.

Maskus, Keith E. 2000. *Intellectual Property Rights in the Global Economy.* Washington, DC: Institute for International Economics.

Masnick, Mike. 2013. "MPAA's Actions, Emails Show That They're Doing Everything Possible to Screw Over the Blind." *Techdirt,* June 24. https://www.techdirt.com/articles/20130624/02222023593/mpaas-actions-emails-show-that-theyre-doing-everything-possible-to-screw-over-blind.shtml.

Mattelart, Armand, and Michèle Mattelart. 1998. *Theories of Communication: A Short Introduction.* London: Sage Publications.

May, Christopher. 2000. *A Global Political Economy of Intellectual Property Rights: The New Enclosures?* London: Routledge.

———. 2002. *The Information Society: A Sceptical View.* Malden, MA: Polity Press.

———. 2007. "The World Intellectual Property Organization and the Development Agenda." *Global Governance* 13:161–170.

McChesney, Robert Waterman. 1993. *Telecommunications, Mass Media, and Democracy: The Battle for the Control of U.S. Broadcasting, 1928–1935.* New York: Oxford University Press.

———. 1999. *Rich Media, Poor Democracy: Communication Politics in Dubious Times.* Urbana: University of Illinois Press.

McCloskey, D. 1972. "The Enclosure of Open Fields: Preface to a Study of Its Impact on the Efficiency of English Agriculture in the Eighteenth Century." *Journal of Economic History* 32 (1): 15–35.

McGirr, Lisa. 2015. *Suburban Warriors: The Origins of the New American Right.* Updated ed. Princeton, NJ: Princeton University Press.

McNally, David. 1989. "Locke, Levellers and Liberty: Property and Democracy in the Thought of the First Whigs." *History of Political Thought* 10 (1): 17–40.

McRobbie, Angela. 2008. "Young Women and Consumer Culture." *Cultural Studies* 22 (5): 531–550. doi:10.1080/09502380802245803.

———. 2016. *Be Creative: Making a Living in the New Culture Industries.* Cambridge: Polity.

Meehan, Eileen. 2000. "Leisure or Labor? Fan Ethnography and Political Economy." In *Consuming Audiences? Production and Reception in Media Research*, edited by Ingunn Hagen and Janet Wasko, 71–92. Cresskill, NJ: Hampton Press.

Menell, Peter S. 2007a. "Intellectual Property and the Property Rights Movement." *Regulation* 30:36–42. https://works.bepress.com/peter_menell/4/.

———. 2007b. "The Property Rights Movement's Embrace of Intellectual Property: True Love or Doomed Relationship?" *Ecology Law Quarterly* 34 (2): 713–754. doi:10.2307/24114639.

Mill, John Stuart. 2002. *On Liberty.* Mineola, NY: Dover Thrift.

———. 2004. *Principles of Political Economy.* Amherst, NY: Prometheus Books.

Mills, C. Wright. 1960. "Letter to the New Left." *New Left Review* 1 (5). http://www.newleftreview.org/?page=article&view=997.

———. 2002. *White Collar: The American Middle Classes.* 50th anniv. ed. New York: Oxford University Press. Kindle.

Mirowski, Philip. 2013. *Never Let a Serious Crisis Go to Waste: How Neoliberalism Survived the Financial Meltdown.* New York: Verso.

Mises, Ludwig von. 1985. *Liberalism: The Classical Tradition.* Irvington-on-Hudson, NY: Foundation for Economic Education.

———. 2000. *Human Action: A 50-Year Tribute.* Edited by Richard M. Ebeling. Hillsdale, MI: Hillsdale College Press.

———. 2001. *Theory and History: An Interpretation of Social and Economic Evolution.* Auburn, AL: The Ludwig Von Mises Institute. internal-pdf://Mises, Ludwig von - Theory and History-2187329281/Mises, Ludwig von - Theory and History.pdf.

Monnat, Shannon M. 2016. "Deaths of Despair and Support for Trump in the 2016 Presidential Election." *Pennsylvania State University Department of Agricultural Economics Research Brief, 5.*

Moore, Barrington. 1967. *Social Origins of Dictatorship and Democracy: Lord and Peasant in the Making of the Modern World.* Boston: Beacon.

Morley, David. 1992. *Television, Audiences, and Cultural Studies.* London: Routledge.

Morley, David, and Charlotte Brunsdon. 1999. *The Nationwide Television Studies.* London: Routledge.

Morran, Chris. 2017. "Supreme Court Rejects 'Dancing Baby' YouTube Copyright Case." *Consumerist*, June 19. https://consumerist.com/2017/06/19/supreme-court-rejects-dancing-baby-youtube-copyright-case/.

Mosco, Vincent. 2004. *The Digital Sublime: Myth, Power, and Cyberspace.* Cambridge: Massachusetts Institute of Technology Press.

Mouffe, Chantal. 2000. *The Democratic Paradox.* London: Verso.

———. 2005. *The Return of the Political.* London: Verso.

Mouffe, Chantal, and Íñigo Errejón. 2016. *Podemos: In the Name of the People.* London: Lawrence and Wishart.

Mullin, Joe. 2016. "'Happy Birthday' Is Public Domain, Former Owner Warner/Chapell to Pay $14M." *Ars Technica*, February 10. http://arstechnica.com/tech-policy/2016/02/happy-birthday-is-public-domain-former-owner-warnerchapell-to-pay-14m/.

Munger, Michael C. 2017. "On the Origins and Goals of Public Choice: Constitutional Conspiracy?" *Independent Institute*, June 29. http://www.independent.org/issues/article.asp?id=9115

Murdock, Graham, and Peter Golding. 1977. "Capitalism, Communication and Class Relations." In *Mass Communication and Society*, edited by James Curran, Michael Gurevitch, and Janet Woollacott, 12–43. London: Sage Publications.

Murray, Charles. 2013. *Coming Apart: The State of White America, 1960–2010*. Repr. ed. New York: Crown Forum.

Nagle, Angela. 2017. *Kill All Normies: Online Culture Wars from 4Chan and Tumblr to Trump and the Alt-Right*. Winchester, UK: Zero Books.

New York Times. 1884. "Papers on Rural Topics: Mr. Parsons Attacks Sharply the Bureau of Agriculture." February 8. http://query.nytimes.com/gst/abstract.html?res=9B0DEFDE1238E033A2575BC0A9649C94659FD7CF.

Noble, David F. 1979. *America by Design: Science, Technology, and the Rise of Corporate Capitalism*. Oxford: Oxford University Press.

Nozick, Robert. 1974. *Anarchy, State, and Utopia*. New York: Basic Books.

Obama, Barack. 2016. "President Obama: The TPP Would Let America, Not China, Lead the Way on Global Trade." *Washington Post*, May 2. https://www.washingtonpost.com/opinions/president-obama-the-tpp-would-let-america-not-china-lead-the-way-on-global-trade/2016/05/02/680540e4-0fd0-11e6-93ae-50921721165d_story.html?utm_term=.0639a1b92628.

Oddi, A. Samuel. 1996. "TRIPS—Natural Rights and a 'Polite Form of Economic Imperialism.'" *Vanderbilt Journal of Transnational Law* 29:415–470.

Olmsted, Kathryn S. 2015. *Right Out of California: The 1930s and the Big Business Roots of Modern Conservatism*. New York: New Press.

Ostrom, Elinor. 2015. *Governing the Commons: The Evolution of Institutions for Collective Action*. Reissue ed. Cambridge: Cambridge University Press.

"Pale." 2007. *Oxford English Dictionary*. Oxford: Oxford University Press.

Parks, Miles. 2017. "Confederate Statues Were Built to Further a 'White Supremacist Future.'" *NPR.org*, August 20. https://www.npr.org/2017/08/20/544266880/confederate-statues-were-built-to-further-a-white-supremacist-future.

Parry, Marc. 2011. "Suttin Hella Koo, Y'all: Regional Dialects Thrive on Twitter." *The Chronicle of Higher Education*, January 13. http://www.chronicle.com/blogs/wiredcampus/suttin-hella-koo-yall-regional-dialects-thrive-on-twitter/28960?sid=at&utm_source=at&utm_medium=en.

Parsons, Talcott. 1937. *The Structure of Social Action: A Study in Social Theory with Special Reference to a Group of Recent European Writers*. New York: McGraw-Hill.

Peet, Richard. 2007. *Geography of Power: The Making of Global Economic Policy*. London: Zed Books.

Peñalver, Eduardo M., and Sonia Katyal. 2007. "Property Outlaws." *University of Pennsylvania Law Review* 155 (5): 1095–1186.

———. 2010. *Property Outlaws: How Squatters, Pirates, and Protesters Improve the Law of Ownership*. New Haven, CT: Yale University Press.

Perelman, Michael. 2000. *The Invention of Capitalism: Classical Political Economy and the Secret History of Primitive Accumulation*. Durham, NC: Duke University Press.

———. 2002. *Steal This Idea: Intellectual Property Rights and the Corporate Confiscation of Creativity*. New York: Palgrave.

———. 2006. *Railroading Economics: The Creation of the Free Market Mythology*. New York: Monthly Review Press.

Phillips-Fein, Kim. 2010. *Invisible Hands: The Businessmen's Crusade against the New Deal*. Repr. ed. New York: Norton.

Piketty, Thomas. 2014. *Capital in the Twenty-First Century*. Translated by Arthur Goldhammer. Cambridge, MA: Belknap Press of Harvard University Press.

Polanyi, Karl. 2001. *The Great Transformation: The Political and Economic Origins of Our Time*. Boston: Beacon Press. Kindle.

Posner, Richard A. 1972. *Economic Analysis of Law*. Boston: Little, Brown.

Poulantzas, Nicos. 1978. *State, Power, Socialism*. London: Verso.

Probyn, Elspeth. 1993. *Sexing the Self: Gendered Positions in Cultural Studies*. London: Routledge.

Qiu, Jack Linchuan. 2012. "Network Labor: Beyond the Shadow of Foxconn." In *Studying Mobile Media Cultural Technologies, Mobile Communication, and the iPhone*, edited by Larissa Hjorth, Jean Burgess, and Ingrid Richardson, 39:173–190. London: Routledge.

———. 2016. *Goodbye iSlave: A Manifesto for Digital Abolition*. Urbana: University of Illinois Press.

Rapport, Mike. 2009. *1848: Year of Revolution*. New York: Basic Books.

Raymond, Eric S. 2001. *The Cathedral and the Bazaar: Musings on Linux and Open Source*. Rev. ed. Cambridge, MA: O'Reilly Media.

Read, Jason. 2003. *The Micro-Politics of Capital: Marx and the Prehistory of the Present*. Albany: State University of New York Press.

Rediker, Marcus Buford. 2004. *Villains of All Nations: Atlantic Pirates in the Golden Age*. Boston: Beacon Press.

Robertson, Geoffrey. 2007. "Introduction." In *The Levellers: The Putney Debates*, compiled by Philip Baker, vii–xxxiii. London: Verso.

Rose, Carol. 1986. "The Comedy of the Commons: Custom, Commerce, and Inherently Public Property." *University of Chicago Law Review* 53 (3): 711–781.

———. 1994. *Property and Persuasion: Essays on the History, Theory, and Rhetoric of Ownership*. Boulder, CO: Westview Press.

Rose, Mark. 1995. *Authors and Owners: The Invention of Copyright*. Rev. ed. Cambridge, MA: Harvard University Press.

Rosen, Ellen Israel. 2002. *Making Sweatshops: The Globalization of the U.S. Apparel Industry*. Berkeley: University of California Press.

Ross, Andrew. 2000. "The Mental Labor Problem." *Social Text* 18 (2): 1–31.

———. 2009. *Nice Work If You Can Get It: Life and Labor in Precarious Times*. NYU Series in Social and Cultural Analysis. New York: New York University Press.

———. 2010. "The Making of Sustainable Livelihoods." *Communication and Critical/Cultural Studies* 7 (1): 92–95.

Ross, Wilbur. 2017. "American Genius Is under Attack from China." *Financial Times*, August 15. https://www.ft.com/content/e283773a-801a-11e7-94e2-c5b903247afd.

Roth, Zachary. 2010a. "Libertarians on Paul's Civil Rights Stance: 'Very Reasonable.'" *TalkingPointsMemo.com*, May 20. http://talkingpointsmemo.com/dc/libertarians-on-paul-s-civil-rights-stance-very-reasonable.

———. 2010b. "Paul: Opposing Civil Rights Act Is 'The Hard Part About Believing in Freedom' (VIDEO)." *TalkingPointsMemo.com*, May 20. http://talkingpointsmemo.com/dc/paul-opposing-civil-rights-act-is-the-hard-part-about-believing-in-freedom-video.

Rothstein, Richard. 2017. *The Color of Law: A Forgotten History of How Our Government Segregated America.* New York: Liveright.

Rucker, Philip, and Robert Costa. 2017. "Bannon Vows a Daily Fight for 'Deconstruction of the Administrative State.'" *Washington Post*, February 23. https://www.washingtonpost.com/politics/top-wh-strategist-vows-a-daily-fight-for-deconstruction-of-the-administrative-state/2017/02/23/03f6b8da-f9ea-11e6-bf01-d47f8cf9b643_story.html.

Sanchez, Daniel. 2017. "What Music Piracy Really Looks Like in 2017." *Digital Music News*, May 11. https://www.digitalmusicnews.com/2017/05/11/music-piracy-looks-like-2017/.

Sarat, Austin, and Jonathan Simon. 2001. "Beyond Legal Realism: Cultural Analysis, Cultural Studies, and the Situation of Legal Scholarship." *Yale Journal of Law and Humanities* 13 (3): 3–32. http://scholarship.law.berkeley.edu/facpubs/151.

Saussure, Ferdinand de. 1961. *Course in General Linguistics.* Edited by Charles Bally and Albert Sechehaye in collaboration with Albert Reidlinger. Translated from the French by Wade Baskin. 3rd ed. London: P. Owen.

Schiller, Herbert I. 1992. *Mass Communications and American Empire.* Boulder, CO: Westview Press.

Schmitt, Carl. 2006. *Political Theology: Four Chapters on the Concept of Sovereignty.* Translated by George Schwab. Chicago: University of Chicago Press.

Schuessler, Jennifer. 2012. "Dictionary of American Regional English Reaches Last Volume." *New York Times*, February 24. https://www.nytimes.com/2012/02/25/books/dictionary-of-american-regional-english-reaches-last-volume.html.

Schwartz, Nelson D., Patricia Cohen, and Julie Hirschfeld Davis. 2017. "Wisconsin's Lavish Lure for Foxconn: $3 Billion in Tax Subsidies." *New York Times*, July 27. https://www.nytimes.com/2017/07/27/business/wisconsin-foxconn-tax-subsidies.html.

Sciabarra, Chris Matthew. 2006. "Libertarianism." In *International Encyclopedia of Economic Sociology*, edited by Jens Beckert and Milan Zafirovski. London: Routledge.

Scott, James C. 1979. "Revolution in the Revolution: Peasants and Commissars." *Theory and Society* 7 (1–2): 97–134.

———. 1990. *Domination and the Arts of Resistance: Hidden Transcripts.* New Haven, CT: Yale University Press.

———. 2012. *Two Cheers for Anarchism: Six Easy Pieces on Autonomy, Dignity, and Meaningful Work and Play.* Princeton, NJ: Princeton University Press.

Seymour, Richard. 2008. *The Liberal Defence of Murder.* London: Verso.

Shirky, Clay. 2010. *Cognitive Surplus: How Technology Makes Consumers into Collaborators.* New York: Penguin.

Smith, Adam. 2007. *An Inquiry into the Nature and Causes of the Wealth of Nations.* Hampshire, UK: Harriman House Publishing.

Smith, Paul. 2007. *Primitive America: The Ideology of Capitalist Democracy.* Minneapolis: University of Minnesota Press.

Smythe, Dallas Walker. 1977. "Communications: Blindspots of Western Marxism." *Canadian Journal of Political and Social Theory* 1 (3): 1–28.

———. 1981. *Dependency Road: Communications, Capitalism, Consciousness, and Canada.* Norwood, NJ: Ablex.

Sonnad, Nikhil. 2014. "Um, Here's an, uh, Map That Shows Where Americans Use 'Um' vs. 'Uh.'" *Quartz*, September 15. https://qz.com/264312/um-heres-an-uh-map-that-shows-where-americans-use-um-vs-uh/.

Springer, Kate. 2012. "#Soda or #Pop? Regional Language Quirks Get Examined on Twitter." *Time*, March 5. http://newsfeed.time.com/2012/03/05/soda-or-pop-regional-language-quirks-get-examined-on-twitter/.

Srnicek, Nick, and Alex Williams. 2016. *Inventing the Future: Postcapitalism and a World without Work*. Rev. and updated ed. London: Verso.

Stahl, Jason. 2016. *Right Moves: The Conservative Think Tank in American Political Culture since 1945*. Chapel Hill: University of North Carolina Press

Sunstein, Cass. 1986. "Legal Interference with Private Preferences." *University of Chicago Law Review* 53 (4): 1129–1175.

———. 1987. "Lochner's Legacy." *Columbia Law Review* 87 (5): 873–919. https://doi.org/10.2307/1122721.

———. 1990. "Paradoxes of the Regulatory State." *University of Chicago Law Review* 57 (2): 407–441.

———. 1993. *The Partial Constitution*. Cambridge, MA: Harvard University Press.

———. 2004. *The Second Bill of Rights: F.D.R.'s Unfinished Revolution and Why We Need It More Than Ever*. New York: Basic Books.

———. 2006. *Infotopia: How Many Minds Produce Knowledge*. New York: Oxford University Press.

Sunstein, Cass, and Richard H. Thaler. 2003. "Libertarian Paternalism Is Not an Oxymoron." *University of Chicago Law Review* 70 (4): 1159–1202.

———. 2008. *Nudge: Improving Decisions about Health, Wealth, and Happiness*. New Haven, CT: Yale University Press.

Supiot, Alain. 2007. *Homo Juridicus: On the Anthropological Function of the Law*. London: Verso.

Sydnor, Thomas D., II. 2008. "Tragedy and Farce: An Analysis of the Book FREE CULTURE." *Progress on Point*, no. 15.5 (April). http://www.pff.org/issues-pubs/pops/pop15.5freecultureanalys.pdf.

Taibbi, Matt. 2014. *The Divide: American Injustice in the Age of the Wealth Gap*. New York: Spiegel and Grau.

Tapscott, Don, and Anthony D. Williams. 2010. *Wikinomics: How Mass Collaboration Changes Everything*. Exp. ed. New York: Portfolio.

Taylor, Sarah. 2017. "Where Is the Outrage for Keeanga-Yamahtta Taylor?" *New Republic*, June 2. https://newrepublic.com/minutes/143064/outrage-keeanga-yamahtta-taylor.

Teles, Steven M. 2012. *The Rise of the Conservative Legal Movement: The Battle for Control of the Law*. Princeton, NJ: Princeton University Press.

Thompson, E. P. 1990. *Whigs and Hunters*. Harmondsworth, UK: Penguin.

———. 1991. *Customs in Common*. New York: New Press. Kindle.

Thrush, Glenn. 2017. "New Outcry as Trump Rebukes Charlottesville Racists 2 Days Later." *New York Times*, August 14. https://www.nytimes.com/2017/08/14/us/politics/trump-charlottesville-protest.html.

Tigar, Michael E., and Madeline Levy. 2000. *Law and the Rise of Capitalism*. New York: Monthly Review Press.

Trachtenberg, Alan. 2007. *The Incorporation of America: Culture and Society in the Gilded Age*. 25th anniv. ed. New York: Hill and Wang.

Travis, Hannibal. 2000. "Pirates of the Information Infrastructure: Blackstonian Copyright and the First Amendment." *Berkeley Technology Law Journal* 15 (2): 777–864. doi:10.15779/Z382D6R.

Tucker, Robert. 1972. *The Marx-Engels Reader.* New York: Norton.

U.S. Government Accountability Office. 1987. "International Trade: Strengthening Worldwide Protection of Intellectual Property Rights." Washington, DC: US GAO.

Vaidhyanathan, Siva. 2001. *Copyrights and Copywrongs: The Rise of Intellectual Property and How It Threatens Creativity.* New York: New York University Press.

———. 2004. *The Anarchist in the Library: How the Clash between Freedom and Control Is Hacking the Real World and Crashing the System.* New York: Basic Books.

———. 2017. *Intellectual Property: A Very Short Introduction.* New York: Oxford University Press.

van Dijck, José. 2013. *The Culture of Connectivity: A Critical History of Social Media.* Oxford: Oxford University Press. Kindle.

Vanguard America. n.d. "Vanguard Manifesto: AMERICAN FASCISM." *Vanguard America.* https://bloodandsoil.org/manifesto/. Accessed August 14, 2017.

Vološinov, V. N. 1973. *Marxism and the Philosophy of Language.* Translated by Ladislav Matejka and I. R. Titunik. New York: Seminar Press.

Wacquant, Loïc J. D. 2009. *Punishing the Poor: The Neoliberal Government of Social Insecurity.* Politics, History, and Culture. Durham, NC: Duke University Press.

Warcutter, Angela. 2007. "Meme Monitor: Dirty Dancing." *Wired*, August 27. https://www.wired.com/2007/08/meme-monitor-di/.

Wasko, Janet. 2001. *Understanding Disney: The Manufacture of Fantasy.* Cambridge: Polity.

Waxman, Sharon. 2003. "With Acquisition, Lions Gate Is Now Largest Indie." *New York Times*, December 16. https://www.nytimes.com/2003/12/16/movies/with-acquisition-lions-gate-is-now-largest-indie.html.

Weber, Max. 2001. *The Protestant Ethic and the Spirit of Capitalism.* New York: Routledge Classics.

Weil, David. 2014. *The Fissured Workplace: Why Work Became So Bad for So Many and What Can Be Done to Improve It.* Cambridge, MA: Harvard University Press.

WENN. 2007. "Dirty Dancing Makers Mount Copyright Infringement Suit." *contactmusic.net*, August 22. http://www.contactmusic.net/news/dirty-dancing-makers-mount-copyright-infringement-suit_1041339.

Whitman, James Q. 2017. *Hitler's American Model: The United States and the Making of Nazi Race Law.* Princeton, NJ: Princeton University Press.

Wilkin, John. 2011. "Bibliographic Indeterminacy and the Scale of Problems and Opportunities of 'Rights' in Digital Collection Building." *Council on Library and Information Resources.* https://www.clir.org/pubs/ruminations/01wilkin.

Williams, Raymond. 1958. *Culture and Society: 1780–1950.* New York: Columbia University Press.

———. 1983. *The Year 2000.* New York: Pantheon Books.

———. 1989. *Resources of Hope: Culture, Democracy, Socialism.* Edited by Robin Gable. London: Verso.

———. 2001. *The Long Revolution.* Orchard Park, NY: Broadview Press.

———. 2011. *Keywords: A Vocabulary of Culture and Society.* Routledge Revivals. London: Routledge.

Winseck, Dwayne Roy, and Robert M. Pike. 2007. *Communication and Empire: Media, Markets, and Globalization, 1860–1930.* Durham, NC: Duke University Press.

Wood, Ellen Meiksins. 1981. "The Separation of the Economic and the Political in Capitalism." *New Left Review* 127 (May–June): 66–95.

———. 1991. *The Pristine Culture of Capitalism: A Historical Essay on Old Regimes and Modern States.* London: Verso.

———. 2002. *The Origin of Capitalism: A Longer View.* Rev. ed. London: Verso.

Wood, Neal. 1984. *John Locke and Agrarian Capitalism.* Berkeley: University of California Press.

Yang, Fan. 2015. *Faked in China: Nation Branding, Counterfeit Culture, and Globalization.* Bloomington: Indiana University Press.

Žižek, Slavoj. 2000. *The Ticklish Subject: The Absent Centre of Political Ontology.* London: Verso.

———. 2008. *Violence: Six Sideways Reflections.* New York: Picador.

Index

Sean Johnson Andrews is an Associate Professor of Humanities and Cultural Studies at Columbia College Chicago. He is the author of *Hegemony, Mass Media, and Cultural Studies: Properties of Meaning, Power, and Value in Cultural Production* and co-editor (with Jaafar Aksikas) of *Cultural Studies and the 'Juridical Turn': Culture, Law and Legitimacy in the Era of Neoliberal Capitalism.*